CONSTITUTIONAL LAW IN THEORY AND PRACTICE

David Beatty draws on more than twenty years' teaching experience to produce a comprehensive introduction to constitutional law, accessible to students of law and non-specialists alike. He reviews the leading cases that have come before the Privy Council and the Supreme Court of Canada concerning the BNA Act and the Charter of Rights and Freedoms. As well, Beatty reviews important decisions made by courts around the world and analyses the function judges perform in liberal-democratic societies when they enforce written constitutions that include bills of rights.

Chapter 1 introduces constitutional law – what it is all about, what its function is, and how it interacts with the constitutional text. The book examines Canadian federalism law and the Supreme Court of Canada's experience with the Charter of Rights. It also looks at significant human rights cases decided by major courts around the world, showing how the same principles and methods of reasoning are used elsewhere to resolve legal disputes. The author concludes that a theory of constitutional law that puts greater emphasis on the social duties politicians must respect than on individual rights should be responsive to the concerns of both those who are sceptical about the virtues of law and the courts and those who fear Western cultural imperialism.

Beatty proposes a radically new way of thinking about 'rights' – one that emphasizes the social duties inherent in the very conception of rights. By reorienting our thinking about rights and the rule of law, we can see that democratic decision-making and judicial review, rather than being in conflict with each other, support a common set of values and ideals.

DAVID M. BEATTY is a professor in the Faculty of Law, University of Toronto. He is the author or editor of several books, including *Human Rights and Judicial Review; Talking Heads and the Supremes; Putting the Charter to Work*; and, with D.J.M. Brown, *Canadian Labour Arbitration.*

DAVID BEATTY

Constitutional Law in Theory and Practice

UNIVERSITY OF TORONTO PRESS
Toronto Buffalo London

Toronto Buffalo London

Reprinted in paperback 2014

ISBN 978-0-8020-0701-8 (cloth)
ISBN 978-0-8020-7650-2 (paper)

Printed on acid-free paper

Canadian Cataloguing in Publication Data

Beatty, David M.
Constitutional law in theory and practice

Includes bibliographical references and index.
ISBN 978-0-8020-0701-8 (bound) ISBN 978-0-8020-7650-2 (pbk.)

1. Canada – Constitutional law. 2. Constitutional law. I. Title.

KE4219.B43 1995 342.71 C95-930143-7
KF4482.B43 1995

University of Toronto Press acknowledges the financial assistance to its publishing program of the Canada Council and the Ontario Arts Council.

FOR NINETTE

A search for a definitive formula for decision in constitutional law is a pursuit worthy of the high political and economic importance of the subject.

Bora Laskin, 'Tests for the Validity of Legislation: What's the "Matter"?' *University of Toronto Law Journal* 11 (1955) 114

Contents

Preface xi

1 Constitutional Law 3
Introduction 3
Constitutions 3
Purpose 3
Style 5
The Dilemma 6
Methods of Reform 8
Constitutional Law 9
Purpose and Method 9
The Controversy 13
The Rules 15

2 Division of Powers 20
Introduction 20
What Do the Words Mean? 21
The Plain-Meaning Approach 21
External Aids: Dictionaries and Precedents 22
Internal Aids: The Intention of the Framers and the Logic of the Text 23
The Federal Principle 25
Guaranteeing Equal Sovereignty 29
Maximizing Equal Sovereignty 39
Constitutional Law 44
The Rules 44

The Rules and the Record of the Court 47
The Possibility of Judicial Review 57

3 Human Rights 61
Introduction 61
What Do the Words Mean? 62
External Aids: American and Canadian Bills of Rights 63
Internal Aids: The Intention of the Framers and the Logic of the Text 64
Defining Rights 66
Fundamental Freedoms: Expression and Religion 66
Reasonable Limits and Maximizing Rights 68
Human Rights and Legal Reasoning 69
Human Rights and the Rules of Constitutional Law 70
Rationality, Proportionality, and the Record of the Court 74
Human Rights and Judicial Exemptions 76
Scope of the Charter: Where Rationality and Proportionality Do Not Apply 76
Human Rights and Judicial Deference 82
The Possibility of Judicial Review 84

4 Comparative Constitutional Law 103
Introduction 103
The United States 106
India 113
Japan 121
Germany 127
The European Court of Human Rights 133

5 Law and Politics 141
Rights and the Rules of Law 141
Rights and Duties 146
Law and Politics 155

Notes 163
Index 201

Preface

This short book on constitutional law has been written with two purposes – and two audiences – in mind. The primary readership, I hope, will be students in law and political science who are coming to the subject for the first time. The pages that follow are drawn from the notes that I have developed to teach constitutional law to first- and upper-year students at the University of Toronto's Faculty of Law. For ten years I have experimented with different approaches and ideas, and this book represents what I believe to be the easiest, most accessible, and most coherent way to introduce students to this subject.

My second objective in writing up the way I have come to understand the rules of constitutional law is to contribute to a lively debate that students and teachers are having about both the conceptual integrity and normative justification of this body of law. Although the book is written in a style intended to make the subject interesting and meaningful to people who have little or no background in the law, the subject matter and content build on and are intended to be responsive to a rich literature that probes both the coherence and the moral basis of the idea of empowering courts – the third branch of government – to sit in judgment on the decisions of the other two branches. Thus, this book is directed also to all of my colleagues who, for one reason or another, and in different ways and degrees, have abandoned the notion that there is an independent, objective, and determinate idea that makes the concept of law intelligible.

Writing any book requires the support and assistance of many people. A book that has been in the making for almost a decade means that my indebtedness is that much greater. My students over these years have been unfailingly tolerant and resourceful in assisting me in finding the best way to approach the material. Allen Rosen single-handedly did almost all of the primary research. My colleagues at the law school have been uniformly supportive in the encouragement and assistance that they have provided. Robert Howse, Patrick Macklem, Dick Risk, and Bob Sharpe in particular all read parts of the manuscript and made many helpful suggestions. Virgil Duff guided the manuscript through to publication with a calmness and kindness for which I am most appreciative. And, once again, friends and family have tolerated all of the interruptions and eccentricities projects like this carry in their wake. Special thanks, for helping out in ways and to degrees that go beyond what either professionalism or friendship could legitimately expect, to Chris Black, Ninette Kelley, Brian Langille, Merril Randell, and Michael Trebilcock.

CONSTITUTIONAL LAW IN THEORY AND PRACTICE

1

Constitutional Law

INTRODUCTION

No one, I am sure, would have any difficulty distinguishing a constitution from either a gopher or a game of golf. Most people, I suspect, would be astonished that anyone would even consider it important or interesting to refer to these three entities in the same breath. Although it is often said that a constitution provides the 'ground' – or foundation – on which the modern nation-state is built, for most people that connection would be too tenuous and remote. The words conjure up such radically different images that to compare them seems quite bizarre.

The reason that we can be so certain that constitutions have nothing to do with gophers or golf is that all three are defined in terms that have almost nothing in common with each other. The core meaning of all three is well settled. For practical purposes, none is a matter of serious dispute or controversy. We know that gophers are members of the rodent family that organize their communities beneath the ground on which the cities and states of North America are built. Golf is a form of recreational activity in which pleasure is derived from hitting a ball into a hole in the ground. Constitutions, by contrast, are universally understood to be all about governments, what institutions they include, how they are structured, and what kind of power they can wield – over gophers[1] as well as the game of golf![2]

CONSTITUTIONS

Purpose

Like gophers and golf, constitutions are known first and foremost by what they do. Rather than being about burrowing or putting balls into holes in the ground, constitutions fix the rules that control people's behaviour when they are entrusted with the powers of government. In the same way that labour agreements create a framework within which people go about their working lives, and separation agreements settle the way relations in families will be conducted after a marriage breaks down, so constitutions are concerned with the way people (politicians, bureaucrats, police, judges, and so on) behave when they occupy positions of state authority.

Like any human artefact, the idea of a state is something that can be put to good use or bad. Because of that, many people have ambivalent feelings about it. While they recognize the real benefits of organizing and subordinating life in a community to the power of some supreme law-making authority, they understand that states cannot act on their own. Governments need men and women to operate the levers of power, and that is where the danger, or dark side, lurks. History is strewn with cases of politicians and bureaucrats who have misused the powers of the state, and so it is that many people consider it essential to find ways to ensure that the abuses that can be perpetrated under any system of majority rule can be stopped before they occur.[3]

Typically, in liberal-democratic societies at least, constitutions impose four broad conditions – or constraints – on how the power of a state can be exercised. First – and perhaps most basic – is the principle of democratic, or popular, rule.[4] Those who actually control the levers of power do so only for as long as they have the confidence and consent of the community. The principle insists that the people have the right to decide for themselves who their governors will be.

If democratic control is the first principle of how modern, liberal nations organize the power of the state, the idea of separation of powers is the second. With this principle, the powers to formulate, enact, and enforce the law are diffused and assigned to three different branches of government: the legislative (House of Commons, legislative assemblies), executive (cabinet, bureaucracy), and judicial (the courts). Although there is wide variation among countries in the degree to which the executive and legislative branches are kept separate and apart, in all liberal-democratic states the judicial branch stands alone and is quite independent of the other two.[5]

In addition to organizing the powers of the state functionally, and assigning them to three separate branches of government, many modern constitutions make use of a third principle – that of territorial division. The authority to regulate and control different parts of a country's life is distributed between a national (federal, central) and various local (regional, provincial, state) orders of government. The power of the state is made to conform to a federal principle[6] as well as to the principles of democracy and separation of powers.

The fourth distinguishing characteristic of most modern constitutions is that, in addition to dispersing the power of the state among different organs (vertically) and orders (horizontally) of government, they place absolute limits on what the state or any of its officials may do. Almost every constitution that has been written since the end of the Second World War contains a long list of basic human rights which no Government is permitted to transgress. Fundamental freedoms of religion, expression, life, liberty, and so on are put beyond the power of the state to control.

Style

Like most other human artefacts and natural objects, then, constitutions are largely known and defined in terms of what they do. However, like gophers and golf, constitutions also have a very distinctive way of going about their business. Constitutions are legal constructs with a style of their own.

Here one can highlight three distinguishing features about the constitutional style or method of organizing and limiting the powers of the state. The first and unquestionably most important feature of a constitution is its claim of supremacy or priority over all other parts of the legal order.[7] Because constitutions control the way people exercise legal authority entrusted to them by (in the name of) the state, they stand above and are superior to all other forms of law. Constitutions are what we use to measure the validity of all other legal acts. Whatever principles and proscriptions a constitution contains, they must take precedence over everything else. Constitutions are the supreme law because they provide the ground on which the legitimacy and integrity of the whole legal order stands. A constitution, to adapt a metaphor made popular by Saddam Hussein, is the mother of all laws.

Not only do constitutions claim supremacy in the legal order, they do so in a very insistent and grandiose way. By nature, constitutions tend to be different from other kinds of laws in their very rigid and very general mode of expression. It is characteristic of constitutions that they are more difficult to alter or change than most other laws. Usually constitutions require the approval of super majorities (e.g., 60, 70 per cent) or multiple majorities (e.g., both national and regional) to amend.[8]

Constitutions also tend to be written with a much grander, at times almost inspirational, flourish. Although every constitution has parts that are written in great detail and in very specific terms, those tend not to be the subject of much litigation and, therefore, are of less concern to the law. The most important and controversial parts are usually those that are written in the sweeping, majestic style with which we commonly associate constitutional texts, and these are the places where the great legal battles are fought. 'Liberté, egalité and fraternité' was the rhetorical idiom characteristic of the first of the modern constitutional texts, and this style continues to predominate today.

Like their claim of supremacy, the rigid and inspirational style that distinguishes constitutions from other parts of the legal order follows logically from the job that they are expected to do. If constitutions are going to serve their purpose of providing a legal foundation for the state, they should be firm and solid and generally resistant to change. Even gophers know that it is a first principle of architecture and engineering that a building is only as strong as the foundation on which it stands.

At the same time, because constitutions are expected to mark off relatively stable boundaries within which the power of the state is to be divided, the language of the text should be large and generous in its style. Typically, governments are given power over vast terrains of 'trade and commerce,' 'criminal law,' and 'property and civil rights,' and citizens are guaranteed basic rights of equality, life, liberty, and the security of their persons as well as fundamental freedoms of thought, religion, expression, association, and the like.

The Dilemma

Although the rigid, elevated style that is characteristic of most constitutional texts follows logically from the purposes constitutions are expected to serve, there is also something quite problematical – paradoxical – in the way these legal artefacts are designed. Precisely because these texts are written in such general terms and are so resistant to change, they run a serious risk of ambiguity and/or irrelevance. There is a danger that the more solid the foundation and the loftier the phrase, the more likely it will be that the document will become less and less able to provide clear direction to resolve the constitutional issues of the day.

When disputes arise as to which (or indeed whether either) order of government has jurisdiction to pass laws about strikes and picketing, Sunday shopping, children's television advertising, pollution, prostitution, pornography, or abortion – to pick just a few contemporary Canadian examples – the conventional mode of constitutional expression may not help very much. All parties can point to something in the text to support their case. On any of these issues the federal government might say that these are matters that fall naturally within the power to enact laws about 'trade and commerce' or 'criminal' behaviour, which the constitution entrusts to them. Provincial governments could respond (and have) that in various ways all of these matters relate either to 'property and civil rights in the province' or are matters of a 'merely local or private nature' and so fall within their jurisdiction.[9] And, against both of these claims, many Canadians would say that neither level of government should be able to proscribe these activities because they have a 'constitutional right' to do these things and behave in these ways.

In the grand and eloquent style in which constitutions are written, they seem to provide no help to the very questions that they are meant to resolve. The constitution seems to say everything and nothing at the same time. The fact is that strikes and picketing can have an intimate connection with both 'trade and commerce' in the country and people's civil rights (in employment) within a province, and they are also closely linked to the fundamental human rights of association and expression. Similarly, prostitution and pornography can fairly be characterized as falling within the power of the federal government to control criminal law, the power of the provinces to ensure that the physical (and indeed metaphysical) environment does not adversely affect the well-being of their residents, and the fundamental rights of people to associate and express themselves in ways of their own choosing.

The dilemma faced by all constitutions is the same. How can the framework or superstructure of the state be constructed in such a way that its foundation will be simultaneously impervious and responsive to the ordinary events and forces of community life? If constitutions are written in a sweeping and inspirational style and made very difficult to change, the danger is that they will become less and less relevant in resolving the nitty-gritty, everyday questions that arise about allocation and organization of power in the state. They will be useless in answering the hard, practical questions about which order or level of government should control specific areas of social policy, such as strikes and picketing, prostitution and pornography, and what kind of control should be allowed. However, if a constitution is designed in a much more detailed way, allowing less room for interpretation – if it is written in the style of a municipal by-law or an income tax act – it may not be able to provide the state with the stability and moral legitimacy that it craves.

Methods of Reform

To resolve this dilemma, generally two types of solutions have been employed – one political, the other legal. Institutionally, processes of negotiation and adjudication have both played a role. Together, political actors and judges try to mould the constitutional framework of the country in ways that will be faithful to bedrock values and, at the same time, responsive to the highly volatile, ever-changing environment in which we live.

In Canada, political practices and institutions have been developed that allow the constitutional framework to be altered informally and in less permanent ways. Politics has been especially central in resolving many questions about how the power of the state is to be distributed, both functionally and territorially, between different branches and orders of government. For example, almost all the rules governing relations between the executive and legislative branches of government, including those that specify when a prime minister – or indeed the whole Government (viz., the cabinet, the executive) – should resign, are fixed by custom and political conventions that the executive and legislative branches establish for themselves. No one would dream of taking the prime minister to court if he or she refused to accept the rejection of one of the Government's policies by the legislature as a vote of 'no confidence.' Similarly, political institutions such as the federal-provincial and first ministers' conferences have been used extensively to modify the federal-provincial division of powers to make it more suitable to our times.[10] Cooperative arrangements between the federal government and the provinces in health care, post-secondary education, social assistance, environmental protection, and the like are the most notable successes of the political approach to constitutional reform.[11]

As important as politics has been (and will continue to be) as an instrument of interstitial, ad hoc constitutional change, it was never expected to do the whole job on its own. Searching for solutions through political negotiation and compromise typically involves significant expenditures of time and energy,[12] and, as Canadians who lived through the failures of the Meech Lake and Charlottetown accords know very well, it cannot always bring success. In the result, on issues that are tightly focused and can be cast into legal terms, as well as those not amenable to resolution by the executive and legislative branches, politics has looked and deferred to the law.[13]

CONSTITUTIONAL LAW

Purpose and Method

The process by which judges adapt the constitutional system of a country to the circumstances of a modern nation-state is really very simple and straightforward, though as a practical matter, terribly costly to the litigants involved. Individuals, interest groups, and even Governments can activate the process and petition the courts to rule on the constitutional validity of any laws whose integrity is suspect.[14] Typically, in Canada, a case will be argued in front of two lower courts before it goes to the Supreme Court of Canada for a final, or definitive, ruling, though it is possible for the federal Government to refer some constitutional questions directly to the nine justices in Ottawa.[15] Once the Supreme Court is seized of a case, it solicits written argument and supporting documentation from the parties and other intervenors who have an interest in the dispute[16] and then schedules a short session (usually between a half and a full day) for oral submissions. After the oral arguments have been made, the Court typically retires to its conference room, where the judges compare their views and make a tentative decision. At the end of the conference, the Chief Justice will select one or more judges to write the decision for the Court and any minority opinions, if there are any dissents.

In reaching their decision, the judges are guided and bound by the law. What the law adds to a constitution can best be described as a set of principles, or tests, developed by the courts, to resolve disputes about how the powers of the state should be distributed and applied when the text of the constitution says either too little or too much. The rules of constitutional law are what the judges have resort to when they adjudicate the competing claims of governments and citizens over the legitimacy of specific laws about strikes, pickets, pornography, prostitution, children's advertising, and so on. In methodological terms, constitutional law is the way in which judges reduce and reformulate the large and sweeping phrases into more manageable terms. It is what tells them whether strikes and picketing or pornography and prostitution are really matters of criminal law or more local matters of provincial concern or basic human rights to which all governments must defer.

In every case in which the constitutionality of a law or an act of some state official is put in issue, the reasoning process is the same. Whether a law is challenged on federalism grounds, as lying outside the jurisdiction of one order of government, or on the basis that it violates someone's fundamental rights, a court will follow the same method of analysis. Indeed, as we shall see in chapter 4, the basic principles of constitutional law are essentially the same around the world, even though there is considerable variation in what guarantees constitutions contain and in the language that they employ.

In general terms, every case in which someone challenges the constitutionality of a law can be divided in two. There are two distinct phases or parts to the process of judicial review.[17] Initially, the court's attention is focused on the constitution. Here the judges endeavour to identify the limits of law-making powers of the relevant institution or official of the state. In the second stage, after the constitutional boundaries have been fixed, the court's attention shifts to the law or bureaucratic ruling that it has been asked to review. At this point, the court looks carefully at the most important features of the challenged law in order to see if it conforms to the limits and restrictions that the constitution contains.

In terms of simple logic, determination of whether a law is constitutional or not closely parallels standard forms of analytical and practical reasoning. Formulating a major premise is what the court does in the first stage of the review process. It particularizes and spells out the relevant rules of the constitution. A finding is made that the constitution gives (or denies) power over a certain interest or activity or area of social policy (like picketing or prostitution) to the federal or the provincial level of government, or to neither, or to both.

The minor premise is based on the court's analysis of the most salient aspects of the challenged law. It takes the form of a judgment of how, taken as a whole, a particular law should be classified and defined. The reasons for which and the ways in which such laws restrict people's freedom to act are examined to determine what they are all about – whether, all things considered, a law prohibiting street solicitation by prostitutes should be seen as an expression, by lawmakers, of a desire, variously, to establish common standards of morality, to protect the character and ambience of local neighbourhoods, or just to impose restrictions on the freedom of people who want to engage in this form of commercial activity. Once the contours of the constitution are clearly defined and the basic character of the law is firmly in view, the court is in a position to pass judgment on the constitutional validity of the latter. Both the ends and the means of the law are held up and measured against rules or tests in the constitution. Combining the two parts of the process of review and the premises they contain leads the court to a conclusion that either or both the federal or provincial level of government has the power to enact the law under scrutiny, or that neither of them does.

Because the two stages of the review process are directed at two different objects of inquiry, they are also distinguishable in the methods of reasoning they employ. In the first phase, when the court is trying to define and give meaning to the constitutional text, the analysis is largely deductive. Though there are a variety of possible sources of meaning available to the courts, as we shall see, more often than not judges tend to rely on the values and assumptions on which the constitution is based – its overriding purposes – to guide them in fixing a meaning for the entitlements and guarantees that it provides. In the jargon of the trade, courts read the constitution 'purposefully,' or 'holistically,' to ensure that all of its component parts are of a single, coherent piece.

In the second phase, deductive reasoning is employed less frequently. In deciding on which side of the line (principle) a particular law should be placed, a court is much more likely to reason analogically – 'horizontally' – than 'vertically,' as thinking deductively requires.[18] To figure out how it should rule on the constitutional validity of a particular law, it is most apt to look back at its prior decisions to see how it has handled laws of this sort in the past. Where it can, it uses its earlier precedents to find the closest analogies and, thereby, to ensure a measure of consistency and equality of treatment in its own decision-making.

As a practical matter, the process of constitutional review is even simpler than this. In reality, the second stage is much more important than the first. As a constitution matures, the interpretive function attracts increasingly less of the courts' attention. Over time, the meaning of the large and sweeping phrases becomes settled. Though the courts may find some words and phrases harder to interpret than others (which may result in some definitions undergoing substantial revision and change), sooner or later the rules of constitutional law get worked out. Each judicial decision, each precedent, provides more detail about what the constitution really means. Eventually, a standard set of basic principles or criteria is drawn from the text, against which all other laws and legal initiatives are tested.[19]

For example, once it is decided that the power of the federal government over 'trade and commerce' does not embrace regulation of contracts in a specific business or industry operating in a single province, that matter is basically settled for all time.[20] Similarly, once the court defines 'freedom of expression' to include any activity designed to convey a meaning – including, on occasion, even parking a car – the scope of protection provided by that constitutional guarantee is more or less fixed. In the result, when a woman challenges a municipal by-law that prohibits prostitutes from soliciting on Calgary's streets or when a children's toy manufacturer in Quebec challenges a law that restricts its freedom to promote its products commercially on television, the case is litigated on the premise that provincial Governments have some authority to control what goes on in local neighbourhoods and in the local advertising business and that both the prostitute and the toy company have some constitutional rights to communicate with their clientele. Those broad boundaries have been firmly settled in earlier decisions of the courts.[21] The difficult question in these (and indeed in all constitutional) cases is whether the particular law that the court has been asked to review goes too far in encroaching on the constitutional powers of (in these cases) the federal government over public morality and broadcasting and in restricting the freedom of the toy manufacturers and the prostitutes to express themselves as they wish.

As time goes by, the focus of the courts shifts more and more from the constitution to the laws whose validity they have been asked to assess. The principles or criteria of review that are embedded in the constitution are taken as given, and the only issue for the judges is how they should be applied in a particular case. Practically all the action takes place in the second stage of the review process.

As it matures, constitutional law becomes like any other area or body of law, in which the role of the court is to apply broad principles such as unconscionability or negligence to the facts of a particular case.[22] Indeed, the practice of constitutional law may even be simpler and more straightforward than how a typical private law case is debated and resolved. Unlike cases in contract or tort, where competing principles are often at play and where there may be real gaps in the law, in constitutional law, in theory at least, the rules and principles should never collide and no gaps should ever appear. As we shall see, in most disputes about the constitutionality of a law there is no disagreement about what the relevant principles are; the question is what conclusion they support in each particular case.

The Controversy

On the account that I have given so far, most students come to see that constitutional law is very much like every other body of legal rules governing a particular area or kind of human activity. Except for the fact that it is addressed to politicians and officials who are entrusted with the powers of the state (rather than to individuals in their more private, interpersonal affairs), there is nothing in this description of what constitutional law is all about that differentiates it from our general understanding of these other areas of law. The idea that, over time, a body of principles and rules is built up around a constitutional text, which gives the legal framework of the state the stability and flexibility it requires, is part of the basic knowledge that is imparted at the beginning of every first-year course in constitutional law. And it is conventional wisdom that, over time, the focus of the courts and of the practice of constitutional law is less and less on identifying the principles and criteria that are required to resolve a dispute and much more on how those rules should be applied.

In the face of this general understanding of what constitutional law is all about and how the courts exercise their powers of review, it comes as a surprise to many students that there is considerable controversy within the legal community about how well the law has gone about its work and indeed about whether it is even capable of accomplishing the task that it is expected to perform. For many scholars, who are generally quite sceptical and critical about almost every aspect of the law, the two-step framework of analysis and doctrinal rulings is not nearly as objective and determinate as many would have us believe. These people argue that in all of the difficult and hotly contested cases, none of the doctrines or principles developed by the courts does the really critical work.

They say that in all of the major, high-profile cases, the rules and prior decisions provide little or no assistance in deciding whether a challenged law or some decision by a state official is constitutional or not. In many – indeed most – cases, they contend, there are conflicting principles or precedents or interpretations available to the court to support the result that it prefers. The law is such that a court can almost always find some legal rule or definition or prior decision on which to base its case. As they say, the cases and principles 'march in pairs.'[23]

In other cases, they will say, the law just 'runs out.' Occasionally it happens, though less and less frequently, that there is just no legal principle (or precedent) that governs the case. In these circumstances as well, the argument is that whether a law is deemed to be constitutional or not really has less to do with legal principles and rules than with how each of the judges personally weighs and ranks the interests and values at stake.

For those who are sceptical and critical of the idea that there are neutral rules and principles of law that can distinguish between laws that are constitutional and those that are not, the whole enterprise of judicial review is highly dubious. If, in the final analysis, judges end up relying on their own intuitions and subjective views about whether a law should be validated or struck down, the sceptics question whether we really need a legal umpire in constitutional disputes. They ask whether it wouldn't be preferable – more honest, more democratic, more effective – to use political institutions and actors rather than hiding behind and relying on the pretence of law.[24] Better to reform the legislative and executive branches of government, they say, than try to deal with the threat of majorities acting excessively by creating a process that is vulnerable to being used as an instrument of subjective (arbitrary) rule by an unelected, legal elite.

Although those who advocate reducing or even eliminating the role of the court in shaping the constitutional framework of government are in a distinct minority, their contention – that rules of law actually play a limited role in deciding whether any legislative or administrative initiative is constitutional or not – is one with which most legal scholars would have some sympathy. Even among those who argue that the judiciary has an important role to play in protecting and developing a country's constitutional framework, there is a widely shared view that, in many of the most controversial and contested cases of constitutional review, legal rules and doctrines cannot provide final answers for a court. Even supporters of judicial review are inclined to concede that in the hardest cases it is the political and/or legal philosophy of the judge and how he or she personally balances the competing visions and values at stake that finally determine whether a law will be held to be constitutional or not.[25] For many people who have studied or practised constitutional law for any length of time, it is conventional wisdom that, in the real world of liberal democracies, a constitution is little more than what the judges say it is.

The Rules

In the rest of this book, I want to examine this conventional wisdom more closely. It seems to me that the claims of the critics cannot be ignored. If the rules of constitutional law do not provide answers in the most controversial and difficult cases, it is hard to see how one can justify a process of judicial review. If the judges are not governed by rules of law – if the rule of law has no definite, determinate meaning that can distinguish laws that are constitutionally valid from those that are not – judicial review should have no place in a society that claims a liberal-democratic pedigree. It would be completely at odds with our tradition of popular sovereignty and personal autonomy to allow decisions about the most controversial and fundamental questions of the day to be made by a small, elite group of unelected officials. If judges were free to decide cases and the limits of legal authority according to their own (considered) views about law, morality, and the state, judicial review would be as much an agent of as a check against arbitrary and autocratic rule. As the critics point out, much more effective – and democratic – solutions could be fashioned in the political domain.

My ambition in this book is to try to resurrect and defend the integrity of law. While acknowledging that the record of the courts has been very uneven, and even woefully inadequate at times, I want to suggest that the decisions of the courts, if they are read carefully, do reveal an overarching, unified method of constitutional review that does distinguish, in an objective and principled way, between laws that are constitutional and those that are not.

In the most general terms, I want to suggest that, for all practical purposes, the rules of constitutional law can be reduced to two basic principles or tests. To establish the constitutional pedigree of a law it must be shown, first, that the public interest or purpose of the law is of sufficient importance that it offsets (justifies) whatever limitation or restriction it imposes on individuals or groups or other orders of government. Some might call this a utilitarian standard of constitutionality, or a test of 'proportionality,' or balance. It requires a court to do a kind of 'cost-benefit' analysis to ensure that the gains to the community that the law is intended to provide outweigh the loss of personal freedom or restriction of another government's jurisdiction that it entails. However, because, as we shall see, courts commonly do this analysis by looking for the closest analogies – by comparing the challenged law with other laws, both at home and abroad, that involve similar interests and ideas – I think that this principle is better described as a rule of 'consistency' or 'anti-discrimination' (equality).

In addition to requiring that the ends or objectives of a challenged law satisfy a basic test of constitutional validation, the courts also insist that the means, or particular method, that it employs meet a basic standard of 'rationality' – or necessity – as well. Regardless of what words are used in a constitution, or indeed whether a challenge is based on grounds of human rights or division of powers, the courts have imposed a burden on those defending a challenged law to show that the means, or the particular policy instrument, that they have chosen for pursuing their objectives was the best available to them. For a law to be validated constitutionally, its supporters must show that no alternative policies or instruments were available that would have allowed them to accomplish their purposes in a way that displayed more respect for the freedom of individuals or the sovereignty of other governments. They must establish that it really was necessary for them to follow the route that they did.

Together, these two basic principles require those who have been entrusted with the powers of the state to act with a measure of moderation and proportion.[26] Politicians and policy-makers are prohibited from madly pursuing some particular agenda without regard for the costs that it entails. No one who controls any power of the state can use any more of it than is required to accomplish his or her purposes. No one can engage in overkill.

Reducing the practice of constitutional law to two basic principles – rationality and proportionality – is not the way the process of judicial review is commonly understood or described. Traditionally, much more emphasis is put on identifying the particular entitlements that the constitution bestows on governments (division-of-powers provisions) and individuals (human-rights sections) alike. Law is usually portrayed as an interpretive exercise in which the role of the court is to elaborate on the meaning of the text.[27] The conventional understanding of constitutional law is that it is directed to specifying exactly what the words of the constitution guarantee and what the various orders of government and individual citizens are free to do. In the area of human rights, the favoured image of a constitution is one in which 'rights ... erect around each individual ... an invisible fence over which the state will not be allowed to trespass.'[28]

Putting principles of rationality and proportionality at the centre of the story of what constitutional law is all about shifts the whole focus of the inquiry 180 degrees. Justification, not interpretation, becomes the leitmotif of constitutional review.[29] Rather than empowering individuals and governments to do various things, the rules of constitutional law actually impose limits on how those (politicians and government officials) who are entrusted with the powers of the state can behave. Duties, it turns out, not rights, are the primary concern of the law. Even in human rights cases, rather than focusing on the claims of the individual who alleges a violation of his or her freedom, the rules of constitutional law are directed to the politicians and their agents, and they speak about the duties and obligations (to act rationally and consistently) they owe to the people whose lives they control.

The novelty of proposing a theory of constitutional law that portrays judges reasoning with rules of rationality and proportionality and invokes a discourse of duties rather than rights will not make it easier for those already sceptical about the integrity of judicial review to reconsider their views. Good lawyers always insist on seeing the evidence before making a judgment about what conclusions they should embrace. To be credible, a theory of constitution law must have both a sound empirical and a sound normative base. It must be able to account for the most important cases in the field as well as providing a normative justification that accords with the values of the society to which it pertains. Accordingly, in the three chapters that follow, I want to show how these two basic principles provide the framework of analysis in virtually every case in which the constitutional validity of a law is at stake.

The story in each of the next three chapters is substantially the same. The actors and interested parties will change, but the basic method of analysis and principles of review reappear again and again. In chapter 2, the focus is on Canadian federalism cases, which, until 1982, were the staple of our own constitutional law. Here we examine how the principles of rationality and proportionality have played themselves out resolving disputes between the federal and provincial governments. In chapter 3, we concentrate on the record of the Supreme

Court of Canada in its protection of basic human rights in the ten years following entrenchment of the Charter of Rights. In chapter 4, our focus extends even further afield, and we see how the same two principles of constitutional law that our Supreme Court has used to exercise its powers of review are at the core of the constitutional jurisprudence of countries around the world. No matter what the legal dispute is all about, or where it occurs, or what language has been used in the constitution, the final decision will be based on how the relevant court applies these two principles of constitutional validation.

After examining the empirical evidence in chapters 2–4, we return, in the final chapter, to the question of whether, with the law in their hands, judges are up to the task of making sure that constitutions provide a durable yet flexible foundation for the state. Reflecting on how the two principles have been used by courts to answer questions about intergovernmental relations (federalism), as well as about relations of a more interpersonal kind (human rights), allows us to draw some normative conclusions about the strengths and the weaknesses of law and what kind of contribution we can reasonably expect it to make. With a clearer appreciation of how law has performed in the past, we should be in a better position to make an informed judgment about whether a process of judicial review can strengthen the constitutional framework of government by ensuring that it is responsive and can adapt to new issues and changing times.

At the end of the day, the story of this book is much more about the possibility and the perfectibility of the law than it is about unremitting triumphs and unalloyed success. As we shall see in the three chapters that follow, it turns out that the evidence of how the courts have actually decided cases is not uniformly flattering and supportive of the virtues of law. As the critics and others have insisted for a long time, the courts have been far from consistent and uniform in how they have exercised their powers of review. Though the two principles of rationality (necessity) and proportionality (consistency) have provided the courts with a basic framework of analysis within which to test the constitutionality of any legal rule or law, many judges all over the world believe that they should not apply these legal tests strictly in every case. Like the critics who question the compatibility of law and democratic decision-making, judges are, as a group, acutely sensitive to the principle of separation of powers and how it differentiates them from the other two, elected, branches of government. Frequently, as we shall see, the courts have been quite uncomfortable insisting that politicians and their agents meet the duties and obligations that these principles of constitutional legitimacy impose.

At the end of almost every course they take, law students are confronted with a gap between the promise and the practice of law. Like any human artefact, law can be only as good as the people entrusted with its development. In light of the common themes that permeate the practice of constitutional review around the world, a serious question remains about what kinds of reforms the sceptics' criticisms recommend. The uneven record that the courts have displayed so far suggests that even if the concept of the rule of law has some coherence and integrity, there is a need to think about what institutional adjustments can be made to reduce the number of occasions on which the principles of rationality and proportionality are misapplied and/or ignored. Any institutional reform that improves the performance of the courts should be a matter of the highest priority to all students of constitutional law, whatever their instinct about its fairness and integrity.

2

Division of Powers

INTRODUCTION

For the first 125 years of its development in Canada, constitutional law was used exclusively to answer questions about where the jurisdictional boundaries of its national and regional governments should be drawn. Historically, federalism cases have been the heart and soul of Canadian constitutional law. Though the courts flirted occasionally with the idea of developing an implied bill of rights, it was not until 1982, when the Charter of Rights and Freedoms was entrenched in the constitution, that human rights came to dominate the attention of the judiciary.

Even though their relative significance may have gradually diminished since the proclamation of the Charter, the cases in which the courts have been asked to resolve disputes between the federal and provincial governments provide textbook examples of how law can protect the basic values and ideas on which a constitution is based and, in so doing, function as an instrument of constitutional evolution and reform. The cases show how the courts, when faced with a text that was written in broad and sweeping terms, have, over time (and, as with any human institution, not without some difficulties along the way), been able to develop a set of mediating principles that allow them to differentiate fairly and impartially between laws that are constitutional and those that are not.[1]

In federalism cases, the question put to the courts is always the same: which level of government is entitled to regulate and set the standards in different areas of social policy? Should the rules governing elections,[2] abortions,[3] strikes and picketing,[4] pornography[5] and prostitution,[6] Sunday shopping,[7] television advertising,[8] and so on be fixed nationally or regionally? Which of these activities of everyday life should be settled uniformly, across the country as a whole, and which should allow for local variation and experimentation? In every case, the essential question is: which community or group of people – national or regional – is entitled to rule? which majority should prevail?

The basic problem for the courts when they are faced with such specific and practical questions is the same interpretive one that bedevils all constitutional texts. The difficulty is that the words of the constitution do not seem to help very much. In the British North America Act, 1867 (now renamed the Constitution Act, 1867), long lists of potentially limitless powers are distributed to both levels of government. In section 91, for example, the federal government was given responsibility for issues of national importance including trade and commerce, defence, the sea coast and inland fisheries, Indians, criminal law, and, in a phrase of conceivably unlimited scope, the general power to enact laws for 'the peace, order and good government' of the country. In sections 92 and 93, the provinces were given jurisdiction over matters of a more local concern. These included all municipal institutions, hospitals, education, natural resources, property and civil rights in the province, and generally 'all matters of a merely local or private nature.'

WHAT DO THE WORDS MEAN?

In dividing the legal powers of the state between national and regional levels of government, the Canadian constitution manifests, quite dramatically, the inherent contradiction identified in chapter 1: it says too little and yet too much. It fails to provide much guidance to the courts. How are the judges to decide whether pornography and prostitution – censorship and anti-soliciting rules – fall within the domain of criminal law? Does the federal government's power over trade and commerce embrace activities such as Sunday shopping or television advertising aimed at young children? Or are all these issues really about 'property and civil rights' in the province, and more matters of a 'merely local or private nature'?

The Plain-Meaning Approach

By themselves, the words of the constitution cannot supply answers to questions such as these. As with so many cases that reach the courts, there isn't a precise clause in the constitution that talks explicitly and specifically to these sorts of interests and activities, and the more sweeping, open-ended heads of power are, by definition, in need of further elaboration and interpretation. There is no one, settled meaning for phrases such as 'property and civil rights' or 'trade and commerce' that would be decisive in any of these cases. Read literally and according to their common meaning, each of the more sweeping allocations of power enumerated in sections 91 and 92 could be read as justifying either federal or provincial control. Prostitution clearly affects a community's moral standards and its health and safety, which have been the traditional concerns of criminal law. At the same time, the practice of the 'world's oldest profession' has a direct (and invariably negative) effect on the environmental quality of municipal neighbourhoods and so can fairly be characterized as a matter primarily of 'local' or provincial concern as well. Similarly, there is nothing in the words 'trade and commerce' or 'property and civil rights' that can tell us where the power to control Sunday shopping or television advertising aimed at young children should fall. On issues such as abortion, strikes and picketing, and so on, the constitution seems silent and expressionless again.

External Aids: Dictionaries and Precedents

Nor are the conventional sources of meaning, to which one might think a court could have recourse, of much help. Typically, when we are confronted with words whose meaning is obscure, we turn to dictionaries for assistance. But in decisions about which order or level of government should have control over issues such as prostitution, Sunday shopping, and children's advertising, neither the standard dictionaries that we all use in our everyday affairs, nor the more specialized legal dictionaries to which the professionals refer, provide much guidance for the courts.

Ordinary dictionaries of common language, such as the *Concise Oxford*, provide virtually no direction for the typical federalism case. The meanings that they stipulate are still far too general to suggest solutions for concrete disputes. 'Crimes' are defined simply as evil acts punishable by law, and 'commerce' as an exchange of merchandise or the solicitation of orders. 'Property' is said to include anything that can be owned or possessed, and 'local matters' could be any interest, activity, issue, or idea that exists in a particular place. Such definitions provide no help to the courts.

Nor can the standard, legal 'dictionaries' help very much. In most areas of law, 'precedents' (prior cases) provide the most reliable guides for a court. If there is some dispute or ambiguity about what a word or phrase means, the natural instinct of every person trained in law is to see if some other judge or court has faced a similar question in the past. Looking for precedents is one of the basic analytical methods in almost every area of law.

But precedents can never be the source from which the primary and most basic definitions are drawn. Precedents and prior cases cannot, by definition, be of any assistance in the first cases heard by the courts. Using precedents to illuminate the meaning of words works only after a system matures. In the earliest federalism cases (and, as we shall see in the next chapter, in the first Charter cases as well), there simply were no earlier decisions to which the judges might refer.

The seminal cases of Canadian federalism law look very different from judgments written today. The earliest decisions of the Judicial Committee of the Privy Council were remarkably uncluttered by comparison with the rulings that the Supreme Court of Canada would hand down a hundred years later. In one of the first important judgments that the Privy Council issued, in *Citizens Insurance v. Parsons* (1881),[9] there was scarcely a reference to prior cases of any kind, and in *Russell v. The Queen*,[10] another landmark case, decided the following year, the only legal authority cited was the earlier decision in *Parsons*.

Internal Aids: The Intention of the Framers and the Logic of the Text

In the absence of any external aids to illuminate the meaning of a text, the instinct of many people, including lots of judges, is to look around the edges of the document, so to speak, and find out what those who actually wrote it thought they were saying. When the text does not make obvious one overriding meaning that might indicate how a particular area of social policy should be distributed or assigned, the idea is to see if perhaps there is a special, particular meaning that was shared by those who negotiated the document. Especially for people attracted by Rousseau's idea of thinking about constitutions as 'social contracts,' it is natural to believe that their meaning is to be found in the intention of those who actually chose the words in the text.

Although one finds repeated references by the courts to the aspirations of the framers, it is generally recognized that intention is as inadequate a source of meaning as are ordinary dictionaries. Invariably, on the kinds of questions that get to the courts, there was no common consensus among those who drafted the document.[11]

On many questions, such as who should control television advertising, no one could even have thought about which level of government should have responsibility, because the technology did not exist in the mid-1860s.[12] Even on issues such as strikes and picketing or prostitution, which were as common in 1867 as they are today, the record shows that no one was thinking at that level of detail. The politicians spent relatively little time on how powers should be divided between the two orders of government. They were concerned more with the general contours and shape of the federal structure than with deciding where particular aspects of community life should be controlled.

Even in the delineation of the most explicit boundaries between the two orders of government, the historical record shows that there was a lot of ambiguity, uncertainty, and even conflicting ambitions.[13] Right from the beginning, French and English Canada have had quite different perceptions about exactly what the constitution allows the national and regional governments to do. French Canadians (including their judges) have consistently read Ottawa's powers much more narrowly than their counterparts in English Canada.[14] Canadians who lived through the debates surrounding the Meech Lake and Charlottetown accords, over what recognizing Quebec as a 'distinct society' really means, will know how easy it is for people who are designing the broad parameters of a constitutional framework to interpret even words that are at the centre of the text in radically different terms.[15]

Even though there has never been a case in which the intention of those responsible for the division of powers in the Constitution Act of 1867 has been either sufficiently pervasive and/or precise to tell the court which order of government has the authority to control contested matters such as children's advertising, Sunday shopping, prostitution, pollution, and pornography, the instinct of the judges to look 'inside' the constitution for direction and guidance has paid off. In the absence of any historical evidence as to how the founding fathers intended that responsibility for such interests and activities should be assigned, the courts tried to draw the meaning of the text from the underlying values and overall structure – the 'inner logic' – of the constitution as a whole. Rather than using linguistic or historical methods of analysis, they tended to rely on deductive – logical – reasoning to provide the most important definitions. More often than not, they sought to read the large and open-ended phrases in sections 91 and 92 purposefully – holistically – so that they would promote the most basic values and ideas that the constitution was supposed to guarantee.

When the courts have approached the various heads of powers that have been assigned to the two levels of government in this way, they have started from a single premise: that the Constitution Act of 1867 created a system of government that was both democratic and federal in nature. It is assumed that these two basic features of modern liberal-democratic states are reflected in the Canadian constitution as well. Democracy and federalism are the purposes that the original constitution was expected to promote.

For most students of constitutional law, the idea that Canada's constitution created a system of government that was both democratic and federal in character would not be seriously contested. These are widely taken as accepted facts about the Canadian state, and both are well-grounded in the text. Right at the beginning, in the preamble, there is a direct reference to the Canadian constitution being 'similar in principle to that of the United Kingdom,' which (even in 1867) was distinguished by its commitment to the principle of democracy and the sovereignty of the popular will.[16] Equally, the two long lists of powers in sections 91 and 92 that give 'exclusive' responsibilities to each order of government over different aspects of Canadian life explicitly recognize and presuppose the independence and sovereignty of both.[17]

THE FEDERAL PRINCIPLE

At one time, some scholars did question whether Canada was truly a federal state, because Ottawa was given powers of disallowance and reservation, which allowed it to control and even overrule the wishes of provincial governments.[18] However, these powers have fallen into disuse over the years, and now everyone recognizes that the 'federal principle' is a central pillar of Canadian constitutional law.[19] Indeed, the view of one of the country's leading political scientists is that the 'federal principle' was the only serious constraint on the exercise of state power in Canada until the entrenchment of the Charter.[20]

Although few have disputed the federal character of the Canadian state, many commentators have questioned how much the federal principle can assist the judges in giving meaning to the constitutional text. For some, simply acknowledging the division of powers between the two orders of government doesn't tell us very much. It doesn't specify with any precision where the lines should be drawn – where responsibility for particular activities such as advertising and abortion should be assigned.[21] For these scholars, the values and political philosophies of the judges, more than any principle of law, determine how such cases will be decided.

Despite this scepticism about the utility of the federal principle, this concept has provided clear directions as to how the judges ought to determine whether a law is constitutional or not. In fact, it has been the source of virtually every important doctrine and rule of law that the courts have devised. As an interpretive device, it has been the lens through which all the grand, sweeping phrases have been read and defined. As a kind of *grundnorm* of Canadian constitutional law, it has been the source from which all of the most important principles and rules of constitutionality have been drawn.

Of course, the federal principle cannot, on its own, tell a court whether a particular interest or activity is the responsibility of the federal or provincial government. What it does do, however, is to ensure that both orders of government are able to enjoy a measure of autonomy and sovereignty within whatever spheres of authority they have been given control. It prevents either level from being subordinated and dominated by the other. It says that there is an irreducible minimum area or jurisdiction for which each government is responsible, even if it is not self-evidently clear what the particulars of that sovereignty might be.

The principle that sovereign power is divided in Canada between two 'equal and co-ordinate' orders of government establishes a starting point from which analysis of the constitutionality of any law can begin. It provides the rules of reading, a framework or method of analysing the constitution, which, if applied impartially and prudently, can lead to determinate results.

In practical terms, the federal principle has given the courts two basic rules of interpretation. First, it has instructed the judges that in deciding what any of the categories or grants of power should be taken to mean, they should never adopt an interpretation or definition that would threaten the autonomy of the other level of government. Implicit in every head of power listed in sections 91 and 92 is the restriction that it authorizes enactment only of laws that are moderate and measured (well-proportioned) and sensitive to the sovereignty of the other order of government. Beyond that, the federal principle directed the courts that, once they were satisfied that the sovereignty of neither government was at stake (viz., that the law met a basic test of balance, or proportionality), they should always read the constitution in a way that guaranteed both orders of government as much room to manoeuvre as possible to pursue the sorts of policies (programs, purposes) that got them elected. The second basic corollary of the federal principle instructed the courts to maximize the jurisdiction of both orders of government as much as the first (proportionality) principle would allow.

As we shall see, both of these interpretive rules have been used again and again by the courts. The first goes by the name of 'mutual modification,' and it uses the idea that the constitution is built on a structure of two independent and autonomous orders of government to rule out meanings and interpretations that might put the sovereignty of either at risk. The idea is to avoid definitions that would allow one government to dominate and overwhelm the others. Governments are obliged to be attentive to the effects their policies have on the sovereignty of other governments. 'Mutual modification' is an interpretive rule that guarantees a measure of balance and proportionality between the authority of Ottawa and that of the provinces. It actually builds a requirement of proportionality right into the definition of the text.

One of the first major cases decided by the Privy Council was *Citizens Insurance v. Parsons*, in which the court upheld the validity of a provincial statute that required all fire insurance policies to contain certain conditions. In explaining why regulation of the fire-insurance industry in a province did not fall within the federal power over trade and commerce, Sir Montague Smith, who wrote the judgment for the Privy Council, explained the rationale underlying the principle of mutual modification in the following terms:

> With regard to certain classes of subjects, therefore, generally described in sect. 91, legislative power may reside as to some matters falling within the general description of these subjects in the legislatures of the provinces. In these cases it is the duty of the Courts, however difficult it may be, to ascertain in what degree, and to what extent, authority to deal with matters falling within these classes of subjects exists in each legislature, and to define in the particular case before them the limits of their respective powers. It could not have been the intention that a conflict should exist; and, in order to prevent such a result, the two sections must be read together, and the language of one interpreted, and, where necessary, modified, by that of the other. In this way it may, in most

cases, be found possible to arrive at a reasonable and practical construction of the language of the sections, so as to reconcile the respective powers they contain, and give effect to all of them.[22]

As a practical matter, this first rule of interpretation functions primarily as a principle of limitation and restraint. 'Mutual modification,' as it is known in the trade, creates a check on what both the federal and provincial governments are authorized to do, what goals and objectives and public interests they can pursue, and what kinds of social policies and programs they can devise, by ruling out of order laws that threaten the sovereignty and independence of other governments. By contrast, the second rule of interpretation that the courts have deduced from the federal principle acts more as a principle of entitlement or empowerment. In a sense, it works in the opposite direction to the first. Known to lawyers as the concurrency rule, it is designed to identify how far governments acting within the scope of their powers can go.

Concurrency is a principle of interpretation that is designed to maximize the law-making power of both orders of government. Within the strictures set by the first rule, mutual modification, this second principle instructs the courts to take a flexible and accommodating approach in defining the jurisdiction and law-making authority of both orders of government. The logic of the federal principle encourages the courts to read the list of powers in sections 91 and 92 as expansively as possible. It says that in all other cases – where enactment of a law by one level of government does not pose any threat to the autonomy of the other (viz., is well balanced and proportioned) – the constitution should be read in a way that supports and respects the democratic will of both national and regional governments. It instructs the courts to accept the legitimacy of whatever public interest causes a government to act. In short, it favours a model of federal-provincial relations in which the law-making powers of both governments are regarded as being integrated and overlapping rather than being cabined in very discrete and highly segregated 'categories.'

Together, the two strategies have provided the courts with a powerful analytical or interpretive framework. Building on these two precepts – of mutual modification and concurrency – the courts have encouraged a division of powers in which almost all commentators – even those generally critical of the courts – can find something to applaud.[23] Even though parts of the text obscure the logic of the federal principle and the interpretive strategies to which it gave rise,[24] the courts have, on the whole, remained faithful to the idea of reading (and defining) the words of the constitution in a way that would respect the sovereignty of both levels of government as much as possible. And, as we shall see, with these two strategies in hand, the courts have been able to play an important – though not a leading – role in keeping the constitution in tune with the times.

The way in which the federal principle has provided the courts with a method of reasoning or framework of analysis, through which they could develop the meaning of the constitution in a coherent way, warrants further explanation and elaboration. Some examples can illustrate how this method of interpretation has actually worked. People who are instinctively sceptical about the objectivity and determinacy of any form of legal reasoning usually want to see the logic of the definitions that the federal principle has produced for the major heads of power listed in sections 91 and 92. Others want concrete examples of how the two rules of 'mutual modification' and 'concurrency' have in fact resulted in a reading that is faithful to the federal structure of the Canadian state which they are designed to support.

Guaranteeing Equal Sovereignty

In any case in which a court is asked to assess the constitutionality of a law or legal regulation, its first job is to determine which parts of community life fall within Ottawa's jurisdiction and which parts are the responsibility of the provinces. The judges must read the text of the constitution and decide if the objectives – the public interest – that underlie whatever law they have been asked to review fall within one of the powers assigned to the government that enacted it. They must break the list of powers enumerated in sections 91 and 92 down into a catalogue of reasons that governments can put forward to justify the exercise of their lawmaking powers.

As noted above, the interpretive approach that has been favoured by the courts in performing this task is known as 'mutual modification.'[25] Mutual modification works through the meaning of words by a method of checks and balances. In defining what areas of public policy fall within the heads of powers assigned to one level of government, the court looks to the list of powers given to the other. Each list serves a dual purpose. As well as describing the primary areas of responsibility of the two orders of government, sections 91 and 92 also mark out limitations and constraints on the powers of the provincial and federal governments, respectively. Mutual modification tries to solve the dilemma presented by the open-ended grants of power by using them as defences against each other – as barricades to the territorial ambitions of neighbouring governments.

Some simple examples will illustrate how this structural, deductive, holistic method of interpretation works. The way the federal government's powers over criminal law have been defined typifies the approach. Though it has been suggested that section 91(27) authorizes Ottawa to impose penal sanctions on virtually any behaviour or activity, this definition has never been attractive to the courts.[26] In order to preserve provincial autonomy, the courts had to devise some limitation on this open-ended source of law-making authority. Ultimately, two separate constraints were imposed. First, the courts insisted that to fall within the criminal law power, the aim of a Government's initiative had to further a particular kind of public purpose – such as peace, order, security, health, or morality – that traditionally fell in the criminal law domain.[27] Ottawa could not rely on this source of sovereignty to justify punishing activities that bore no relation to the traditional jurisdiction of criminal law.[28] Second, and perhaps more important, the courts also ruled that the criminal law power authorized the federal government only to pursue these objectives with policies that used the traditional means of prohibition and punishment. The courts have always been quite firm that section 91(27) did not authorize Ottawa to develop more modern and extensive methods of social control.[29]

Other important tracts of federal jurisdiction were fenced in a similar way. For example, while the federal power over the 'seacoast and inland fisheries' was defined to include rules controlling the time and manner of fishing, regulations about recognition of fishing rights or processing and marketing of fish were said to be matters of provincial responsibility.[30] Federal treaty-making powers were also modified to protect the autonomy of the provinces. Though the Privy Council ruled that the federal executive could enter international treaties and agreements with other independent states, it said that Ottawa could not guarantee their performance where the subject-matter of the international instrument dealt with an area of provincial responsibility.[31] Similarly, in its interpretation of the federal power over marriage and divorce, the rules and criteria of marital validity and legitimacy were reserved to the provinces.[32] Here again, the courts read the list of provincial powers as implying limits on the purposes that Ottawa could pursue under its law-making powers.

The technique of implying limits on the powers of one government by looking to the jurisdiction assigned to the other has also been used to ensure that definitions of provincial powers were compatible with the federal principle. For example, in one well-known line of cases, the courts developed a doctrine of 'interjurisdictional immunity' that restricted provincial laws, wherever they were grounded, from interfering with the vital status or essential powers of such federally incorporated institutions as Bell Canada and Via Rail.[33] Similarly, in an effort to maintain a balance of power between the two orders of government, the Supreme Court has defined the provinces' power over the administration of justice (section 92[14]) as including authority to regulate matters of criminal justice but not to set up public inquiries into the commission of a specific crime.[34] The Court saw that purpose as cutting too close to the core of the federal power over criminal law and so beyond the jurisdiction of the provinces to pursue. Another narrow, but clear, example of this interpretive strategy at work is the way the courts have read the provincial power to incorporate companies (section 92[11]) as excluding power to incorporate banks, which was expressly assigned to the federal government in section 91(15).[35]

Even the 'property and civil rights' clause, which is one of the most potent sources of provincial power, has been defined by a logical or deductive method of analysis, though here the courts worked back from both the democratic character of the constitution and the principle that the status of the national and regional governments was coordinate and equal. The most famous cases in which the Supreme Court was asked to rule on the meaning of the property and civil rights clause concerned the constitutional validity of several laws enacted by the Quebec government of Maurice Duplessis in the 1950s to control use of property and distribution of literature that attacked the spiritual values and beliefs of many Quebecers.[36] The Court struck down all these laws on the ground that the property and civil rights clause did not give the provinces jurisdiction to restrict people's basic civil liberties, such as freedom of speech and religion. In effect, the Court derived a constitutional bill of rights restricting the powers of the provinces from the preamble of the Constitution Act of 1867 and from Ottawa's power over criminal law.

The development of an implied bill of rights is unquestionably one of the most dramatic examples of how the courts have reasoned logically, or deductively, to imply limitations in a part of the constitution that, on its face, seemed all-encompassing. In these and other cases,[37] the courts insisted that the power to enact laws about property and civil rights could not be used by the provinces for purposes that were fundamentally at odds with the democratic character of the Canadian state. However, perhaps the most powerful demonstration of how the courts have reasoned deductively, to work the federal principle and the idea of proportionality into the definitions of the powers of government, has been their reading of the federal power over 'trade and commerce,' and 'peace, order and good government.' These are among the largest and most all-inclusive grants of power and posed the most serious threats to the federal structure.[38] Read literally, and perhaps even according to the intention of some of those who were responsible for their inclusion in the constitution, either source of authority could have justified Ottawa's legislating on pretty much whatever it pleased.

In the minds of some of Canada's most distinguished scholars of constitutional law, the power that Ottawa was given in the preamble to section 91 – to make laws for the 'peace, order and good government' (POGG) of the country – was the most pervasive and all-encompassing in the whole constitution. For commentators such as Bora Laskin, W.P.M. Kennedy, Donald Creighton, and MacGregor Dawson, POGG was the source of all the federal government's law-making powers, including – but not limited to – those set out in the 29 enumerated paragraphs that section 91 contains. In their view, POGG was the residual, catch-all clause for the constitution and it justified federal legislation on any issue that was not explicitly assigned in section 92 to the provinces.[39]

One of the most frequently recounted stories in Canadian constitutional law concerns how the courts have struggled to find a meaning for the POGG clause that wouldn't compromise the nation's federal character. A definition that would respect and give effect to the federal principle was not transparently obvious and did not come easily to the courts. Over the course of 125 years, the courts' record has been the subject of extensive comment and criticism.

On their own, the words 'peace, order and good government' did not admit of one obvious meaning. Nor was there any historical evidence to suggest that those responsible for creating the constitution had any specific list of purposes in mind. In an early case, which was decided just before the turn of the century, the Privy Council, in reflecting on what sorts of policies the POGG power authorized the federal government to pursue, did recognize that its interpretation could have a critical impact on the autonomy of the provinces. The case is known as the *Local Prohibition* case, and in it the Privy Council was asked to consider the legitimacy of a provincial liquor licensing scheme that was very similar to a federal temperance law that it had upheld 15 years earlier. In explaining the decision to validate the provincial law, the Law Lords of the Privy Council's Judicial Committee addressed the threat that Ottawa's POGG power posed for provincial autonomy. The Law Lords wrote:

> There may, therefore, be matters not included in the enumeration, upon which the Parliament of Canada has power to legislate, because they concern the peace, order, and good government of the Dominion. But to those matters which are not specified among the enumerated subjects of legislation, the exception from s. 92, which is enacted by the concluding words of s. 91, has no application; and, in legislating with regard to such matters, the Dominion Parliament has no authority to encroach upon any class of subjects which is exclusively assigned to provincial legislatures by s. 92. These enactments appear to their Lordships to indicate that the exercise of legislative power by the Parliament of Canada, in regard to all matters not enumerated in s. 91, ought to be strictly confined to such matters as are unquestionably of Canadian interest and importance, and ought not to trench upon provincial legislation with respect to any of the classes of subjects enumerated in s. 92. To attach any other construction to the general power which, in supplement of its enumerated powers, is conferred upon the Parliament of Canada by s. 91, would, in their Lordships' opinion, not only be contrary to the intendment of the Act, but would practically destroy the autonomy of the provinces. If it were once conceded that the Parliament of Canada has authority to make laws applicable to the whole Dominion, in relation to matters which in each province are substantially of local or private interest, upon the assumption that these matters also concern the peace, order, and good government of the Dominion, there is hardly a subject enumerated in s. 92 upon which it might not legislate, to the exclusion of the provincial legislatures.[40]

Such sensitivity was not, however, always forthcoming, and the logic of the federal principle did not fully prevail until the courts had worked with the clause for over a century. Actually, the first time the Privy Council passed on the meaning of POGG, in *Russell v. The Queen*, it proposed a definition that, if allowed to stand, would have completely compromised provincial autonomy. In confirming Ottawa's power to pass temperance laws (the Canada Temperance Act), the Court ruled that POGG authorized the federal government to pass laws – in this instance, empowering local municipalities to prohibit the sale and public consumption of liquor in their communities – whenever it was felt that uniformity of legislation was desirable.[41] In later years, other members of the Privy Council tried to explain away this decision on the ground that it was based on a set of factual assumptions that bore no resemblance to those reported in the original judgment[42] and eventually accepted its continuing authority only because it had stood so long without expressly being overruled.[43]

Forty years after its decision in *Russell*, the Privy Council, led by Richard Haldane, went to the other extreme and ruled that POGG empowered the federal government only to pass laws on issues that were normally within provincial jurisdiction when there was an emergency, such as a war or the outbreak of a contagious disease,[44] and then only if the law was temporary in nature.[45] On this reading, no new issues of social policy that did not fall within one of the enumerated clauses of section 91 could ever be regarded as matters of national concern and within Ottawa's jurisdictional domain.

After Haldane stepped down from the Bench, both the Privy Council and the Supreme Court of Canada gradually resurrected the idea, recognized by William Watson in the *Local Prohibition* case, that there were issues of national concern, going beyond the exigencies of temporary emergencies, that called for regulation by the federal government – including aeronautics[46] and the organization of a region for the national capital.[47] However, it was not until 1988, in a case in which the logging giant Crown Zellerbach challenged a federal law controlling marine pollution, that the Supreme Court stood back and made a concerted effort to think logically – and publicly – about what the POGG power must mean in terms of the federal principle and the dictates of proportionality.[48]

In upholding the federal *Ocean Dumping Control Act*, the Supreme Court defined the words 'peace, order and good government' in terms of two basic rules, of rationality (necessity) and proportionality (balance). According to Justice Gerald LeDain, who wrote the judgment for the majority,[49] POGG empowered Ottawa to pass laws in those circumstances in which the provinces were restricted, either legally (constitutionally) or practically (politically), in their capacity to deal with a matter (such as marine pollution) and when the initiative did not range too broadly or impinge too deeply into areas of provincial responsibility. POGG authorized the federal government to act where it could show that there was a need for national solutions and where those solutions did not threaten provincial autonomy. As a practical matter, the Court identified, in addition to responding to emergencies affecting the country as a whole, the provinces' inability to manage effectively an issue of public policy as another legitimate rationale for the exercise of federal law-making authority.

Translating the words 'peace, order and good government' as implying a 'provincial inability' and 'scale of impact' test struck a balance (a measure of proportionality) between the two orders of government that was much more in keeping with the federal principle than were any of the earlier definitions. Although the Court did not define these tests with absolute clarity and precision and in a way that removed all ambiguity in the boundaries they drew,[50] its judgment in *Crown Zellerbach* reflected a more sophisticated and sensitive understanding of the federal character of the Canadian constitution than it had ever demonstrated in the past.

The way in which the Supreme Court has come to favour a deductive approach to defining what purposes or objectives Ottawa can pursue when it invokes its power to make laws for the peace, order, and good government of the country parallels very closely the story of how the courts have interpreted the federal power over trade and commerce. As in its reading of POGG, here again one finds a history of erratic interpretation and extreme definitions before the Supreme Court embraced the deductive approach and the logic of the federal principle.

As with the courts' reflections on what the POGG clause should be taken to mean, there were few explicit signposts available to the judges as to how to draw the boundary between the trade and commerce clause and the provinces' control over property and civil rights. Neither the words themselves, nor the intentions of those who drafted the act, gave very precise directions. In the beginning, the Privy Council was actually quite sensitive to the danger posed by the trade and commerce power.[51] As we have already seen, in the first major case in which it reflected on the meaning of section 91(2), the Privy Council endorsed the idea of interpreting the constitution holistically and deductively in order to protect the autonomy and the law-making powers of both orders of government. It was in *Citizens Insurance Co. v. Parsons* that Sir Montague Smith wrote that the lists of powers assigned to the national and regional governments 'must be read together, and the language of one interpreted, and, where necessary, modified, by that of the other.'[52] Applied to section 91(2), this approach meant: 'The words "regulation of trade and commerce," in their unlimited sense are sufficiently wide, if uncontrolled by the context and other parts of the Act, to include every regulation of trade ranging from political arrangements in regard to trade with foreign governments, requiring the sanction of parliament, down to minute rules for regulating particular trades. But a consideration of the Act shows that the words were not used in this unlimited sense.'[53] In the result,

> Construing therefore the words 'regulation of trade and commerce' by the various aids to their interpretation above suggested, they would include political arrangements in regard to trade requiring the sanction of parliament, regulation of trade in matters of inter-provincial concern, and it may be that they would include general regulation of trade affecting the whole dominion. Their Lordships abstain on the present occasion from any attempt to define the limits of the authority of the dominion parliament in this direction. It is enough for the decision of the present case to say that, in their view, its authority to legislate for the regulation of trade and commerce does not comprehend the power to regulate by legislation the contracts of a particular business or trade, such as the business of fire insurance in a single province.[54]

The idea that both orders of government had a toehold in the constitution to regulate economic and commercial activity was not one, however, that attracted the support of everyone who sat on the Bench. Richard Haldane, for example, took as decentralized and provincialist a view of this aspect of Canadian life as he did about Ottawa's power to legislate for the peace, order, and good government of the country. Soon after his arrival on the Judicial Committee, Haldane spearheaded what came to be known as the 'ancillary theory' of the trade and commerce power, which stripped section 91(2) of any independent authority and allowed it to be used only in conjunction with some other source of federal law-making power. In the same judgments in which he reduced Ottawa's power to enact laws for the peace, order, and good government of Canada to temporary interventions to relieve or prevent emergencies of national proportions, Haldane created almost insuperable constitutional impediments against the federal government's ability to act effectively in what was widely regarded as one of its primary areas of responsibility.[55]

After Haldane's departure from the scene, the courts' approach to the trade and commerce clause closely parallels the jurisprudence on

POGG. Over time, there was a conscious effort to find a definition of this power that was compatible with the federal character of the constitution. At first, the judges focused on the interprovincial part of the definition that the Privy Council had laid out in *Parsons*. In several cases, the Supreme Court reconsidered its earlier approach of erecting virtually impenetrable barriers around the provinces' jurisdiction over their local industries. Occasionally, it showed some tolerance for federal initiatives aimed at some aspect of interprovincial or international trade, even when they affected private property and civil rights in a province.[56] Where it could be shown that regulation of local trade was necessary to ensure that Ottawa could deal effectively with interprovincial and/or international matters that were within its jurisdiction, the Court displayed more understanding and sympathy for the federal position.

Rethinking their stance on the interprovincial part of federal jurisdiction over trade and commerce has not been easy for the courts. As we shall see shortly, the courts have not always been clear or consistent in saying when the powers of the two levels of government can overlap and when they cannot. However, for a long time, the courts had an even harder time reviving the 'general regulation of trade' part of the original definition propounded by Montague Smith in *Citizens Insurance Co. v. Parsons.* Until 1989 in fact, there was only one occasion when the Privy Council or Supreme Court was prepared to validate a piece of federal legislation (establishing national labelling standards) as a general regulation of trade affecting the country as a whole.[57]

The second time the Supreme Court upheld a federal initiative as a law concerned with the 'general regulation of trade affecting the whole dominion' occurred in a case called *General Motors v. City National Leasing*,[58] which was decided just a year after *Crown Zellerbach.*[59] In *General Motors*, the Court was invited to elaborate on what the power 'to regulate generally' might possibly mean, and, in responding, it turned once again to the federal principle, and in particular to the ideas of rationality (necessity) and proportionality (balance), which figure so prominently in *Crown Zellerbach.*

In *General Motors*, the Court was asked to strike down a provision in the federal *Combines Investigation Act* that allowed people injured by anti-competitive practices that were proscribed in the act to sue the perpetrators for their losses. In upholding this law, the Court breathed life into the general-regulation part of the trade and commerce power by, once again, building the principles of rationality (necessity) and proportionality (balance) right into the definition of section 91(2). For a law to be characterized as a 'general regulation of trade affecting the whole dominion,' Ottawa would have to show that both the ends and the means satisfied a basic test of necessity and reflected a measure of proportionality with the powers of the provinces to control their local economies. In the same way that it approached the federal power to pass laws for the peace, order, and good government of the country, the Court defined the scope of the trade and commerce power in terms of the provinces' inability to deal effectively with issues for which national solutions were required. Indeed, in *General Motors*, the Court pushed the logic of the federal principle one step further and insisted that not only did the purposes or objectives of the law have to meet a rule of rationality (necessity), but so did the means as well. Though the Court acknowledged that the connection between the ends and means of federal trade policy might vary with the circumstances of the case, it stressed that if a law penetrated deeply into provincial jurisdiction, it would insist on a strict linkage between the objectives pursued by the federal initiative and the particular policy instrument it employed.

Crown Zellerbach and *General Motors* are landmark cases because they show that when the courts have read the constitution purposefully, and have reasoned deductively from the federal principle on which it is based, they have been able to identify a set of criteria that can differentiate laws that are legitimate from those that are flawed, and do so in an objective and reasonably determinate way. They show the courts stretching the logic of the federal principle as far as it can reach. They say that, to be validated constitutionally under either POGG or section 91(2), not only must a law be drawn with a measure of balance, it must also meet an elementary test of rationality. Provincial autonomy is protected because both powers are defined in terms of principles of 'subsidiarity,' as the Europeans would say.[60]

Notice that, even though the actual words 'trade and commerce' and 'peace, order and good government' have nothing in common, as a practical matter they have been read by the Supreme Court to mean the same thing. To be grounded in either, a law must meet the same two criteria of rationality and proportionality. The fact that a major piece of macro-economic policy, such as the federal anti-inflation legislation of the 1970s, was upheld under POGG, rather than as a legitimate exercise of the trade and commerce power, shows how relatively unimportant the specific phrases and particular choice of words in the text really are. The Court's reading of the trade and commerce and the POGG clauses makes it clear that it is the principles of rationality and proportionality, rather than the words of the text, that do most of the work. They are the real litmus tests that tell the courts whether a law or any other government activity is constitutional or not.[61]

In *Crown Zellerbach* and *General Motors*, and indeed in all the cases considered so far, our focus has been on what the different heads of powers listed in sections 91 and 92 permit each government to do. We have seen how the courts have for the most part defined these sections in terms of the purposes or policy objectives that each order of government can legitimately pursue. Reasoning deductively, from the principles and values (viz., federalism and democracy) on which the constitution is based, the courts have identified limits on how far a Government can push these interests when it intervenes in some aspect of community life.

Maximizing Equal Sovereignty

Deciding what goals, objectives, public interests, and so on that each government can validly pursue is an essential part of the way the courts give meaning to a constitution. But it is not the only question of interpretation or definition they have to resolve. At the same time that they were laying out jurisdictional borders between Ottawa and the provinces, the courts had to come to grips with a second, equally basic interpretive question: what should these lines of legal demarcation be taken to mean? In addition to deciding where the boundaries should be drawn, the courts had to decide what effect they would have – what kind of sovereignty they would confer. Identifying the purposes and objectives – the areas of responsibility for which each order of government could exercise its law-making powers – was not enough. The courts also had to make a decision about what kind of sovereignty governments would enjoy in the territory or jurisdiction over which they had been given control.

Because the lists of powers assigned to each level of government are so extensive, even when they are read deductively and made to reflect the federal character of the Canadian state, more often than not both the federal and provincial governments can advance some interest or objective to justify their intervention in almost every aspect of community life. Frequently, both orders of government can point to valid reasons (purposes) that would justify their taking action, and when that happens the courts have had to decide how the two sets of law-making powers could best be reconciled and resolved.

Unlike with the location of the jurisdictional boundaries, on the issue of what kind of sovereignty the heads of powers conferred, the courts' options were much more constrained. As a practical matter, there were only two models of federal-provincial relations from which to choose. Either each government would be the sole and absolute ruler over the areas that fell inside its boundaries, or else their sovereignties would be defined in a more interpenetrating and integrated way. Either certain areas of social policy, such as prostitution, pornography, Sunday shopping, television advertising, elections, and abortions, would be treated as completely separate and independent categories of law-making authority, and assigned exclusively to Ottawa's control, or they could be characterized as matters of concurrent and joint responsibility, on which provincial governments might initiate local initiatives as well.

In the end, the constraints on the judges' choices in defining the limits of the law-making powers in Ottawa and the provinces did not make much difference in the performance of the courts. The judges struggled here as much as they did identifying the policy objectives that each level of government could pursue. Both conceptions of intergovernmental relations had some support in the constitution. The words in the text favoured the idea of each order of government being absolute master in its own, separate domain. The logic of the federal principle, in contrast, pointed to a system of more cooperative, overlapping responsibilities.

The document offers all kinds of evidence that, in the minds of those who actually worked out the terms of Confederation, federal-provincial relations were expected to be quite segregated and very much at arm's length. In half a dozen places, sections 91 and 92 describe the powers assigned to both Ottawa and the provinces as being 'exclusive' or 'exclusively' within the jurisdiction of one or the other. By contrast, when the drafters intended that both governments should have the power to enact laws with respect to other areas, such as agriculture and immigration, they said so quite explicitly.[62] Read literally, and at face value, the actual words of the constitution strongly supported the view that each head of power marked out distinct and discrete categories of public policy, over which one government or the other would enjoy an unfettered monopoly.

Notwithstanding the strong textual evidence that Canada's constitutional framework was originally intended to create a highly segregated system of federal-provincial relations, there was a problem with reading the constitution in this way. The difficulty is that it substantially reduces the law-making powers of both. It runs counter to the most basic values and assumptions that the federal principle is designed to promote. Rather than maximizing the sovereignty of the two orders of government over as wide an area of social policy as possible, the literal, 'originalist' interpretation portrays the division of powers as a 'zero-sum' game, in which the authority of either government can grow only through imposition of limits on the other.

The literal, categorical approach does not permit a law enacted by one level of government to have any effect on issues and policies that are within the jurisdiction of the other. The lists of subjects in sections 91 and 92 serve not only to define the powers of both orders of government but also as absolute and impenetrable constraints on the sovereignty and autonomy of the other. For example, once it is decided that street solicitation by prostitutes is a matter of criminal law, the concerns of provincial and municipal authorities for the well-being of local neighbourhoods count for nothing and are completely ignored.[63]

Even when it is recognized that a Government is pursuing an objective that is within its area of responsibility, under the categorical approach it could never act in ways that would trench even slightly on institutions and areas of community life under the control of the other level of government. For example, in *King v. Eastern Terminal Elevator* (1925), a leading case on the trade and commerce power in which the categorical approach carried the day, the Supreme Court ruled that federal authority to regulate international trade in Canadian wheat did not give it a licence to legislate on purely local – intraprovincial – transactions, even if the latter were unavoidably entangled with the international trade and accounted for only a small proportion of the grain.[64] On the view that the legislative responsibilities of the two governments were absolutely separate and distinct, considerations of balance and proportionality were dismissed as fallacious and irrelevant. According to Lyman Duff, a future chief justice of the Court, it was wrong to think of the federal principle as a rule of law, the application of which could be governed by percentages.

Despite the strong historical and textual evidence suggesting that the law-making powers of the two orders of government covered very separate and discrete areas of responsibility, reading the constitution in this way could not survive against the logic of the federal principle. The essence of the federal principle – to protect the autonomy and sovereignty of both levels of government as much as possible – directed the courts to recognize large areas of joint or concurrent responsibility. Paradoxically, defining the sovereignty of both orders of government in less absolute and categorical terms than a literal or historical reading of the text would suggest promoted the basic idea underlying the federal principle by enlarging the sovereignty of both. Concurrency was a more reasonable – rational – alternative because it allowed the popular sovereignty of both governments to grow without threatening the independence or autonomy of either.

Once the concepts of jurisdiction and sovereignty are given a softer, more permeable definition, border crossings do not automatically result in findings of constitutional invalidity. The laws of each government will, in principle, be allowed to spill over into the domain of the other. Governments will be able to pass laws that affect interests and activities normally falling outside their jurisdiction where they can show that it is essential (rational) to the effectiveness of the law to do so. In principle, it would be perfectly legitimate for both orders of government to pass identical laws regulating exactly the same areas of social policy, so long as they did not conflict with each other.[65] On a model of cooperative, concurrent, federal-provincial relations, in all these cases the law-making powers of both governments would be respected by the courts. Unless a law seriously threatened or compromised the sovereignty of the other government over policy issues that lay at the core of its jurisdiction, the logic of the federal principle would argue for its constitutional validation.

An environmental issue – such as controlling pollution in rivers and lakes and oceans – provides a good case study of how significant the difference in the two approaches can be. When the lists of powers in sections 91 and 92 are analysed deductively and defined in a way that is faithful to the idea that the two orders of government are coordinate and equal in their sovereignty, it is apparent that both orders of government have legitimate interests in protecting the environment. Ottawa's responsibilities for fisheries, navigation, and the criminal law, and provincial control over matters of health, municipal affairs, and property and civil rights, make environmental protection a matter of concern for both levels of government.[66] The difficult issue for the courts is how the legitimate aims and ambitions of each government can be accommodated so as to respect the independence and autonomy of the other.

The Supreme Court faced precisely this issue in a pair of cases – *Fowler* and *Northwest Falling*[67] – in which the constitutionality of different parts of the federal Fisheries Act was attacked. In the 1970s, when politicians began to be more conscious of environmental issues, Parliament amended its fisheries law to prohibit people putting various substances into waters inhabited by fish. The problem with the new federal rules was their potential impact on the property and civil rights of important interests and groups – especially in the forest and paper-products industry – in the provinces.

On the categorical, arm's-length approach that is supported by a literal reading of the text, this external aspect of the fisheries law would be enough to tie Ottawa's hands. If the Court had used the same reasoning that it used in *Eastern Terminal Elevator*, there would be nothing that the federal government could have done. By contrast, if the logic of the federal principle were allowed to prevail, Ottawa would have constitutional authority to do whatever was necessary (rational) to protect this important national resource, so long as it used a measure of moderation and proportionality and did not impinge too deeply into the capacity of the provinces to develop their own policies of land use control. It could act to prohibit activities known to be harmful to fish life, even though in doing so it imposed significant restrictions on what people could do with their property.

The Supreme Court had no doubt that the latter approach was the one that it should follow. However, it was equally certain that there were limits on how far Ottawa could go. Thus, at the same time as it upheld a provision that made it unlawful to put substances in water that were 'deleterious' to fish, the Court also ruled that another section of the act that purported to prohibit putting any debris into any water that was inhabited by fish, whether or not it was actually harmful, went too far. A provision as pervasive as that could not pass the proportionality test. In the Court's mind, not only was such a sweeping interdiction not linked sufficiently with the purposes of the Fisheries Act, but it would have had enormous implications for the logging industry as well. No one on the Court was prepared to say that protecting fisheries against every conceivable risk, no matter how improbable and insignificant, was more important – counted more – than provincial control over harvesting and managing of forestry resources.

Although *Fowler* and *Northwest Falling* might not qualify as landmark cases in terms of the national importance of the federal policies under attack, the decisions are instructive from a conceptual or jurisprudential point of view. They reveal a good deal about the substance and method of Canadian constitutional law. Reading the two cases together, one can see the Supreme Court avoiding an all-or-nothing, categorical approach and trying to reconcile the interests of the two orders of government in a more sensitive and accommodating way. Even though the Court never expressed its thinking in so many words, the cases show how the principles of rationality and proportionality can be used not only to define the goals and objectives that each level of government can legitimately pursue but also to establish a framework of analysis for those situations in which both levels of government can point to different aspects of the public interest to justify their intervention. As a practical matter, the lesson of the Court's judgments in these two cases is that Ottawa can pass laws that promote valid federal purposes, even though they impinge on matters under provincial control, so long as the overlap is necessarily incidental to the realization of federal policy (rationality) and does not cut too deeply (proportionality) into the provinces' sovereignty over their own affairs.

The example of how the courts have come to assign jurisdiction between Parliament and the provinces with respect to protecting the environment illustrates how the logic of trying to maximize the sovereignty of both orders of government argues for defining their jurisdictions as concurrent and overlapping and countermands the words of the text, which suggest a more arm's-length, segregated system of intergovernmental relations. It is part of the larger story of how, in conflicts between a logical and a literal or historical reading of the constitution, logic has gradually prevailed. Bit by bit, more and more areas of social policy have come to be regarded as matters of shared responsibility. In doctrinal terms, the courts have shown a strong preference for rules and standards derived from and giving expression to ideas of rationality and proportionality.

CONSTITUTIONAL LAW

The Rules

Unquestionably the best-known and most important of these tests is what has come to be called the 'double aspect' rule.[68] According to this doctrine, an area of social policy or human activity may have one feature – or aspect – that brings it within the jurisdiction of one level of government and another feature that brings it within the sphere of the other. Sunday shopping, pornography, children's advertising, and environmental protection in fact are all matters that the courts have said have both a federal and a provincial dimension. These are issues where the courts have recognized that the federal and provincial interests are so equally balanced (well proportioned) that both have good reason to regulate them.

Though the double aspect doctrine has been applied by the courts from the beginning,[69] its use has grown exponentially over time. Even though the constitution talks of powers being assigned 'exclusively' to one order of government or the other, and specifically earmarks only four areas where their jurisdiction overlaps and is shared,[70] the courts have championed a scheme of cooperative federalism that complements parallel initiatives by the politicians to develop their own institutions and processes of constitutional reform.

Criminal law, though formally assigned to the federal government, has practically become a matter of shared jurisdiction.[71] The courts have come to recognize that provincial governments, as well as Ottawa, have the power to pass laws proscribing and punishing pornography, sharp and unethical business practices, as well as socially unacceptable behaviour in public places (for example, reckless driving on highways). The Sunday shopping, television advertising, marketing board, and labour relations cases show that trade and commerce has also become an area of joint jurisdiction. On other matters that are not expressly allocated by the constitution, such as the environment and communications, we have already seen that the courts have opted for a concurrent approach as well. In his locus classicus, Peter Hogg lists insolvency, temperance, interest rates, support of spouses and custody of children, entertainment in taverns, and fisheries as other domains where the two orders of government are allowed to exercise their law-making powers concurrently.

Double aspect has been an important analytical tool, by which the courts have been able to harness the idea of balance or proportionality to strengthen the federal principle's commitment to the independence and autonomy of both levels of government. Across a wide range of issues they have designated the national and local perspectives as being equally worthy of recognition and respect. However, the double aspect doctrine was not the only legal rule developed by the courts to enlarge the scope of both federal and provincial powers. Closely allied with it are the 'pith and substance' rule and the 'ancillary' (or 'necessarily incidental') doctrine.[72] Like 'double aspect,' these are labels used by the courts to describe their assessment of the laws that they have been asked to review – to say what they think – overall and on balance –

a law is all about. According to these principles, if a law rationally pursues a set of objectives that are within the law-making powers of that government, the courts will affirm its constitutional integrity, even though it affects interests and activities that normally fall within the jurisdiction of the other level of government, so long as it can be shown that any cross-border effects are necessarily incidental to the efficacy of that law (rationality) and do not impinge on the sovereignty of other governments in a way that threatens their autonomy (proportionality).

Though some scholars have argued that there is no need for a separate, ancillary doctrine because it is part and parcel of the pith and substance rule,[73] there is no dispute that whatever label one wishes to use, this line of reasoning extends the areas of concurrent sovereignty. Together the pith and substance rule and the ancillary doctrine have strengthened the federal character of the constitution by enlarging the fields of social policy over which both levels of government have some authority to act.

In addition to developing doctrines to validate laws that affect matters that are normally within the jurisdiction of the other order of government, the courts also devised a rule to promote the federal principle in those cases where both levels of government actually exercise their sovereignty and pass laws covering the same issue or area of public policy. In such cases, a court must decide if the two laws should be permitted to live together, or if one should fall in the face of the other. If the court decides that the two laws cannot live together, it must then pick a rule to determine which law – or government – should prevail. This is the so-called paramountcy rule.[74]

The question whether two laws are so incompatible that they simply cannot, as a matter of practice, both operate simultaneously is an important one for the courts to get right. If the judges adopted too loose a definition of what constituted conflicting positions between the two orders of government, the federal structure could be seriously weakened. Once it is accepted that the constitution allows for a lot of overlapping and concurrent powers, a definition of conflict that was too open-ended and easy to meet might allow Ottawa (whose laws are deemed paramount whenever a conflict is found to exist) to usurp provincial powers in a way that would undermine the federal character of the Canadian state.[75]

Fortunately, on virtually every occasion on which they have addressed this question, the courts have consistently favoured a narrow and stringent definition of inconsistency.[76] They have adopted a rule that results in the validation of both sets of laws except in the extreme case where compliance with one defeats the purpose of the other. Unless it is impossible for those affected by the laws to comply with both simultaneously, or unless one law frustrates the purposes of the other, the courts have respected the sovereignty of both levels of government to address the interests and activities that are the subject of the legislation in whatever way they see fit.

Doctrines such as double aspect, pith and substance, and paramountcy, which the judges developed to help them classify and reconcile the laws that they have been asked to review, are among the most basic and well-known rules of Canadian constitutional law. They have been of critical importance to the courts in their effort to promote a constitutional structure in which the sovereignty of both orders of government is allowed to range over as wide a territory as possible.

Alongside these rules, which are the staples of every first-year course in constitutional law, we should take note of two other doctrines that the courts have developed to encourage the federal and provincial authorities to work through informal, ad hoc adjustments to the constitution. First – and even though again it initially seemed to the courts that it was inconsistent with the intentions of the framers and the language of the text – the judges were able to work through a doctrine of 'delegation,' which effectively allows one level of government to ask the other to take charge of an area of public policy that would normally be its responsibility.[77] Similarly, and perhaps of even more practical significance, the Supreme Court has upheld the constitutionality of Ottawa's 'spending powers,' whereby it makes grants of money (or taxes) available to the provinces for programs in health, education, and welfare – areas primarily within provincial jurisdiction – on condition that these services are provided in a way that meets basic federal objectives.[78] Like the other interpretive doctrines, the delegation decisions and the rule of conditional grants give expression to the federal principle and the idea that unless the sovereignty and autonomy of either government are at stake, (constitutional) law should respect and accommodate the wishes of the people as much as it possibly can.

The Rules and the Record of the Court

So far, all our energies have been devoted to description. My concern has been to get as accurate a picture as possible of the method that the courts have favoured when they have been asked to read the constitution and give meaning to its text. From our review of the cases, we have seen that 'mutual modification' and 'concurrency' have been the most important doctrines or devices for both the Privy Council and the Supreme Court. Following logically from the federal principle and the idea that the two orders of government enjoy equal and coordinate status, these two interpretive axioms have provided the courts with a framework of analysis that gives expression to principles of rationality and proportionality and allows them to distinguish laws that are constitutionally valid from those that are not.

With this picture of the courts' framework of analysis and process of reasoning clearly in view, we should stand back and reflect for a moment on what the courts' experience teaches us about the day-to-day practice of constitutional law. What should we make of the jurisprudence that we have reviewed? As a practical matter, unquestionably the most important lesson is the recognition that all of the most vital rules and doctrines of constitutional law reflect and give effect to two simple, straightforward tests of legitimation. Generally laws will be judged to be constitutionally valid if they can pass two basic tests, of rationality and proportionality. As we have seen, these principles have been built right into the definitions of the most significant grants of federal power. Rationality and proportionality are what the words 'trade and commerce,' and 'peace, order and good government' are now understood to mean. It is these principles, not the words of the text, that tell the courts whether a law is constitutional or not.

Similarly, the double aspect, pith and substance, necessarily incidental, and paramountcy rules have allowed the courts to bring the principles of rationality and proportionality to bear in the second stage of the review process in the same way in which ideas of mutual modification and concurrency introduced them in the first. Once it is established that a law serves an aim or objective (aspect) that is within the power of the government that enacted it to pursue, it should be validated as constitutional unless it can be shown to fail the tests of rationality and proportionality in some way. Only those parts of a law that cannot be shown to be 'necessarily incidental' to legitimate purposes will be struck down by the courts.

In suggesting that all the major rules and doctrines of federalism law give expression to two basic tests of constitutional validation, one must resist two temptations. On the one hand, even though the principles of rationality and proportionality are very accommodating of the 'will of the people' and their elected representatives, it would be wrong to assume that they do not provide any meaningful protection against one government's acting in a way that compromises the jurisdiction of another. On the other hand, one must guard against the equally naive belief that the protection that the law can provide is infallible and 'fail-safe' in every case. In fact, as we have seen, the simplicity and coherence of the operative principles of constitutional law are no guarantee that they will always be applied sensitively and sensibly by the courts.

The fact that the basic rules of constitutional law that have been developed by the courts have generally marked out a pretty broad range of territory in which both governments can roam does not mean that politicians can do whatever or go wherever they please. Even though it is usually quite easy to point to one of the heads of power to identify some valid aspect that a legislature is allowed to pursue, the principles of rationality and proportionality are meaningful monitors of the law-making powers of both orders of government. They are standards with a critical edge.

We have already seen, in cases such as *Fowler* and *Northwest Falling*, that the federal interest in protecting the environment will not justify policies that cut too deeply into provincial jurisdiction, especially when it is unclear just how much good they will do. Similarly, the Supreme Court has struck down parts of Ottawa's food and drug standards that were not related to health and safety, when they were seen to threaten provincial sovereignty over the terms and conditions on which local trade was conducted and when alternative, less invasive policies could have been used to accomplish Parliament's purposes.[79]

Rationality and proportionality have also reined in provincial governments that have acted overzealously in pursuit of local agendas. Earlier, we saw that the Supreme Court has not been hesitant to strike down provincial laws that significantly restricted Ottawa's power to conduct its own elections and guarantee people's political and civil rights, especially when the property interests the provincies promoted were marginal or tenuous at best.[80] Similarly, where it was thought that provincial governments had been overly aggressive in using their powers to tax[81] or conduct public inquiries into the administration of justice,[82] and not sufficiently sensitive to the federal interests at stake, the Court has acted decisively to protect the sovereignty of the federal government.

Such decisions should dispel any thought that the rules of constitutional law permit governments to do whatever they please. *Labatt Breweries* and *Dominion Stores*, *McKay* and *Starr* make it clear that constitutional standards of rationality and proportionality really do have some bite. However, in cataloguing the cases where either federal or provincial laws have been struck down as insufficiently attentive to the sovereignty of the other, It is important to acknowledge that the courts have not proven to be an absolutely reliable check.

The fact is, as we have seen, the record of the courts is far from perfect. I have referred to various cases in which, in giving meaning to some of the most important clauses of the constitution, the courts' performance has been erratic and inconsistent. In fixing the boundaries around the POGG clause and Ottawa's power over trade and commerce, the judges have been all over the map. The definitions of these powers have fluctuated radically between those that would permit the federal government to do pretty much whatever it pleased, and those that would add practically nothing to its power to pass laws in the national interest.

Even today, commentators complain that the current definitions are still too loose and open-ended to provide objective and determinative criteria that can distinguish laws that are in conformity with the constitution from those that are not.[83] Questions remain, they say – about whether the 'inability of the provinces' refers to legal, constitutional impediments on provincial powers, or also to political unwillingness or incapacity to act; about the scope of Ottawa's authority to assert jurisdiction on the basis that some matter is beyond the provinces' (legal and/or practical) control; and about what kind of evidence is required to prove that federal legislation is necessary to fashion an effective solution for the policy area to which the law is directed. Because the courts have yet to provide clear answers to such questions, these commentators argue that indeterminacy and indefiniteness continue to plague the most important federal grants of power and still permit each judge to decide each case on his or her own views of what will be best for the country, rather than on the basis of some fixed or settled rule of law. From their perspective, the fact the Supreme Court divided 5:4 in applying the provincial-inability test in *Crown Zellerbach* illustrates how malleable the definitions of rationality and proportionality remain even now.

Unevenness and ambiguity have also plagued the courts' position on the reach of the powers of the federal and provincial governments when they are pursuing policy objectives that fall within their areas of recognized responsibility. As we have seen, the courts have struggled on this second interpretive question as much as they have delineating which goals and objectives each level of government can pursue under the different heads of power in sections 91 and 92. Though the cases reveal that, over time, the courts have shown an unmistakable preference for characterizing the law-making powers of both orders of government as concurrent and overlapping, judges continue on occasion to draw very bright lines around the jurisdiction of both orders of government and to regard the sovereignty of each as operating over very discrete and mutually exclusive domains.

Whenever the courts have defined the areas of responsibility of the two orders of government in terms of mutually exclusive, watertight categories, they have implicitly abandoned the tests of rationality and proportionality in favour of criteria of constitutional legitimacy that are much more demanding and much more difficult to meet. On the highly segregated, arm's-length relationship that the categorical approach implies, a law will be invalidated without regard to the public interest that it promotes or to the fact that the 'border crossing' is relatively trivial and insignificant. Regardless of how well a law might measure up in terms of rationality and proportionality, on this approach it can be struck down just because it crosses over into territory usually regulated by the other level of government.

Some of the most highly criticized rulings that the courts have handed down over the years are cases where they have embraced this stricter, all-or-nothing standard. We have already seen how the Supreme Court blocked Ottawa's attempt to establish a comprehensive system of grading and cleaning grain in order to enhance the saleability of Canadian wheat in international markets. *Eastern Terminal* remains one of the most notorious examples of the Court's insisting on a stricter standard of review than what the principles of rationality and proportionality imply.[84] Constitutional law is not made up of principles, said the Court, in which percentages can carry the day.

The federal government's treaty-making powers are widely thought to have been undermined in a similar way.[85] Even when major national interests are at stake, the courts have been adamant that Ottawa has no licence to pass laws on subjects that fall within the provincial domain in order to live up to international obligations that they have incurred.

Many provincial policies have suffered a similar fate. Attempts by provinces – to control production of their natural resources by quotas and price restrictions;[86] or to stabilize conditions in the farming community by establishing marketing boards for the sale and distribution of agricultural products;[87] or to license cable operators in the province[88] – have been struck down when the Court invoked the more rigid, categorical standard of *no* cross-border effects. We have seen how legitimate provincial interests in regulating the quality of life on the streets were ignored by the Supreme Court when it ruled that every aspect of prostitution was a matter of criminal law and exclusively within Ottawa's domain. As well, provincial desires to have local labour laws applied uniformly throughout their jurisdiction have been frustrated by decisions of the courts that provide immunity to federal institutions and companies (such as Bell Canada, and Via Rail) even when core issues of federal sovereignty are not at stake.[89]

Typically, the difficulties that the courts have had in deciding the extent to which the powers of the two levels of government can overlap and operate concurrently have manifested themselves in the second stage of the review process, when the judges' attention is focused on the law itself. So far, I have said very little about this second phase, even though, as we saw in chapter 1, interpreting the constitution typically represents a small part of the courts' work in cases that are litigated today. In most cases, the definitions are taken as a given, and almost all the energy of the courts is expended in the second stage, when the focus is on the law whose constitutionality is in dispute.

At this point in the review process, the courts really have only one task to perform. The job, very simply, is to size up the law. The court must make a judgment about how the statute in question can best be characterized or described. The judges must say what they think the law is all about – what it is trying to do. Examining both its purposes and its effects, the court must decide whether, on balance (in 'pith and substance'), the law is directed to one of the purposes or goals that are within the domain of the government that enacted it and whether it impinges too deeply into the powers assigned to the other order of government (viz., meets the test of proportionality).

As we saw in chapter 1, in the second phase, the line of reasoning followed by the court is different than in the first. In the first stage, the court typically reasons deductively, interpreting each grant of power to give expression to the federal principle. In the second stage, in contrast, the court relies much more on reasoning by analogy. For the most part, the courts examine how laws of a similar kind have been slotted in the past. The judges look to earlier cases to see where, in the constitution, laws that are most like (analogous to) the one under review have been grounded before. At this stage, their primary concern is to ensure that their analysis of a law is consistent with their own past decisions. As a check on the integrity of their own characterization of the law being reviewed, the courts turn to earlier precedents to ensure that their treatment of the law-making powers of the two levels of government is more or less consistent over time.

Though this comparative exercise might not appear especially problematic for the courts, many judges have experienced even more difficulty here than in the first phase when they face what seem to be much larger and more open-ended interpretive questions about how the two long lists of powers should be reconciled and defined. In many cases, the courts' evaluation of the challenged law has been much too one-sided and radically incomplete. Too frequently, the interests and objectives of one level of government are simply avoided and ignored. In other cases, the courts have handed down rulings that seem entirely inconsistent with earlier precedents, without making any attempt to explain or reconcile their decisions. As more than one scholar has remarked, the principles and the cases seem to march in pairs.[90]

Examples of both kinds of failures abound in the reports. In cases such as *CIGOIL* and *Potash*,[91] where the Court struck down efforts by the Saskatchewan Government to conserve its natural gas and potash resources by complex schemes of taxation, price controls, and quotas, and in its decision in *Westendorp*,[92] where the Court invalidated Calgary's attempt to control prostitution on its streets, the judges looked solely at the federal interests affected by these laws and paid almost no regard to the legitimate interests – policy objectives – that had prompted Saskatchewan and Calgary to act. The Court's assessment of Calgary's anti-solicitation by-law typifies this approach. Rather than using the double aspect doctrine or the pith and substance rule, the Court reverted to the classic all-or-nothing, categorical approach and characterized the city's initiative as an illegitimate attempt to invade federal jurisdiction over criminal law. Rather than openly and fairly trying to evaluate the concerns of both governments about activities of this kind, the Court studiously ignored the provincial interest in regulating the quality of life in its neighbourhoods and on its streets, and played down its minimal effect on federal jurisdiction to regulate the legality of prostitution itself. Rather than acknowledging that the by-law regulated only one place where this activity might be conducted, and that the core of the federal government's power over prostitution remained largely intact, the Court insisted on giving Ottawa a complete monopoly over this aspect of city life.

The erratic and inconsistent way in which the courts have sometimes treated social policies and legislative initiatives that seem to have a lot in common with one another is notorious in Canadian constitutional law. Across the full spectrum of cases touching on trade and commerce, criminal law and morality, politics and elections, civil liberties and human rights, one can find decisions that, if not fundamentally in conflict with each other, are very poorly explained. Over the years, for example, the provinces have been told that they may enact laws to regulate prices of inputs of products destined for interprovincial markets but not prices of the products themselves;[93] to regulate activities of trade unions and their own public servants in federal elections but not the freedom of ordinary citizens to put up election signs on their lawns;[94] and to control solicitation and display of sexual activities in nightclubs and bars but not on a city's streets.[95] So pervasive has the courts' inconsistency been that many leading scholars of constitutional law have concluded that there is no 'principled basis' on which the rulings can be justified or explained.[96]

However lamentable the courts' record, the idea that judicial review is inherently an unprincipled (and therefore illegitimate) method of differentiating laws that are consistent with the constitution from those that are not seems much too pessimistic and extreme. First, it ignores the fact that over time the courts have demonstrated that they are getting better at the job. Especially in the first phase of the review process, when they decide what the words of the constitution should be taken to mean, we have seen the courts showing increasing sensitivity to the federal principle and the rules of mutual modification and concurrency that it logically entails. More than ever before, the Supreme Court has embraced the federal principle and the method of deductive, or purposeful interpretation to give meaning to the constitution.

Those who would challenge the integrity of judicial review and argue that disputes between the federal and provincial governments should be resolved politically by negotiation and compromise also ignore the fact that many of the cases that they correctly condemn for the judges' failure to explain adequately their conclusions could have been justified if the courts had remained faithful to the principles of rationality and proportionality. The fact that the courts have not always written their judgments in these terms doesn't mean that the decisions cannot be justified in this way.

In *McKay v. The Queen* (1965), for example, which has been roundly condemned by commentators and judges alike,[97] the Supreme Court's decision that municipalities cannot prohibit the display of political posters in federal elections can be defended as a sensitive reconciliation of the federal and provincial interests involved. Even if the Court was not as explicit and forthcoming as it might have been, it seems quite reasonable to say that, when a by-law allows some people, such as real estate agents and physicians, to post signs advertising their wares, the local interest in keeping neighbourhood lawns free of election posters for six weeks every four or five years pales by comparison to the federal interest in allowing citizens to express their political preferences in what, in Canada at least, is a common and widely accepted method of political participation. When the by-law already accommodates the interests of doctors and realtors, it is impossible to argue that the interests of ordinary citizens to express themselves politically for very brief periods of time are not as important or that their signs would have a significant impact on the municipality's interest in protecting the aesthetics of its neighbourhoods.

Similarly, a case such as *Saumur v. Quebec* – where the Supreme Court has been fairly taken to task for failing to give any weight to the genuine offence that was felt by a large segment of Quebec society vis-à-vis the religious pamphlets and tracts that were being published and distributed by the Jehovah's Witnesses – can be defended on principles of rationality and proportionality. Even if proper weight is given to the purposes that motivated enactment of the by-law, the way it was drafted, which gave police officers virtually unfettered discretion to prohibit the publication and distribution of any literature or pamphlets, seems much more sweeping and heavy-handed than was necessary to ensure that Quebecers' moral sensitivities were not subjected to ridicule and abuse.

Other controversial and contested cases can be explained in a similar way. For example, though critics have condemned the Court's failure to explain why Quebec was allowed to set up a marketing scheme fixing the price of inputs for milk products destined for interprovincial trade, while Manitoba was prohibited from creating a provincial marketing board to control the production and sale of eggs within its borders, the two cases can be reconciled if one pays close attention to the extra-provincial interests at stake. In the *Carnation* case, the effect of Quebec's Agricultural Marketing Act on the interests of consumers outside the province was insignificant compared to the welfare of the local farming community, which profited by the program, and to the extra-provincial interests that could be adversely affected by Manitoba's marketing scheme.[98] In the latter case, even though the Court expressly played down this factor, there was a significant chance that local producers could have used the legislation to discriminate against egg producers outside the province and, in so doing, to impose significant losses on a group of individuals that had no opportunity to participate in the development and the operation of the scheme.

In many cases, then, even though the courts' treatment of the relevant interests and prior decisions can be criticized as superficial and inadequate, it does not follow that the process of judicial review is inherently subjective and unprincipled. To the contrary, close attention to the facts of the cases shows that many of the most notorious decisions can be defended and explained in a principled and objective way. Moreover, even cases such as CIGOIL, *Potash*, and *Westendorp*, where the principles of rationality and proportionality cannot be advanced to rescue the decisions, do not provide any support for the conclusion that judicial review is a flawed institution, prone to generating subjective and arbitrary results. Quite the contrary, in fact. These cases, as much as those that can be salvaged in terms of rationality and proportionality, offer still more evidence that law and legal reasoning can produce objective and determinate results. It is precisely because decisions such as CIGOIL, *Potash*, and *Westendorp* cannot meet the standards of rationality and proportionality that we know they are wrong. We are certain that the Supreme Court erred badly in striking down the provincial laws in these cases only because, when we measure the decisions against principles of rationality and proportionality, it seems so clear that the local interests at stake dominate any national, pan-Canadian interests that may have been involved.

In *Westendorp*, the municipal by-law that outlawed street solicitation by prostitutes served a compelling provincial interest in protecting the quality of life in local neighbourhoods in a way that respected Ottawa's sovereignty and its decision not to make prostitution an offence. The mistake in *Westendorp* was human error, not a failing in the conceptual apparatus available to the Court. If the judges had embraced the principles of rationality and proportionality and if concurrency had been applied in the usual way, the Court would have validated the by-law and supported the legitimate efforts of Canadian cities to control the quality of their neighbourhoods and streets. It would have supported the expression of the popular will in Calgary without impairing the federal government's power to make prostitution illegal when and as it saw fit.

It would have ruled in a way to maximize the sovereignty of the Canadian people at all levels of government.

Similarly, the lesson to be learned from the criticisms that can fairly be levelled at cases such as *CIGOIL* and *Potash* is that, had the Supreme Court applied the principles of rationality and proportionality impartially and even-handedly, it would have validated the efforts of Saskatchewan's government to conserve and manage its natural resources. This is especially true in the *CIGOIL* case, where the provincial tax had no net effect on out-of-province consumers and international trade.[99] Once again, we can be confident in our criticism of the Court's treatment of provincial attempts to control their own natural resources because it is possible to say, as a matter of rationality and proportionality, what is right. Once again, popular sovereignty is being sacrificed even though no federal interest is enhanced as a result.

THE POSSIBILITY OF JUDICIAL REVIEW

As students read through these federalism cases in their courses in first-year law, it is not uncommon for them to feel a sense of dissatisfaction. Some are disturbed by the fact that there are cases in which the principles of rationality and proportionality do not seem to provide any clear answers where there are sharp differences between themselves and the rest of the class on whether a law should be upheld as being constitutional or not. For them, the idea that two principles of review can explain all constitutional law will be badly overstated. Others will have exactly the opposite reaction. For them, the fact that there are so many cases where the reasoning is faulty and the principles of rationality and proportionality are ignored is cause for despair. Whatever the logic and coherence of understanding constitutional law in this way, they believe that history makes it clear that it is not a lesson that the judges are likely to embrace.

Both reactions are entirely natural. After reading the cases that we have reviewed so far, students have good reason to respond in either or both of these ways. Fortunately, the reality is not as desperate as either of these initial perceptions would suggest, and on reflection most students come to see that both the integrity of the law and the efficacy of the courts are still within our power to control.

For the first group of students, relief usually comes when they contemplate how infrequently sharp divisions in the class actually occur. In most cases, the 'right' answer is evident to virtually everyone. The hard cases, where reasonable people can disagree about what rationality and proportionality require, are the exceptions which prove the rule.

The fact that there are hard as well as easy cases does not prove that constitutional law is fatally subjective or radically incomplete.[100] The numerous cases we have just reviewed, in which the principles of rationality and proportionality do provide clear answers, prove that judicial review is not a process in which each judge just evaluates the competing interests at stake according to his or her own (political) views about what division of powers would be best for the country. Constrained by the principles of rationality and proportionality, the judges should not decide cases such as *Westendorp* or *McKay* by ruling in favour of the level of government that they believe can address the underlying social-political issues best, as many students are taught. To the contrary, the role of the court is to decide whether the law meets the standards of rationality and proportionality and not whether it conforms to its vision of how power should be divided between Ottawa and its provincial counterparts. The role of the court in such cases is to make a judgment about how important the municipal by-laws were to the legitimate interests of the federal and provincial governments, in terms of the way related interests were treated in the by-laws and the relevant federal legislation and not as a matter of crudely assigning weights to the competing interests in the abstract.

In applying these principles, each judge will have a certain amount of discretion in deciding how these two principles should be applied, but that is not fatal to the integrity of the law. No rule or principle in any area of law is self-enforcing, and constitutional law is no exception. There are close cases when the decision could go either way. But even here, the principles constrain the reasoning process and direct the judges to analyse the rationality and proportionality of the challenged law and preclude them from giving effect to the political values and visions they care about most.

The reaction of those who worry about the failure of the law to provide crystal-clear answers in every case is actually much less acute and easier to assuage than those who look at the erratic record of the courts and wonder whether constitutional law can ever be done right. The scepticism of the latter is much more extreme. Their despair is based on the fact that not only do judges have a discretion on how the relevant principles and doctrines should be applied, they seem to have the final say on whether this method of analysis and process of reasoning will be followed at all.

On reflection, however, the thought that one should simply abandon the law because the judges have not been as faithful to its most basic precepts as they should seems much too extreme. That the courts have not always applied the principles of rationality and proportionality as faithfully and even-handedly as they should is cause for concern, but not for despair. It certainly does not argue for replacing judicial review with some other institution or process of dispute resolution. The moral of Canadian federalism law is that in every case in which the constitutionality of a law is challenged, the judges should apply these two basic criteria as vigorously and consistently as they can.

To rectify the courts' uneven performance, one must improve the institution – the process – not the law. One must look for ways to ensure that the judges will apply the principles of rationality and proportionality more faithfully than they have in the past. To be able to tell a more positive story of constitutional review, we need to pay more attention to the law, not less. Calls for political institutions to perform the function of interstitial constitutional reform instead of the courts ignore the very real contribution that law has made to adapting the structure of federal-provincial relations to meet the modern needs of the Canadian state. Even if their role has been a supporting one, and even if their performance would not win them any international awards, the judges on the Supreme Court of Canada and the Privy Council have developed a set of principles and doctrines and an analytical method that have added strength and substance to the federal character of the Canadian state.[101]

The fact that the courts have failed to apply the principles and method of analysis as consistently and even-handedly as they could does not undermine the integrity of the process or take away the contribution that law can – and has – made. The problem is not with the rules of constitutional law but in how they have been applied. To ensure that the courts stop writing judgments that are poorly reasoned and interfere with the process of constitutional adjustment and reform requires more attention and fidelity to the core principles of constitutional law, not less. The solution is to ensure that only people who are committed to the federal character of Canada, and the legal principles that that implies, are appointed to the courts.

In the past, the system by which judges have been selected for the highest courts has allowed for the appointment of people whose commitment to one level of government or the other is so strong as to compromise their ability to apply the principles of rationality and proportionality impartially and even-handedly. In the pantheon of judges who have sat on Canada's highest courts, it is easy to identify those who consistently applied the principles of constitutional validation in favour of one order of government or the other. Ironically, some of the worst offenders are among the most celebrated and powerful legal thinkers who have sat on the Bench. For all their understanding and learning in law, Richard Haldane and Bora Laskin, perhaps more than anyone else, applied the principles of rationality and proportionality with their thumbs on the scales.[102]

Law is not one of those human artefacts, such as computer programs, that are capable of automatic, mechanical application. In this, law is a lot like playing golf. It is not self-enforcing. Only if the judges apply the basic principles and doctrines rigorously and impartially will law be able to play its part in maintaining the federal character of the country and to silence the relentless criticisms that have been levelled at the courts. When they have adhered to such rules as the double aspect doctrine and the provincial inability test, the courts have been able to maximize popular soverignty in the country and, at the same time, promote the kind of cooperative federalism that many critics believe should be the primary method of informal constitutional reform. When they have remained faithful to the precepts of rationality and proportionality, courts have encouraged a highly integrated system of federal-provincial relations, in which the legislative authority of politicians at both levels of government is allowed to flourish as much as possible.

The rigorous enforcement of rationality and proportionality should appeal to the critics because it promotes a system of intergovernmental relations and informal constitutional adjustment in which the political branches of government have considerable latitude in structuring their relations to suit their needs. It should also find favour with people who believe that government works best when the will of the people and the power of the state are made subordinate to the rules of law. Appointing people to the Supreme Court who are absolutely committed to the principles of rationality and proportionality would ensure that although governments could adjust and adapt to meet the needs of the times, those who exercise the powers of the state would always be obliged to respect the most basic principles of justice which inhere in the rule of law.

3

Human Rights

INTRODUCTION

Until 17 April 1982, the only constitutional cases that Canadian courts had heard were arguments about which order of government had authority to rule. These were disputes between those who claimed to speak on behalf of all Canadians, in the national interest, and those who were elected to serve people in one of the ten provinces that make up the Canadian state. The rules of constitutional law were developed to decide which of these two groups of people – which majority – should control different areas of public policy and issues of social concern. Constitutional law adjusted the boundaries between the Government acting for the country as a whole and those whose mandate was to represent more local and regional communities. With the law, the courts could ensure that the division of powers between the two orders of government would be carried out in a way that maximized the sovereignty of both.

On 17 April 1982, a bill of rights was entrenched in the Canadian constitution, and two years later the Supreme Court of Canada heard its first 'Charter' case. In addition to mediating disputes about the sovereignty of two interdependent communities, the courts were given the task of defining the limits of law-making powers within each. As well as reconciling the claims of competing majorities, the courts were now being asked to develop rules to coordinate relations between the majority and various minority groups in both the political life of the country as a whole and in the more local affairs of the provinces.

In the very first cases that the Court heard under the Charter, the judges recognized that, despite all the fanfare that had surrounded its entrenchment,[1] the basic nature of their role had not really changed. In Charter cases, the courts would be required to evaluate laws passed by either order of government against the strictures of the new constitutional text, just as in federalism cases they had had to define the limits of the law-making powers in Ottawa and the provinces. In the Court's mind, the only change was that the Charter extended the range of values that the constitution guaranteed and that it would be responsible for defending.[2] In addition to protecting the federal character of the Canadian state, courts were now being asked to develop rules of (constitutional) law that promoted the idea of personal autonomy and the concept of human rights.

WHAT DO THE WORDS MEAN?

The Court also discovered very quickly that it faced exactly the same sorts of problems developing rules to settle relations between majorities and minorities in a single province, or in the country as a whole, as it had in resolving disputes between the federal government and its provincial counterparts. Here again, the words of the constitution seemed to provide little guidance as to where the line between the will of the majority and the rights of minorities ought to be drawn. Once again, the inspirational and elevated style of the text seemed to say too little and too much.

The words of the Charter, like the broad phrases of the original BNA Act (now called the Constitution Act, 1867), shed little light on the hard, practical questions about the kinds of human-rights violations that the Court was asked to address. The phrases themselves were quite opaque. How could the Court distinguish between interests and activities that qualified as constitutional rights and those that did not, simply by reading the text? How could the judges tell whether prostitution, pornography, picketing, or children's advertising were modes of expression that enjoyed the protection of the Charter? Is the right to strike or join a union included in the guarantee of freedom of association? Does liberty or personal security include the right to have an abortion or a job? Do Sunday shopping laws interfere with the religious freedom of those who do not adhere to the Christian faith? On specific and concrete questions such as these, the words of the Charter seemed to provide virtually no help at all.

Once again, the Supreme Court had to provide definitions for words and phrases of potentially limitless and infinite scope. Like their colleagues who had decided the first federalism cases 125 years earlier, the judges needed good dictionaries – sources of meaning – to assist them in marking out the boundaries of the rights and freedoms that the Charter guaranteed. Once again, in the first Charter cases, the judges had to find their way pretty much on their own. It was impossible for them to benefit from the wisdom of those who had preceded them on the Court, and so they had to look elsewhere for help.

As a practical matter, the Court faced the same choices that it confronted when it began to read the large and open-ended grants of power that were embedded in the Constitution Act of 1867. It could look for assistance from sources either inside the Charter or outside it. It could either adopt an internal, holistic – deductive – approach in trying to specify exactly which interests and activities fell within the rights and freedoms that the Charter guaranteed, or it could rely on more historical and/or literal analyses or have reference to external sources for the definitions that it had to provide.

External Aids: American and Canadian Bills of Rights

External aids, it turned out, were as unhelpful here as they were in deciphering the Constitution Act of 1867. Ordinary dictionaries could not identify which interests and activities would qualify as one of the rights or freedoms the Charter guaranteed,[3] and early on, the Court rejected two professional possibilities as equally unhelpful.

It might appear, at first blush, that the judges' situation in 1982 was not as desperate as had been the case for those who sat on the courts soon after Confederation. After all, when it began to interpret the Charter, the Supreme Court could have recourse to two major precedents – the Canadian Bill of Rights, of 1960, and the U.S. Bill of Rights, ratified as a series of amendments to the American constitution. The two documents used many of the same words and phrases to express almost exactly the same values and ideas; indeed, many parts of the Charter had actually been drafted with them in mind. Especially in the case of the U.S. Bill of Rights, there was a rich history of judgments in which the U.S. Supreme Court had already grappled with the meaning of many of the same rights and freedoms that the Charter guaranteed.

On reflection, however, the Supreme Court of Canada came to the conclusion that neither its own prior jurisprudence on the Canadian Bill of Rights, nor that of its counterpart in Washington, could be of much assistance. Quite quickly, in fact, the Court dismissed both as having little practical utility. It rejected its own definitions of the rights and freedoms listed in the Canadian Bill of Rights because, unlike the Charter, it was just an ordinary act of Parliament.[4] The Court took the position that the rules of interpretation for statutes were generally much more conservative and historical than was appropriate for the elucidation and elaboration of constitutional texts.[5] From its experience resolving federalism disputes, the Court had no hesitation rejecting interpretive approaches that would inhibit the capacity of the Charter to grow and evolve so as to adapt and remain relevant to the changing social and economic conditions that it would confront.

Similarly, and though the Court agreed with the U.S. Supreme Court that a constitutional bill of rights should be interpreted in a large and liberal fashion, for the most part it was reluctant to embrace specific doctrines and definitions that the Americans had developed to give meaning to their constitution. The Court stressed that because the two countries have quite different political, legal, and social histories, and because the two constitutions were organized quite differently, one could not assume that the way in which the U.S. Supreme Court had defined a particular right or freedom would be appropriate for the Canadian context. Virtually from the beginning, the Court made it clear that blindly following the decisions and doctrines worked out by the Americans was not an approach that it would endorse.[6]

Internal Aids: The Intention of the Framers and the Logic of the Text

In the absence of external aids to assist it in identifying where the boundaries between personal autonomy and state authority should be drawn, the Supreme Court adopted the same approach as it had used to decipher the division of responsibilities between the federal and provincial governments. It shifted direction, changed its focus, and looked inside the Charter for help.

This time, and with the benefit of its experience reading the Constitution Act, 1867, the Court made it clear, right from the outset, that adopting an internal, contextualist approach did not mean searching out the intention of those who drafted the Charter. Such an 'originalist,' intent-based approach, said the Court, was both empirically and normatively flawed. Empirically, it was quite impossible to find any evidence of what the 'fathers' of the Charter were thinking about how the Court should exercise its powers of review when they entrenched basic human rights in the constitution. On most questions, given the huge number of people involved in bringing the Charter to life, the idea of there even being a single, collective will was absurd.[7] The fact is that those who were responsible for entrenching the Charter almost never turned their minds to the kinds of cases – Sunday shopping, children's advertising, abortion, prostitution, and pornography – that the Court would be asked to resolve.

Normatively, there were problems as well. In addition to the fact that there was little empirical evidence to support it, the Court did not think that a historical method of searching for some original, common intent was appropriate for a constitutional text. It was backward-looking, and it would not be conducive to allowing the Charter to evolve to meet the needs of a changing social and economic environment. No one dared to flirt with a method of interpretation that had led the Court, just over half a century earlier, to deny that women were 'persons' who were 'qualified' to sit in the Canadian Senate. Again, right from the beginning, the judges recognized that to keep the Charter relevant and responsive to the role that it was expected to play, they should flesh out its meaning with an eye to the future rather than glancing backward to the past.[8] Even when there was some evidence of a common understanding of what a particular right and freedom was intended to protect, the Court did not feel bound to give effect to it.[9]

Rather than looking inside the Charter for the intention of those who were responsible for its entrenchment, the Court focused its search for interpretive sources on the logic and structure of the Charter itself. In the same way in which the Court read the Constitution Act of 1867 to give effect to the federal principle, it looked to the underlying purposes – the most basic values – on which the Charter was grounded to provide guidance as to how the specific rights and freedoms that it guaranteed should be defined.[10] And approaching the text in this deductive, holistic way paid off just as handsomely here as it had a hundred years earlier.

Within two years of hearing its first Charter case, in the landmark decision of *Regina v. Oakes*,[11] the court was able to catalogue the most essential values and ideas that underlay the Charter and that would anchor its whole interpretive approach. In *Oakes*, the Court was asked to rule on the constitutional validity of certain provisions of the Narcotics Control Act that reversed the usual onus of proof in criminal proceedings and, for example, required people who were found in possession of illicit drugs to prove that they were not engaged in the more serious offence of trafficking. In striking down these provisions, the Court began its ruling by identifying 'respect for the inherent dignity of the human person, commitment to social justice and equality, accommodation of a wide variety of beliefs, respect for cultural and group identity, and faith in social and political institutions which enhance the participation of individuals and groups in society' as the final standards, the ultimate purposes, that all the rights and freedoms in the Charter were meant to serve. It was these overarching norms that would give the Court the necessary guidance and orientation to define the reach of specific entitlements in the Charter and the sorts of interests and activities where the will of the individual could roam free in the absence of some compelling, overriding interest of the state.

Although the Court relied on the same logical, deductive process of reasoning to interpret the Charter as it had to delineate the divisions of powers between the federal and provincial governments, it is important to notice how employing the same methodology produced quite different results. In contrast with the federal principle, which required the list of powers assigned to each level of government to take account of and be modified by the law-making authority of its neighbours, the values and principles that lay at the root of the Charter argued for large and liberal definitions of the guaranteed rights and freedoms. The logic in respecting the inherent dignity of every person, defending social justice and equality, and promoting pluralism and political participation instructed the Court to read the guarantees of expression, religion, association, equality, and life, liberty, and security of the person as very broad and all-encompassing terms.[12]

DEFINING RIGHTS

Fundamental Freedoms: Expression and Religion

The way in which this purposeful, deductive approach led the Court to adopt large and liberal definitions can be seen most vividly in the cases in which issues of freedom of expression and/or freedom of religion were at stake. The connection between these two long-standing, traditional, 'first-generation rights' and the values and ideals that the Court identified in *Oakes* is especially clear. Fidelity to values of equality, pluralism, and human dignity directed it to read these two guarantees as broadly as possible.

To give effect to these values (which distinguish all liberal-democratic forms of government), freedom of expression was defined to include anything – including purely physical behaviour – that was done to convey a meaning. Even the act of illegally parking a car, if done to protest or make a statement, could fall within the ambit of its terms.[13] Commercial, artistic, and political statements were all recognized as being intimately linked with personal autonomy and self-fulfilment and so were included on the list of protected activities. Only behaviour that was physically violent was excluded as being at odds with the spirit of the Charter.[14] Picketing,[15] pornography,[16] prostitution,[17] advertising aimed at young children,[18] and even lies[19] were seen to be directly related to the Charter's commitment to equality, pluralism, and respect for the dignity of each human person and so to be entitled to the protection that the Charter provides.

Guided by the same purposeful approach, the Court defined the Charter's guarantee of religious freedom in an equally large and liberal way. In the Court's mind, the logic of the fundamental values on which the Charter was based meant that everyone must be free to form their own moral and spiritual ideas for themselves. To further the Charter's goal of respecting the dignity of every human being, freedom of religion was interpreted to guarantee that everyone would be allowed 'to hold and manifest whatever beliefs and opinions his or her conscience dictates,'[20] so long as they showed similar respect for the belief systems of others.

Two of the earliest cases that the Court heard in which the question of religious freedom was raised involved challenges to federal and provincial laws prohibiting shopping on Sunday, and, in both, the Court made it clear that it intended to read this constitutional guarantee comprehensively as well. Freedom 'of' religion, said the Court, had two sides. Not only did it include the positive freedom 'to' join and participate in the activities and affairs of any religion,[21] but it also guaranteed the negative entitlement to be free 'from' being told by the state to embrace interests or ideas antithetical to what one believes.[22]

The Court also insisted that the guarantee protected people against laws that indirectly and unintentionally interfered with their right to work through their own belief system for themselves, as well as those that quite deliberately and directly forced people to submit to particular religious ideas or practices. In *Edwards Books and Art Ltd. v. Queen*,[23] although the Court upheld the validity of Ontario's Retail Business Holidays Act which, with minor exceptions, outlawed all Sunday shopping, it had no doubt that the law seriously restricted the freedom of those whose sabbath fell on some other day to practise their religion. In *Big M Drug Mart*,[24] the Court actually struck down the federal Lord's Day Act because it was expressly enacted to force everyone to submit to the Christian definition of a sabbath or holy day.

The way the Court read freedom of expression and religion to include virtually any statement and every belief system is an important example of the holistic, deductive method of interpretation at work. The expansive definitions that the Court has given to these and other human rights shows clearly how reading a constitution purposefully promotes the fundamental values on which it is based.[25] The link between people's freedom to express themselves and formulate their most intimate beliefs and the idea of human dignity and personal autonomy is immediate and direct. To protect and encourage the former is to enhance the possibility of the latter.

Reasonable Limits and Maximizing Rights

Reading the rights and freedoms guaranteed in the Charter in a large and liberal way was one strategy that the Court followed to promote the purposes and values that the Charter was meant to serve. Reading the kinds of restrictions that could be imposed on people's constitutional rights very strictly was another. To maximize the protection that the Charter could provide, the Court did both.

In the first section of the Charter, the text expressly contemplates the possibility that the rights and freedoms that it guarantees can be restricted by 'reasonable limits' that 'can be demonstrably justified in a free and democratic society.' According to the Court, these words, no less than the rights and freedoms that the Charter guarantees, had to be read in light of the Charter's larger purposes.[26] To determine what constitutes a 'reasonable limit' on someone's constitutional rights, one must reason from the same set of underlying values and ideas. Human dignity, autonomy, equality, social justice, and political participation would provide the same sources and premises from which both the limits and the rights would be identified and defined.

When the Court read section 1 purposefully, in *Regina v. Oakes*,[27] it identified two principles of justification that would have to be met by any law that interfered with people's constitutional rights. One focused on the ends – the public interest – promoted by the statute or regulation under review, the other, on the means – the particular policy instrument – chosen by the Government to translate its political program into law. Both insisted that all powers of the state must be exercised with a degree of moderation and sense of proportion.[28]

To be consistent with the spirit of the Charter, the Court said, no law could interfere with people's constitutional guarantees unless it served 'pressing and substantial' community interests that 'outweighed' the restrictions on the rights and freedoms that it entailed. Nor would it survive if it were established that there was some less restrictive policy available to the Government to accomplish its objectives. The logic of human dignity, autonomy, equality, and social justice meant that no politician or public servant exercising any power of the state could act in ways that imposed gratuitous, unnecessary limitations on people's constitutional rights and that the more serious the invasion of rights, the more powerful and pressing the Government's explanation would have to be. The first rule – of least drastic means – operates like the concurrency principle in division-of-powers cases and gives expression to the idea of rationality, while the second functions, like the doctrine of mutual modification in federalism cases, as a standard of moderation and proportionality.

Human Rights and Legal Reasoning

Working through a definition of what would qualify as 'reasonable limits' on people's constitutional rights was an important event for the Court. Once it had identified the tests that a Government would have to meet, the basic analytical framework that the judges would follow was in place. From that point on, the Court had a logical, systematic process of reasoning to follow whenever it exercised its powers of review.

In *Oakes*, the Court spelled out how it expected the review process to unfold. According to the Court, there were two distinct phases in the process of deciding whether a law violated someone's constitutional rights. Each part was entirely separate from the other and, as the Court stressed, was analytically quite distinct. In the first phase, the individuals or group who challenge the validity of a law have the floor. In the second, it is the Government's turn to talk. At each stage, there are two questions that the Court has to address.

In the first stage, there is both an interpretive and a factual question. In order to prevail, anyone who challenges the constitutionality of a law must first demonstrate that the interest or activity for which protection is being sought falls within one of the rights or freedoms that the Charter protects. It is here that the interpretation takes place and the scope of the right or freedom (such as expression or religion) is defined. Then the challengers must show that the law that they are challenging really does limit their freedom in the way they describe. They must establish the 'factual' foundation of their case.

In the second stage, supporters of the law must satisfy the Court on two matters as well. First, they must show that the public welfare that is promoted by the law will outweigh and compensate for whatever limitations are imposed on people's rights – that it will do more good than harm (proportionality). As well, they must show that whatever restrictions the law imposes on the rights that the Charter guarantees are necessary to realizing the lawmakers' purposes (including goals of fiscal responsibility) – that there is no other, less drastic policy available that would interfere less with people's rights and freedoms (rationality).

The way in which the Supreme Court developed this two stage analytical framework was really quite remarkable. Barely two years after it had heard its first Charter case, the Court was able to identify a method of reasoning embedded in the logic of the Charter which it has followed ever since. After its decision in *Oakes*, the process was always the same. First, the Court addresses the interpretive and factual dimensions of a challenger's case. Then, where it is established that the law did in fact limit an interest or activity that falls within a Charter guarantee, the Court moves on to measure the means and ends of the law against the 'proportionality principles' it enumerated in *Oakes*.

Human Rights and the Rules of Constitutional Law

The story of how committed the Supreme Court has been to enforcing the Charter, and protecting human rights, is really an account of how each judge, and the Court as a whole, have applied this two-stage sequence of analysis. The tale has two prominent features, both of which we have seen before. First, following the pattern observed in chapter 2, as time has gone by, everyone's attention has focused more and more on the second stage of the analysis and less and less on the first. Protecting people's rights ends up being much more about testing the objectives and methods of disputed rules and regulations than about plumbing the meaning of a constitutional text. Second, as in its federalism jurisprudence, the Court has failed to apply the standards of review that it developed in *Oakes* in a very consistent and principled way. Even though the judges have spent most of their time working with the same two principles, they have had as much difficulty using them to reconcile the competing interests of individuals and groups within a community as they did trying to resolve disputes between the federal and provincial governments.

Reading the Court's Charter jurisprudence chronologically, one finds it striking how quickly the 'proportionality principles' developed in *Oakes* came to dominate centre stage.[29] In contrast with its experience in organizing relations between Ottawa and the provinces it took the Court very little time to define the broad parameters of protection provided by each right and freedom that the Charter guaranteed, and these became fixed points of reference for all future litigation. Especially where the Court gave a holistic, or purposeful, reading to the text, as it did when cases involved questions about freedom of expression and of religion, the interpretive hurdle was never very difficult to clear. Evaluating whether a law conformed to the Charter became increasingly a test of the ends and means of rules and regulations promulgated by the state against principles of moderation and balance, and less and less a matter of reading and teasing out the nuances of the constitutional text.

In less than a decade, the Court mapped out the major boundaries of the rights and freedoms that the Charter guaranteed and identified what kinds of interests and activities they would protect. Testing the constitutionality of a law under the Charter came down to determining whether legislation and administrative rulings could pass the 'proportionality principles' that the Court had laid down in *Oakes.* Very quickly, judicial review under the Charter came to mirror the way the Court mediated relations between the federal and provincial governments.

Substantively, the 'proportionality principles' synthesized in *Oakes* were identical to the principles of rationality and proportionality we examined in chapter 2. The content of the rules and their relational nature (between ends and means and costs and benefits) were precisely the same. The line between the autonomy of an individual or some minority group and community control was defined with the same yardsticks the Court used to stake out the jurisdictional domains of the federal and provincial governments. In the same way that the major doctrines of federalism law, such as concurrency, mutual modification, double aspect, and the pith and substance rule, maximized the sovereignty that Ottawa and the provinces could enjoy as equals, the 'proportionality principles' were designed to ensure that everyone enjoyed the greatest amount of personal autonomy possible.

Though the standards that the Court developed under the Charter were the same as those that guided its analysis of the Constitution Act, 1867, the relative importance of the two criteria were quite different. In the federalism cases, we saw how proportionality played a critical role both in the method of mutual modification that the Court used to define the scope of the powers listed in sections 91 and 92 and in the principles and doctrines that it developed to reconcile the law-making powers of the two orders of government. By contrast, in virtually every case in which a law was struck down as violating the Charter of Rights, it was the means-oriented principle of rationality (or necessity) that did all the important work.

Only three times in the first ten years of deciding Charter cases did the Court invalidate a law because of the ends or objectives that it sought to achieve. The first occasion occurred in the *Quebec Protestant School Board* case, where the Court struck down an important part of Quebec's language law because it was aimed directly at denying some English-speaking people a right to have their children educated in their mother tongue that the Charter explicitly guaranteed.[30] A year later, the federal government's prohibition of Sunday shopping in the Lord's Day Act was ruled unconstitutional because, as its title made clear, its basic purpose was to insist that people of all religious faiths conform to the Christian definition of a weekly, spiritual day of rest.[31] In between these two decisions, the country's rules for people claiming refugee status fell in *Singh v. Minister of Employment and Immigration* because the Court was not persuaded that the financial savings that could be made by restricting the number of people who would be given an oral hearing to make their claim were weighty enough to offset the threat to the lives, liberty, and security of those who might be improperly denied refugee status as a result.[32] In a country in which everyone who gets a parking ticket has the right to a hearing, proportionality (equality) requires that refugee claimants whose lives may be at risk have the same opportunity to plead their case.

In every other case in which the Court struck down a law because it violated someone's constitutional rights, it was the means (the method), not the ends (the objective), that was found to be problematic. All other rulings of constitutional invalidity were based on the Court's finding that the means adopted by the Government to carry out its program were not proportional to the ends. The law was seen by the

Court to be too heavy-handed for the objectives that it was trying to achieve. In some cases, the law was written in terms that were overly broad; in others, the law was unnecessarily rigid and absolute. On other occasions, the defect was that the law was more discretionary and uncertain than it needed to be. Whatever the reason, in each case the Court could identify alternative ways in which the law could be redrafted or reformulated in narrower, more moderate terms, without compromising any of the legislature's objectives.

In all the most highly publicized and well-known instances in which the Court has invalidated some law or regulation, the principle of rationality or alternate means has carried the day. The defect in Canada's abortion laws, for example, was (for the majority at least) strictly of a methodological kind. In its view, parts of the process by which hospital committees were required to approve therapeutic abortions had been designed in a way that actually frustrated the objectives of Parliament.[33] Laws used to regulate speech that is intended to incite people to hate were also struck down when they were drafted in terms that were too sweeping and all-encompassing.[34] Similarly, another provision of Quebec's language code – which effectively prohibited all written communication of a commercial nature other than in French – was invalidated because the Court believed that the Government's objective of preserving a 'visage linguistique' in the province could have been secured by less draconian measures that would have allowed some discrete and subordinate use of English on signs and other kinds of commercial messages.[35]

In other high-profile judgments, in which the Court struck down rules disqualifying people over 65 from unemployment relief,[36] provincial restrictions on the freedom of people qualified in law and health care to practise and publicize their professional wares,[37] federal laws that made it unlawful for practically every public servant to engage in virtually any form of political activity,[38] and regulations prohibiting political picketing and leafleting in all areas of Canada's airports,[39] it was the means-oriented principle of least drastic means (rationality) that did all the work. In a series of cases touching the question of regulating 'professional' occupations, the Court came to the conclusion that those (lawyers!) responsible for formulating various rules on competence, advertising, firm organization, and so on had used policies and instruments that were much more restrictive and zealous than they needed to be. Similarly, with respect to the virtually absolute ban on all political activity imposed by the federal Government on its own employees, the Court responded that neither the competence nor the independence of the public service (which were the objectives the law was trying to promote) would be compromised by a more permissive law that took account of the different kinds of functions and tasks that public servants perform and the different kinds of political activities in which they might take part. And again, the Court's decision striking down the absolute ban on political picketing and leafleting in airports was justified on the basis that some activities of this kind could be accommodated in appropriate places in the terminals without compromising the Government's legitimate interest in ensuring the expeditious and safe movement of travellers. Common to all these cases was the judgment of the Court that there were alternative, less heavy-handed ways in which Governments could have achieved their objectives without any additional costs and which would have allowed the challengers considerably more freedom to pursue interests and activities that the law curtailed.

Rationality, Proportionality, and the Record of the Court

Cataloguing the decisions in which the Supreme Court struck down an act of some legislature or government official as violating the rights that the Charter guarantees runs the risk of conveying the impression that the Court was more consistent and committed to the protection of human rights than it actually has been. In fact, the judges have displayed just as much ambivalence towards the basic principles of constitutional law in their work with the Charter as they exhibited supervising the division of powers between Ottawa and the provinces. Once again, individual judges and the Court as a whole have had a lot of difficulty applying these standards and tests in a consistent and uniform way. Sadly, the Court's performance protecting human rights has been as uneven as its record in policing intergovernmental affairs.[40]

At various times and on specific issues, the Court has exercised its powers of review with considerable energy and enthusiasm. During the first two years in which it worked with the Charter and developed the principles and analytical framework set out in *Oakes*, the Supreme Court exercised its powers of review vigilantly. Parts of Quebec's language code,[41] a provincial motor vehicle licensing law,[42] and various sections in federal laws touching competition policy,[43] Sunday shopping,[44] immigration,[45] and drug trafficking[46] were found to offend these principles and were declared to be unconstitutional.

After the first two years, however, the Court became much more selective in the kinds of laws it would subject to strict and searching review. Usually only criminal laws and regulations governing the practice of 'professional occupations' such as medicine and law were subjected to a really rigorous evaluation. Only in these two areas has the Court been confident that it had a comparative advantage over the other two branches of government in its understanding of the issues.[47] For example, in criminal law, the Court has invalidated parts of Canada's abortion law,[48] the Narcotics Control Act,[49] homicide rules,[50] the system of automatic detention of people acquitted on grounds of insanity,[51] rape shield rules,[52] laws on sexual offences,[53] and methods of criminal investigation.[54] In the area of laws governing the practice of professional occupations, the Court has struck down rules imposing citizenship[55] and geographical[56] qualifications for acquiring a licence to practise, as well as restrictions on the freedom to advertise commercially,[57] by using the proportionality principles established in *Oakes* to their full.

Once the judges stepped outside the domain of criminal law and professional practice, however, their attitude changed quite dramatically. As the Court gained experience working with the Charter and as its membership changed,[58] the framework of analysis developed in *Oakes* was applied more cautiously and laws were declared to be unconstitutional much less frequently. In doctrinal terms, the Court added a set of very restrictive and qualifying provisos that limited the protection that the principles of rationality and proportionality could provide.

Over the course of the eight years following its decision in *Oakes*, the Court's thinking moved along two parallel lines, both of which restricted the reach of the principles of review that it established in that case. In some cases, the Court ruled that the type of law that it was evaluating was immune from Charter review. Sometimes whole areas of law were said to be beyond the Charter's reach. On other occasions, particular interests or activities were identified as not being the sort that the Charter was meant to protect. In either situation, the effect was the same: laws could be validated even though they failed the tests of rationality and proportionality.

At the same time that it was compiling a catalogue of laws, interests, and activities that fell beyond the Charter's reach, the Court also put a gloss on the two-stage analytical framework to deal with those cases that did fall within the scope of the Charter that has allowed the judges to soften and mute the force of their powers of review when and as they see fit. Essentially, the Court has adopted a different attitude towards each of the two stages in the review process, which has had the effect of further reducing the protection that the Charter can provide. In the first phase, the Court has come to take a relatively hard line about what challengers must prove to meet the factual and interpretive hurdles they face. By contrast, in the second, it has adopted a much more deferential and conciliatory attitude to what a Government must do to justify a law that is under attack.

HUMAN RIGHTS AND JUDICIAL EXEMPTIONS

Scope of the Charter: Where Rationality and Proportionality Do Not Apply

Most of the laws that the Supreme Court has exempted from all manner of judicial review are in the area of 'private' law. These are the rules the courts themselves have developed to regulate the personal, private relations of individuals. The Court has in effect declared that all the common law rules of contract, property, and tort (delict) lie outside the courts' powers of review when they govern relations between two private individuals and do not involve any other branch of government. Though its position has been widely criticized by commentators of quite different political and legal persuasions, the Court has continued to insist that the Charter would apply only when either the legislative and/or executive branch of a government was directly involved. Where the only intervention by the state was the judicial creation and application of a (common law) rule that governed a dispute, the Court has said that that was not sufficient to attract constitutional review.

The idea that, for a law to fall within the Court's powers of review, it must be directly connected to the legislative or executive branch has had the effect of removing large parts of Canadian law from having to comply with the Charter. Based on this reasoning, the Court has said that it will not review tort laws developed by the courts to regulate picketing;[59] rules of mandatory retirement contained in contracts of employment between public universities and their employees;[60] provisions of labour agreements between unions and private employers compelling payment of dues to or membership in a union;[61] or judge-made rules governing the relations of a husband and wife concerning the birth and custody of their child.[62]

The idea that there must be a sufficient degree of state or Government action to attract the Court's powers of review has also influenced the Court's thinking in cases where relations with a foreign Government are involved. In several cases where a person has challenged a law or an order of the Canadian Government extraditing him or her to a foreign state, the Court has taken the position that the essence of these complaints is really with some aspect of the foreign law that is seen to be in conflict with the Charter's guarantees. Where the Court perceives the foreign law as posing the real threat to an individual's constitutional rights, invariably it has concluded that the involvement of the Canadian Government is too peripheral to warrant review. Only, the Court has said, in 'extreme' cases, where the foreign law 'sufficiently shocks the conscience,' where it is 'simply unacceptable' (for example, in sanctioning or tolerating torture), will the Court hold up the law or order in question to review under the principles in *Oakes*.[63] On the basis of this kind of reasoning (and in contrast with the approach followed by the European Court of Human Rights),[64] the Court has rejected the claim of people who raised constitutional challenges to their being extradited to foreign states that sanctioned the death penalty as a method of criminal punishment.[65]

When the Court is of the opinion that there is not enough 'state action' involved in a challenger's complaint, either because the law in question is purely a matter of judicial creation and enforcement, or because it is really a foreign law that is involved,[66] the tests of constitutional validation laid out in *Oakes* have no application whatsoever. These laws are completely immune from any form of judicial review. Though, as we have seen, this line of analysis has removed important areas of law from the reach of the Charter, in most cases that have come to the Court, the question of 'state action' is not in issue. The involvement of the federal or one of the provincial governments is clear. In these cases, the model in *Oakes* will be applied, but even here the Court has developed its thinking in ways that further reduce the protection that the Charter can provide. As noted above, in applying the two-stage model of review established in *Oakes*, the Court has insisted that challengers satisfy a burden of proof that is in fact much more rigorous and demanding than what many Governments have been asked to meet.

In the first phase of the review process, it will be recalled, challengers must establish two parts to their claims. They must demonstrate a real factual basis to their complaint and show that the interest or activity for which protection is being sought falls within one of the enumerated rights or freedoms. On both criteria, the Court has proceeded in a way that can make it difficult for many individuals and groups to make out a case. First, the Court has made it clear that establishing the factual foundation of a case is not an automatic, pro-forma requirement. In several leading cases, the Court has refused to review a challenged law or administrative act because, in its view, the challengers were unable to or did not prove that their rights or freedoms had actually been limited in the way in which they claimed. The Court has shown strong aversion to 'taking judicial notice' of facts essential to the success of a claim. For example, in a case involving a challenge to Ottawa's decision to allow the testing of U.S. cruise missiles over Canadian territory, it went so far as to declare that it would be impossible for the challengers ever to establish that their 'lives' or the 'security of their persons' would be threatened by the Government's action.[67] In another case, the Court refused to review provisions of an election financing law that provided public assistance only to the major political parties for the reason that the challengers (who were members of a small, fringe party) had not put forward affidavit evidence to prove that their constitutional right to be treated equally had actually been infringed.[68] Though the Court has said on a number of occasions that a challenger need prove only that a law or Government action threatens his or her constitutional rights and need not actually suffer the deprivation,[69] these and other cases[70] show that proof must be adduced to show that the threat is real.

Though it has not been common for the Court to refuse to test the rationality and proportionality of a challenged law on the ground that it did not, as a factual matter, interfere with the complainants' freedom, many challengers have been tripped up trying to clear the interpretive hurdle that the analytical framework worked out in *Oakes* requires them to surmount. In many cases, the Court has abandoned the deductive, holistic method of reading the constitution, which has made it more difficult for claimants to establish that the interest or activity for which protection is sought falls within one of the Charter's guarantees. Sections 2(d), 7, and 15, in particular, have been cut down in this way. In the years since its decision in *Oakes*, the Court has identified a wide range of interests and activities which, in its opinion, fall outside the scope of these guarantees. When, for example, groups of workers have sought the benefit of section 2(d), which guarantees freedom of association, to protect their right to strike,[71] to bargain through the union of their choice,[72] or to shield them from having to pay dues to allow a union to pursue projects and policies unrelated to collective bargaining,[73] they have been met with the response that these interests and activities do not fall within that constitutional guarantee.[74] In the words of one commentator, these decisions have rendered freedom of association 'barren, protecting nothing of positive importance to the union movement.'[75]

Section 7's guarantee of life, liberty, and security of the person has been shrunk in a similar way. No corporations, the Court has said, are protected by this entitlement.[76] More serious, and in contrast with its definition of what kinds of expression section 2(d) protects, the Court has ruled that section 7 does not reach purely commercial activities.[77] In sharp contrast with the way in which 'liberty' has been interpreted by other courts around the world, the Supreme Court of Canada has resisted the idea that this universal guarantee of human freedom protects people's interest in being able to control their own destinies in the economic and social spheres of their lives. Although the Court has been generally quite receptive to defining the 'principles of fundamental justice' in a broad and expansive way,[78] the judges have been more reluctant to embrace the deductive, purposeful approach that they used to read sections 2(a) and 2(b) when they defined the parameters of 'life' and 'liberty' that section 7 was entrenched to protect.

The equality rights in section 15 have suffered a similar, perhaps even more dramatic, demise. Because it misunderstood the way in which the formal, Aristotelian definition of equality works, the Court rejected what in human rights circles is often referred to as the 'similarly situated' test.[79] As a result, the Court has said that section 15 protects only those 'discrete and insular minorities' that have traditionally been the victims of prejudice and abuse, and other groups in analogous circumstances, from discriminatory treatment by Governments and their officials.[80] On this interpretation of the equality guarantee, the Court has said that the interests of workers in being able to sue those who have harmed them in the same way as others who are victims of misfeasance[81] and the claims of various individuals caught up in the (federal) criminal justice system to be dealt with according to the same principles and procedures across the country[82] fell outside the scope of section 15 and so beyond its competence to protect.

Other sections of the Charter dealing with democratic rights (to vote and to stand for office – in section 3), and language rights (sections 16–23) have been defined in a similar way. Here again, the Court has abandoned the purposeful approach and has made no effort to reason deductively, from the larger values and ideas on which the Charter is based. For example, in dismissing a challenge to a provincial electoral-boundary law, which allowed for as much as 15 per cent variation in the population of different constituencies, the Court reasoned that the right to vote in section 3 did not guarantee that each person's ballot would have exactly the same weight or influence.[83] Similarly, in interpreting the Charter's guarantee to French and English linguistic minorities to be able to speak in their mother tongue in the federal and some provincial courts, the Court concluded that the protection guaranteed only the opportunity to express oneself and not necessarily the right to be understood.[84] More broadly still, various judges have suggested that none of the rights and freedoms enshrined in the Charter will protect interests or activities that they designate as relatively trivial or unimportant.[85]

In many of these cases in which it was held that the interest or activity for which protection was sought did not fall within one of the rights and freedoms that the Charter guaranteed, the Court followed a similar pattern of reasoning. Instead of reading the Charter in a purposeful, holistic way, as it had in defining freedom of expression and religion, as often as not the Court switched to a 'balancing' approach, in which the public interest promoted by the law being reviewed was compared to the limit that the law imposed on the challengers' freedom to act.[86] At critical moments, on some of the most important rights and freedoms in the Charter – freedom of association, equality, life, liberty and security of the person – the Court simply stopped reading the Charter deductively and with a view of promoting the values of pluralism, equality, and human dignity on which it was based. Instead, the Court used a kind of utilitarian, cost-benefit test to determine which interests and activities were protected and which were not. Where the public interest promoted by a challenged law was seen to substantially outweigh the constraint that it imposed on people's freedom to act, the Court would imply a limit in the right or freedom that put the interest or activity that the challenger wanted recognized outside the Charter's guarantees.

A clear example of the balancing approach is the Court's recognition of a *de minimis* rule. Putting an interest or activity beyond the reach of the Charter on the grounds that it is too insignificant or trivial to merit being reviewed is just another way of saying that, when the challenger's interest is weighed against the public interest promoted by the law and the Court's limited time and resources, it is not substantial enough to warrant close attention by the judges.[87] Voting rights provide another striking illustration of where this method of constitutional interpretation has carried the day. In defining the meaning of a citizen's voting rights in section 3, the Court struck a balance between the principle of parity and equality of political participation and the practical imperatives of effective representation.[88]

Other examples of the Court's using a balancing approach to distinguish interests that would fall within the Charter from those that do not include its decisions dismissing challenges to laws providing for the indeterminate detention of dangerous offenders;[89] excluding routine customs and border searches from the Charter's guarantee against 'unreasonable searches and seizures';[90] and outlining how accessible a Government must make the (public) property that is under its control to those who want to use it to express their views.[91] In the last case, a majority of the Court decided that whether people can claim access to a piece of public property, as a matter of constitutional right, in order to propagate their views would vary, depending on the nature of the property; the use to which it is normally put; the extent to which the access claimed by the challengers could be reconciled with those uses; and the degree to which the challenged law actually impaired the challengers' ability to communicate their views.

In many of these cases, the Court justified its balancing approach by what might be characterized as a 'separation of powers argument.' For example, in the labour and language cases, it reasoned that because laws that affect these kinds of interests are inherently matters of compromise and accommodation of competing and often conflicting interests, and because legislatures are usually better informed and more expert in resolving such issues, the legislative branch is uniquely suited for resolving them. Again, in the extradition cases noted earlier, the Court made a similar separation-of-powers argument and stressed the enormous benefits that all countries derive from an effective system of extradition and from every country's adhering to the principle of comity (respect) among independent nations.

These cases, in which the Court has used a balancing approach to define the limits of the Charter's guarantees and to identify interests and activities that can be regulated without regard to any standard of rationality (necessity) and proportionality (consistency), form an important part of the Court's jurisprudence. Quantitatively, the number of cases in which the Court has reasoned in this way is substantial. And, as we have seen from the broad range of interests and activities that a Government can restrict in any way that it sees fit, collectively these cases represent a significant limitation on the Court's powers of constitutional validation and on the relief that the Charter can provide. They underscore just how cautious and conservative the Supreme Court of Canada has been in using the Charter in the defence of human rights.

Human Rights and Judicial Deference

Together, the cases in which the Court found that challengers did not prove the factual bases of their claims and those in which it ruled that an interest or activity did not fall within one of the Charter's guarantees show that the burden of successfully establishing a human rights violation in Canada is not a light one. Added to the cases in which the Court has ruled that whole areas of law are beyond the reach of the Charter has meant that many challenges have been dismissed without the Court's ever reaching the second stage of the review process. When, however, the Court did pass to the second stage of the review process, its attitude seemed to shift 180 degrees.[92] Rather than rigorously and strictly applying the standards that challengers have been obliged to meet, it has given Governments considerable latitude and discretion in showing that their laws meet the tests of constitutional validation set out in *Oakes*. In some areas of social policy, the Court has qualified these principles by saying that it would apply them only in a deferential and passive way.

The most striking examples of this differential treatment are those cases in which the Court characterized the law being reviewed as one involving a compromise or accommodation of competing interests and policy objectives. In cases of this kind, the Court repeatedly has applied the principles in *Oakes* only with caution and restraint. Even though a challenger has met the interpretive and factual hurdles of the first stage of the review process, the Court has muted the force of the proportionality principles in *Oakes* by saying that it would apply them only with considerable deference. In the Court's words, with respect to such laws, legislatures are not required to choose the 'best possible means' to accomplish their objectives. In these circumstances the Court does not 'insist on perfection.' Instead, it requires only that a legislature or Government have a 'reasonable basis' for choosing the policy it did.[93]

According to the Court, the reason for adopting this posture of deference is, once again, to show proper respect for the separation of powers between the judicial and the elected branches of government. In the Court's view, the democratically elected branches of government are designed to let everyone participate in deciding how compromises should be effected, so that in reviewing such laws it should 'be mindful of the legislature's representative function.'[94]

For the most part, the Court invoked this line of reasoning in cases involving challenges to social and economic policies, where, according to the Court, the legislature acts as a mediator between conflicting interests and groups. In the Court's view, the legislature's role is different in these areas of community life than in criminal law, for example, where the Government is characterized as one of the protagonists to the dispute, representing the interests of the community as a whole against those who are alleged to have violated some aspect of its criminal code.

The importance to the Court of the distinction between these two kinds of laws can be seen in its decisions affirming the constitutionality of a series of provincial laws that severely curtailed shopping on Sunday[95] and commercial advertising aimed at young children[96] as well as various laws which required people to retire and give up their jobs at a specified age.[97] Characterizing these laws as essentially matters of compromise and accommodation, the Court recognized a wide 'margin of appreciation' for the legislatures involved and applied the principles in *Oakes* with great restraint. In fact, in most cases in which the Court has adopted such a posture, it has upheld the constitutional validity of the law under review.[98] Deference, like the principle of 'minimal scrutiny' in American constitutional law, has, more often than not, meant no review at all.

Although the Court has frequently emphasized the distinction between social and economic policies on the one hand and criminal law on the other hand, the line is not absolute and inflexible. The fact is that most, if not all, parts of our criminal law involve the compromise of competing interests, just like any other area of social or economic policy. Consider a law on abortion or pornography or rules about what evidence, concerning a victim's past, should be admissible in a rape trial and the competing interests they affect. In addition, we have just seen that in some areas of social and economic policy, such as professional regulation, where the law attempts to mediate different interests and groups, the Court has been quite willing to apply the principles of rationality and proportionality forcefully. Conversely, in several instances, the Court has invoked a posture of deference and given a wide margin of appreciation to the legislature, even when it was reviewing rules of criminal or quasi-criminal law. Thus, when it tested laws regulating gun control,[99] extradition,[100] pornography,[101] soliciting (prostitution),[102] the presumption of sanity,[103] and (in the highly publicized Rodriguez case) assisted suicide,[104] the Court explicitly invoked the principle of deference to sustain its decision upholding their constitutionality. Still, and despite this blurring of the distinction between social or economic laws and criminal law, the division is an important one to the Court. On one occasion it resulted in the Court invalidating Canada's 'rape-shield' law, even though it recognized that the law was very similar to social and economic laws in striking a balance between the interests of two different groups (complainants and accused) in the community.[105]

THE POSSIBILITY OF JUDICIAL REVIEW

The first decade of Charter jurisprudence is now history. Commentators are generally agreed as to how the Court has gone about its work and what results have been achieved. All law students learn that after an early flirtation with a highly activist, interventionist approach, the Court settled down and became much more cautious and deferential in its views. What remains a more open and hotly contested question is what one should make of the jurisprudence that the judges have crafted.

Critics who are instinctively sceptical about the integrity of law will want to argue that this body of case law offers still more empirical evidence to support their views.[106] Indeterminacy and subjectivity abound. Glaring inconsistencies already mar the landscape. Early on, as we have seen, the Court divided quite openly between two contending schools of thought. The radically different approach that the Court has taken to particular rights and entitlements (freedom of religion and expression v. freedom of association and equality) makes a credible case of class bias on the part of the Court.[107] The concept that there are different degrees of review, that the principles of rationality and proportionality are applied more vigorously in some cases than others, allows each judge to do whatever he or she wants in each individual case.

On the record that we have just reviewed, there can be no quarrel with the critics' description of the Court's work. The mistake of the critic is in the conclusion that it is inherent in the nature of law and legal reasoning to be open-ended and indefinite and subject to personal manipulation and control. As we saw in their response to an equally uneven body of federalism law, those who are sceptical about law tend to react very strongly when the legal process is seen not to be doing its job as well as it should.

Anyone who is inclined to doubt the integrity of law after reading the first few years of the Court's Charter jurisprudence should read the cases again. Every student can profit by trying to analyse the substance – the merits – of the two lines of cases or two schools of thought that are said to illustrate the subjectivity and indeterminacy of the law. It is not enough to point out that there are competing lines of authority that provide judges with a substantial measure of freedom and choice in how to decide any particular case. The critics must be even more critical than they have generally been so far.

If one examines the jurisprudence more closely, it turns out that the decisions of the Supreme Court, over the first decade of the Charter, do support the integrity and viability of subordinating democratically elected Governments to the rule of law. If one reads the Court's judgments with a more discriminating eye, it is possible to identify serious logical and/or empirical mistakes in all the major cases in which it has refused to apply the rationality and proportionality principles to their full force and effect.[108]

The cases in which the Court insulated state institutions, and indeed whole areas of regulation, from any form of review are the easiest to criticize. A generation of lawyers has cut its teeth writing critical comments about *Dolphin Delivery* and its progeny.[109] In *Dolphin Delivery*, the Court had ruled that the common law (judge-made) rules that regulate strikes and picketing in many parts of the country did not fall within or have to conform to the standards of rationality and proportionality on which the Charter was based. The justification that was offered for this conclusion did not persuade many and failed in a number of fundamental respects.

First, and most important, the idea that there are areas of law that lie outside the scope of the constitution and the Court's powers of review is based on a logical impossibility. It is fundamentally at odds with the fact that the constitution is supreme in the legal order. As we saw at the beginning of chapter 1, the idea of supremacy is inherent in all constitutions, and section 52 of the Charter could not be any clearer on the point. It says quite explicitly that the constitution is the supreme law in Canada and that *any* law that is inconsistent with its provisions is of no force or effect. Putting entire bodies of law and legal relations outside the scope of the Charter means that the constitution is not in fact supreme when state powers are exercised in these areas. Here legal authority does not have to be exercised in a way that satisfies the tests of rationality and proportionality.

Sometimes students advance a 'privacy' argument to support their claim that there are limits on the reach of the Charter. The idea is that if the principles of rationality and proportionality were applied to every action that was taken by government or an official of the state, law would penetrate too deeply into people's personal affairs[110]. The concern is that if every rule and regulation were subject to review by the courts, the notion of privacy would be destroyed, and every corner of our lives would be subject to the rule of law and scrutiny by the state.

It is surprising how many people worry that if the Charter is applied too rigorously and extensively it will pose a threat to the most personal aspects of our lives. The fear is actually quite irrational and has no basis in fact. Constitutional review is never directly concerned with the behaviour of individuals, except those who are empowered to develop and execute the law. As we saw at the very beginning of chapter 1, the rules of constitutional law regulate the content of other laws, not the way people deal with each other in their everyday affairs. (The latter is now commonly the subject of statutory regulation in the form of human rights codes.) In those aspects of our lives, such as who we invite to dinner,[111] where no legal rule limits what we can do, the Charter simply has no application. It is only when a law is at issue that the courts intervene, and then only to test the rationality and proportionality of the rule.

It is true that laws can seriously restrict what people can do in the most intimate aspects of their lives. Laws regulating abortion or sexual activities are laws of that kind. But that does not provide any reason why they should be immune from review by the courts. Quite the contrary. If anything, given their importance to personal autonomy and self-actualization, such laws should be the first to be reviewed under the Charter, whether they are enacted by the legislature or handed down by a court. There is nothing in the Charter that says that laws that regulate the 'private sphere' can be reviewed when they are enacted by a legislature but not when they are formulated by a court.

Although the Supreme Court has ruled that section 32 of the Charter limits its reach to action taken by the legislative and executive branches, it is widely accepted that this interpretation can not withstand even the most superficial analysis.[112] There is nothing in the words or history or underlying values of the Charter that supports the

Court's 'deconstruction' of the text. Read purposefully, deductively – to give effect to the values underlying the Charter – and in a manner that accords with the way in which 'government' is normally understood, section 32 must refer to all three branches of government, including the judiciary.[113] The fact is, there is no textual support for the idea that when the courts develop and apply some rule of common law, they can do so free of the obligations and principles that the Charter contains.[114]

Most students have little difficulty understanding how the Court's interpretation of section 32 is inconsistent with the principle of constitutional supremacy and the larger purposes (values) of the Charter. Many, however, have more problem seeing that the limits that the Court has read into such substantive guarantees as sections 2(d), 7, and 15, and the idea that judges have a discretion in deciding how vigorously the 'proportionality principles' will be applied in any case, constitute just as serious infringements of section 52 and the supremacy clause. Inevitably one encounters some hostility to the idea that every time someone exercises a power of the state they have a duty to respect the basic precepts (rationality, consistency) that underlie the rule of law. In a postmodernist age, absolutes and claims of universality are not easy for many people to accept.

Resistance to the idea that the supremacy of the constitution is pervasive and all-encompassing is not grounded in anything in the text. There is not a single word or phrase that supports the idea that rights and freedoms such as those set out in sections 2(d), 7, and 15 contain unwritten limitations or that there are levels or degrees of intensity with which the 'proportionality principles' can be applied. The inhibition of most students relates to concerns about institutional competence and the proper role of the Court. Students fear that the Court will be flooded with cases and the judges will be 'in over their heads.' Restricting the circumstances in which and the intensity with which different laws will be reviewed is defended as prudent judgment about how the Court should best use its scarce resources and what its strengths and institutional capacities are.[115] The Supreme Court would be swamped if it ruled that every interest or activity qualified as a constitutional right, and this would stretch the Court's policy-making role beyond all reasonable limits.[116] It would trivialize the really important rights and freedoms, such as religion and expression, say some, to treat all aspects of human freedom the same.[117] Others worry that judicial review of every legislative initiative, or action taken by some state official, ignores the comparative advantages of the three branches of government and asks the Court to rule on matters of social policy about which it is neither well-informed nor well-equipped to resolve.

Before considering what we should make of these pragmatic concerns about the competence of the courts and the most efficacious use of their resources, it is important to recognize that whenever a court rules that a law need not be measured against the principles of rationality and proportionality or that these tests of constitutional validation need be applied only in a very tentative and deferential way, it invokes a line of argument or reasoning that compromises the supremacy of the constitution. Reading limits into the rights and freedoms that the Charter guarantees is the antithesis of the 'large and liberal,' 'purposive' approach that constitutions demand. Any time a court designates some interest or activity as falling outside the Charter's guarantees, there is a danger that laws will be validated that impinge unnecessarily on people's freedom to act out their own lives, and/or do so in a way that is out of all proportion with how others have been treated elsewhere and in the past.

That is what happened, for example, in the *Labour Trilogy (1987)*, where the Court, in a 4:2 split, ruled that a series of federal and provincial laws limiting workers' freedom to strike and bargain collectively were constitutionally sound. As the dissenting judges, Brian Dickson and Bertha Wilson, were at pains to point out, in all these cases laws were validated that restricted people's freedom to live their lives autonomously, even though the restrictions were gratuitous and unnecessary. In each case, alternative policies were available to the Governments concerned that could have allowed them to accomplish their purposes in ways that would have shown more respect for the people whose lives they controlled.

In the case of Alberta's collective bargaining law, which denied all public servants the freedom to strike, the Government could have drafted its legislation in a more focused fashion and still realized its objective of guaranteeing essential services – police, health, and fire – in the province. The prohibition on concerted activity could have been aimed specifically at workers in these sectors, and public servants working in less urgent areas or jobs could have been allowed to go free. Similarly, in *PSAC*, the federal Government could have pursued its inflation-restraint program without banning all bargaining in the public service. As Bertha Wilson pointed out to her colleagues, the Government's program would not have been sacrificed in any way if it had been made to continue to bargain on non-monetary matters of employment such as seniority, management rights, and grievance procedures.

It bears repeating that there is nothing in the text of the Charter that suggests that rights and freedoms should be read in a way that validates laws that restrict people's freedom gratuitously (unnecessarily) and/or in a manner out of all proportion with the way others in similar circumstances have been treated. No words or phrases authorize the Court to compile one list of interests and activities that fall within one or other of the rights and freedoms that the Charter guarantees and another list of human behaviours that do not. As noted above, in most cases when the Court has excluded some form of human enterprise from the scope of the Charter, it has used a kind of balancing approach in which the public interest that is promoted by a law and the institutional resources of the Court are weighed against the ambit of personal freedom that it curtails.

'Definitional balancing,' however, is as much at odds with the principle of constitutional supremacy as the rules that put whole categories of law and state institutions beyond the Charter's reach. As a practical matter, important areas of law, such as labour law, have been effectively immunized from meaningful review by the courts. As the *Labour Trilogy* demonstrates so dramatically, the supremacy of the constitution and the rule of law are compromised when laws are validated that cannot meet one of the most important principles that the Charter contains. These bodies of substantive law stand above the constitution, immune to the duties that lawmakers are ordinarily required to respect. In the words of one commentator, the combined effect of the *Labour Trilogy* and *PIPS*[118] is nothing short of a 'national embarrassment.'[119]

Nothing in the constitution supports the idea of weighing the costs and benefits of a challenged law as a way of defining which interests and activities fall within the rights and freedoms that the Charter guarantees and which do not. Cost-benefit – prudential – analysis is as inappropriate a method of reading the words in a constitution as searching for some historical or literal meaning. As the Court itself recognized in the first Charter cases, the constitution instructs the judges to read the Charter deductively, 'purposefully,' to give effect to the basic principles and values on which it is based. The principles of rationality and proportionality oblige the Court to maximize the protection that the rights and freedoms can provide.

The logic of respecting such values as human dignity, equality, and personal autonomy requires the Court to read the rights and freedoms in the Charter in a 'large and liberal' way, rather than imposing restrictions and limitations on the protection that they can provide. From the standpoint of human dignity and personal autonomy, virtually every form of human activity can fairly be characterized as an act of expression, association, conscience, or liberty. The larger lesson of the hate propaganda cases such as *Keegstra* and *Zundel*,[120] and the court's validation of the sections in the criminal code dealing with pornography in *Butler*,[121] is that no matter how harmful and disruptive a behaviour or an activity may be, for the person engaged in it, it is at the core of the personal history he or she wants to project.

Even acts of killing – for example, an abortion or a political assassination – can be characterized as important aspects of personal liberty or political expression that fall within the larger purposes that these constitutional guarantees are designed to promote. The fact that some of these interests or activities may cause more harm than good does nothing to change their character as matters of fundamental, intensely personal, importance to the people who commit them. The issue of the weightiness or harmfulness of the activity involved and how it should be balanced against the interests of others in the community is not a matter of constitutional interpretation; it is a matter of justification under section 1.

As a method of interpretation, of reading the Charter, 'definitional balancing' is conceptually flawed. It inverts the hierarchical ordering implicit in the idea of constitutional supremacy and uses an ordinary statute or law to give meaning and fix the parameters of the constitutional text. It parallels the now-discredited 'frozen concepts' approach that was used to drain the original Canadian Bill of Rights of any force or effect[122] and would prevent the Charter from being able to adapt and adjust to the times.

Analytically, definitional balancing is equally untenable. Contrary to the Court's own admonitions, it collapses the two stages inherent in the process of review and runs them together.[123] It fails to respect the analytical distinction that separates the two stages of the review process. It uses a standard that is designed to measure the content of the rules and laws that the Court is asked to review as a way of giving meaning to the constitutional text.

Though not quite so dramatically, the doctrines that allow the Court to shield politicians and policy-makers from the full measure of the rationality and proportionality tests suffer the same logical contradiction as do those that purport to immunize whole areas of law and human activity from review. It is true that when the Court applies the 'proportionality principles' deferentially, the criteria of constitutional validity do have some role to play. It is not, as in cases such as *Dolphin Delivery* and *Labour Trilogy*, saying that there is no room for any form of review.

However, though it may appear that a principle of tiered, discretionary review is more benign than a rule that results in complete immunity, it is no less defective in the end. There is no more justification for applying the tests of constitutional legitimacy deferentially in some cases than in refusing to apply them at all. Once again there is no support for this doctrinal gloss, either in the text or in the history of the constitution. Nowhere does the Charter say that judges have the authority to differentiate between types of law in the intensity of review to which they will be subjected. Section 52, proclaiming the supremacy of the constitution, refers to 'any' law and speaks in absolute terms.

By definition, applying the principles of rationality and proportionality tentatively and deferentially means that the constitution is not being enforced to its full effect. Its supremacy is being compromised, even if only partially and not as crudely as in cases such as *Dolphin Delivery* and the *Labour Trilogy*. When the rules of constitutional law are applied partially and/or deferentially, laws are upheld that would be struck down if the constitution, including its two most basic precepts, were acknowledged to be supreme.

The idea that there are different levels or tiers of review available to judges to evaluate different types of laws poses the same threat to the principle of constitutional supremacy as cataloguing a group of interests and activities that fall outside all the rights and freedoms that the Charter guarantees. Whenever the Court decides to apply the principles of rationality and proportionality deferentially, and not to their maximum effect, it runs the risk of upholding laws that restrict people's freedom to control their own destinies unnecessarily, or more than the way in which the freedom of others in similar circumstances has been restricted elsewhere and/or in the past.

That is what happened, for example, when the Court validated a series of provincial laws that forced some people to retire from work at age 65 against their will and to pay dues to unions to pursue political and social causes that were unrelated to collective bargaining and to which they were personally opposed. In *McKinney*,[124] the court upheld a law that permitted people to be terminated from their jobs at age 65 even though there was considerable evidence that alternative policies could have accomplished the same purposes, including rules of retirement that were tailored to particular occupations and work environments, were gender-neutral, and even (as in some U.S. and Canadian jurisdictions) that avoided age discrimination entirely. Similarly, in *Lavigne*,[125] the Court refused to interfere with an Ontario law that allowed unions to compel payment of dues from those they represent for any cause they chose to support, even though there was evidence before it that in other jurisdictions laws had been enacted that restricted the uses to which the dues could be put to those that were related to their role as bargaining agents, without harming the unions in any way.

The Court's highly publicized decision rejecting Sue Rodriguez's plea for someone to be allowed to assist her in controlling the termination of her life provides a particularly powerful example of where deferentially applying the 'proportionality principles' allowed the judges to skip over other policies that the federal government might have adopted very superficially. Because it required Parliament only to prove that it had a 'reasonable basis' for concluding that its law satisfied the principle of rationality or necessity, the Court refused to consider whether alternative policies, developed in other free and democratic societies, could have accomplished all the Government's objectives but in a way that showed more respect for Rodriguez's right to control her own destiny.

Creating a flexible, multi-level framework of tiered review and implying limits on the reach of the Charter and its rights and freedoms were unquestionably the two doctrines developed by the Court that were most destructive of the principle of constitutional supremacy and the criteria of rationality and proportionality. As we have seen, these two strategies have shielded large areas of law and community life from any independent, impartial assessment. Before moving on to consider the pragmatic reasons that the Court and others have advanced in support of these doctrines, it is important to take note of one other major interpretive failure committed by the Court, which resulted in the reach of the Charter being reduced even further.

The shrinkage occurred in the Charter's equality clause, and the difficulty arose the first time the Supreme Court was asked to turn its mind to section 15. We have already seen how the Court struggled with what meaning should be given to the words 'without discrimination' and the list of enumerated grounds on which classification and differentiation are proscribed. Rather than interpreting these words – like those in section 15(2) – as inspirational, hortatory parts of the text, underscoring and reinforcing the idea of equality as a measure of consistency and proportion, the Court adopted the view that 'without discrimination' is a limiting phrase, restricting the protection that section 15 can provide. According to the Court, inclusion of the words 'without discrimination' means that section 15 can be invoked only by groups that are specifically enumerated in the text (racial, national, ethnic, religious, and so on) or that have suffered adverse treatment on analogous grounds.

In addition to reading the words of the text in a very limiting, restrictive way, the Court also had a lot of difficulty understanding how the idea of equality works. By its own admission, the Court, like many in the legal community, found equality to be an 'elusive concept;'[126] whose meaning was the subject of vigorous contest and debate.[127] It is not surprising therefore that on the very first occasion on which it was required to interpret section 15, in *Andrews v. Law Society of British Columbia*, it stumbled rather badly. Even though the Court struck down the provisions in British Columbia's Barristers and Solicitors Act that required all lawyers in the province to be Canadian citizens, it did so in a way and for a set of reasons that demonstrated a deeply flawed understanding of what equality really means.

Outside the legal community, it has been known for a long time (going back at least as far as Aristotle) that equality is a relational concept, or a measuring device, that requires that those things that are alike should be treated alike, and (therefore) other things that are unlike should be treated differently, in proportion to their differences. So described, equality is really a very simple idea. In legal discourse, it is often referred to as the 'similarly situated' test.

Properly understood, equality – or the 'similarly situated' test – is just a restatement of the proportionality (consistency) principle.[128] However it is described, the rule requires that whenever politicians formulate any law or regulation they must treat everyone who is similarly situated the same. If a law provides compensation to people who lose their jobs involuntarily and through no fault of their own, they must not exclude any person or group who suffers this fate. They could not, for example, arbitrarily deny anyone over age 65 the benefits that the law provides.[129] Similarly, if a law condemns certain behaviour as harmful to the physical health and psychological well-being of certain sectors of the community, everyone who commits the offence should be made to face the consequences it prescribes. No individual or group should be privileged to inflict the kind of harm that the law is meant to prevent.[130] Equality insists that politicians respect a basic measure of consistency when they infuse the planks in their political platforms with the coercive force of the law.

The difficulty that many people (including members of the Supreme Court) have with the principle of equality is not so much in comprehending the basic idea as it is in figuring out how to apply this standard or measuring device. Many students worry that a definition of equality that is built on a principle of proportionality or consistency would allow lawmakers to pass rules and regulations that discriminate against minority groups such as Jews, Blacks, and Aboriginal people, so long as everyone in the group were treated the same. It was, in fact, precisely this concern that caused the Court to reject the 'similarly situated' test in the seminal case of *Andrews v. Law Society of British Columbia.*

Though the fear of the Court is one that many students also feel, it is not one that has any basis in fact. As we saw in the analysis of the operation of section 1, that is not how the proportionality principle works. That principle is much more than Dicey's traditional formulation of the rule of law as the 'equal administration' of the law. In testing whether a law satisfies the equality, or consistency test, the idea is not to judge the classification used by the law in terms of itself. Rather, the Court is expected to evaluate the classification – the means – in terms of the larger purposes that the law is meant to serve.

The 'similarly situated' test is supposed to be applied in the same way as the principle of proportionality under section 1. Both ensure that everyone affected by a set of circumstances that the law is meant to redress or engages in behaviour that the law is designed to curtail will be treated consistently – no differently from – others whose circumstances are essentially the same. Understood in this way, neither the anti-Semitic laws passed by the Nazis in Germany nor the racist laws that Ottawa has enacted, singling out Aboriginal people for special regulation and control,[131] could satisfy the test of proportionality. A law that is passed to deter drunk and disorderly conduct should not be validated unless it treats both Aboriginal and non-Aboriginal offenders the same.

With this description of the Court's misunderstanding of the equality clause, we can finish our discussion about the scope of the Charter and the principle of constitutional supremacy. We have analysed the most important doctrines developed by the Court that have restricted the reach of the Charter and compromised its supremacy.[132] The constitutional defect – of validating laws that cannot meet basic standards of rationality and proportionality – is always the same and should now be clear. In every case where the judges recognize a limit on the reach of the Charter or one of the rights and freedoms that it guarantees, the Court fails in its role as 'guardian of the constitution.' To maximize the protection that the Charter can provide imposes an obligation on the Court to develop doctrines and modes of reasoning that enhance personal autonomy and human dignity as much as possible. This is a constitutional imperative that no state official, not even a judge, can ignore.

In fact, no one I know disputes the principle of constitutional supremacy and the logic that it entails. Those inclined to defend the record of the Court rarely, if ever, address the constitutionality of its practice of implying restrictions on the scope of the Charter and the principles of rationality and proportionality. For the most part, both the text and the logic of the constitution are conveniently ignored. Instead, typically, they defend the Court's implying of limits on the reach of the Charter and its muted application of the 'proportionality principles' with pragmatic arguments about expediency and social utility. Two arguments in particular are thought to justify the Court's thinking about its powers of review. One is the familiar 'floodgates' argument; the other is about the Court's 'institutional competence' and the functions that it can effectively perform.

Though policy arguments – that scarce resources or institutional competences require constitutional supremacy to give way – often have an initial attraction for some, on reflection they eventually persuade very few. The Court itself has recognized that administrative costs cannot justify laws or rules that seriously interfere with important aspects of people's lives.[133] Moreover, given the huge expense involved in pressing a constitutional challenge all the way to the Supreme Court, and the fact that if a limit on someone's personal freedom is relatively small it can usually be justified under section 1, the idea that long queues will develop along Wellington Avenue seems alarmist in the extreme! No potential litigant will find much encouragement in being told that the interest or activity that the law restricts is one that falls within one of the Charter's guarantees if he or she is also advised that the Court will almost certainly find that the law can satisfy the tests in section 1. Few people are eager to push forward cases that will cost them enormous sums if they are likely to lose. Certainly, as it stands, there is little reason for the Court to worry that it will be flooded with cases if it holds Governments and their officials to account every time they exercise the powers of state. Compared to that of other major courts around the world, the caseload of the Supreme Court of Canada is actually quite light.[134]

Nor is there much substance to the argument that doctrines of deferential or tiered review or definitional balancing help courts to avoid becoming too deeply enmeshed in policy-making. The argument about the institutional competence of the Court misconceives the way the principles of rationality and proportionality work. As we saw in the federalism cases, and again here in the area of human rights, when courts apply the principles properly, the judges are really not engaged in an act of balancing or policy formation at all.

The lesson of the cases we have just reviewed is that, as a practical matter, the Court's primary job is ensuring that no person (or minority group) is burdened (or ignored) gratuitously (unnecessarily) or in a way that is out of all proportion with the way others have been treated elsewhere and in the past (consistently). Contrary to the beliefs of some, the Court's task is not to balance the policy of legislation against 'the policy of the Charter.'[135] As the Court itself has repeatedly stressed, its role is not to 'second guess' the wisdom or the merits of whatever it is asked to review. Judges should never rank the relative worth of the various interests affected by a law according to their own personal views or by what they believe to be the prevailing mood in the community. To reason from personal and popular beliefs is the way to do politics, but not law. Law proceeds from the overriding purposes of the constitution and the tests of rationality and proportionality to which it gives rise. As we have just seen, in virtually every case in which the Supreme Court has ruled that a law offends the Charter, it did so simply because the Government that enacted it could not prove that the policy that it devised was the least drastic means available to accomplish its objectives.

When a court adheres to the framework of analysis that the rationality and proportionality principles create, the function of the judges is basically a comparative one. Just as in federalism cases, the essence of the job is to review a series of alternative policies, looking for the best analogies. The critical search is for policy instruments (alternative means) that might accomplish the purposes of the law under review in ways that either interfere less with the freedom of those adversely affected by the law or are at least more consistent with how they, or other 'free and democratic' governments, have restricted other people's freedom elsewhere and in the past. As in virtually every other major area of law, the Court's reasoning process is primarily analogical, looking to see how the law that is before it compares to other laws and policies that those challenging and defending the law say are most like the one being reviewed. The rules of rationality and proportionality guide the Court in evaluating the competing interests that are affected by a challenged law. They are measures of necessity and consistency against which the Court can test any legal rule or decision.

Whether the rule or regulation that is challenged is a matter of criminal law or is related to social and economic life in the community does not affect the job of the Court or the role it will play. In the *Labour Trilogy*, Bertha Wilson and Brian Dickson did not need any special expertise to recognize that a law that restricts the right to strike of workers who perform essential services (such as health, police, and firefighting) is a more rational and reasonable policy than one that indiscriminately restricts the rights of all public servants, no matter what kind of job they do. Similarly, in *PIPS*, it was clear to Peter Cory, who dissented in the case, that the standard procedure that is part of every collective bargaining regime across the country and that allows employees to select whatever union they want to be certified as their bargaining agent promotes both the constitutional freedom of workers to associate with each other in organizations of their own choosing and the policy objectives underlying our collective bargaining laws better than one that allows the employer to usurp that choice and designate one union for everyone, no matter what their preferences might be.

Out of an abundance of caution, it is perhaps appropriate to repeat a point that was made at the end of our review of federalism law. To say that the process of enforcing constitutional rights is not about judges' subjectively balancing the competing interests or values that are raised by a case, or that concepts such as tiered review and definitional balancing are not legitimate expressions of constitutional law, is not to say that judges have no discretion in deciding cases. In every case, each judge must make up his or her own mind on the evidence – on the facts – that are before the court. One judge may be satisfied that there is enough evidence to establish that the public welfare was at risk or that there were no alternative policies available to a Government to realize its objectives, while another judge may want more. As we saw in the federalism decisions, constitutional law is not like a computer program that can be operated mechanically and without any possibility for human error or choice. It is inherent in the concept of law that an adjudicator must make a fresh decision – a judgment – on the facts of each case. Each judge must determine for him- or herself how the law under review measures up against the tests of necessity and consistency.

Discretion in deciding what conclusions the rules of rationality and proportionality call for in any case is, however, altogether different from recognizing a discretion in the judge as to whether a rule of law should be applied or, if it should, how vigorously it ought to be enforced. The former is, as we saw in the last chapter, inherent in the nature of law. The latter denies law any meaningful substance or coherence.

At the end of the day then, it turns out that the critic is only half right. It is true that, as in its federalism jurisprudence, the law that the Supreme Court has built up around the Charter is badly flawed. But it doesn't have to be that way. Had the Court remained faithful to the principle of constitutional supremacy and the logic that it implies, its record would not be as uneven and inconsistent as it is. The real protection that the Charter can provide against state powers' being exercised in an arbitrary and abusive way could be extended much further afield.

Even if the Charter jurisprudence could be used to persuade sceptics and critics to reconsider their views, it is likely that another group of commentators will remain pessimistic about the judiciary's commitment to protecting human rights. When one stands back and reflects on all the ways in which the Court has abandoned and/or qualified the proportionality principles in so many different areas of law, it is quite natural to experience a sense of disquiet and even despair. It seems that we are back in exactly the same space we found ourselves at the end of our analysis of Canadian federalism law. The way the Court has read the Charter and applied the proportionality principles has been very uneven, even quite arbitrary at times. When you read the judgments of the Court chronologically, there is no avoiding the conclusion that the constitutional protection of human rights in Canada has become weaker and weaker over time. Large parts of the most basic aspects of people's lives, related to their work, social and economic well-being, and ordinary, interpersonal relations, already have been put completely outside or substantially shielded from any meaningful kind of review. Within ten short years, those responsible for guarding the constitution have encrusted it with a series of qualifications and provisos that has seriously compromised the principles of justice that it contains.

As discouraging as the Court's record of human rights protection has been, however, it is too early to give up hope. Civil libertarians and social activists whose instinct might be to abandon constitutional litigation in favour of more political strategies of liberation should remember that the Court's record resolving federalism disputes was uneven and unpredictable at times but that eventually, and on the whole, the judiciary has helped preserve the autonomy and law-making authority of both the federal and the provincial governments. It is important to put the Court's performance on rights in the context of its experience shoring up the federal structure of the country. The fact that the jurisprudence that the Court has written in Charter cases is so similar to how it settled disputes over the division of powers gives reason to hope that, sooner or later, the Court will get things right on human rights as well.

Human rights activists must also see that the way the Supreme Court has been able to derive the same standards and tests of constitutional validity from two radically different texts provides compelling evidence about the integrity and the possibility of law. Reading the Court's Charter and federalism decisions together provides a powerful account of the unity and coherence of law. The common analytical framework the Court applies to both kinds of disputes tells a strong story about the neutrality and universality of 'the rule of law.'

Against this, some people might want to question the soundness of my instinct to encourage human rights activists to look on the bright side of things. The most discriminating students sometimes say that the juxtaposition of federalism and human rights law actually undercuts the idea that there is a universal, objective way of determining the constitutionality of law. Rather than conjuring up an image of constitutional law as an all-encompassing, unified system in which the same principles are applied in every case, they point out that the way I have described the rules of constitutional law seems to result in the powers of the courts being applied deferentially and with considerable caution and restraint in federalism law but vigorously and enthusiastically when they are enlisted in the cause of human rights. For these students there is a sharp – potentially fatal – tension in the way I have portrayed these two domains of constitutional law.

On reflection, however, it can be seen that the apparent inconsistency in the way the constitution directs the principles of rationality and proportionality to be applied in federalism and in human rights cases is just that – apparent. Even though the principles seem to require the courts to be much more actively involved in human rights cases than in federalism disputes, this is not because the judges are applying them differently in the two sets of cases. The differences in the results of the federalism and the human rights cases are not caused by the courts applying the principles of rationality and proportionality deferentially in the former and more aggressively in the latter. Rather, the outcomes diverge because in federalism cases the overarching commitment to the independence and sovereignty of two levels of government usually argues for upholding the law, while, when human rights are at stake, the logic of equality, personal autonomy, and human dignity on which the Charter is based results in more findings of constitutional invalidity.

In federalism cases, the principles of rationality and proportionality are derived from and give expression to the federal principle and the idea that there are two orders of government that are coordinate and equal. As we saw in chapter 2, to respect and give effect to the federal principle argues in favour of allowing both Ottawa and the provinces as much room to manoeuvre as possible. To ensure that the federal principle operates to its full effect, the Court must apply the tests of rationality and proportionality in a way that will maximize the law-making powers of both levels of government and that results in many findings of constitutional validity. As we saw in chapter 2, concurrency is the vehicle through which the logic of maximizing the sovereignty of both orders of government is operationalized and the principle of rationality (necessity) made to govern the resolution of federalism disputes.

In Charter cases, by contrast, the contest is between individuals and groups (majorities and minorities) within the same community, and the 'proportionality principles' are enlisted in aid of a different set of values, including human dignity, personal autonomy, and pluralism. In these cases, the logic of maximizing such rights as equality and liberty acts as a check on the idea of popular sovereignty and the principle of majority rule. The values underlying the Charter do not argue in favour of always trying to broaden the law-making powers of government the way the federal principle did. Here the competing interests cannot as easily be maximized by enlarging the authority of both. In human rights cases it is the principle of least dramatic means that is the agent for maximizing constitutional values (of personal autonomy, pluralism, and so on) and through which rationality extends its rule.

In Charter cases, the values of equality, human dignity, personal autonomy, and so on must be reconciled with the values of democracy and popular rule. Human rights cases, more than federalism disputes, are 'zero-sum games.' Rather than using rationality and proportionality to promote the law-making authority of two orders of government, here judges are required to identify solutions that will give as much recognition to the freedom of ordinary citizens as to the law-making powers of governments.

The idea that the principles of rationality and proportionality and the framework of analysis that they create may produce different results in different circumstances and when different interests and values are at stake will seem less foreign and unsettling to students who have some familiarity with other systems of constitutional law. As we shall see in the next chapter, though the ideas of rationality and proportionality are at the centre of the constitutional jurisprudence written by all the major courts around the world, the judgments that they write on similar issues may be dramatically opposed in the conclusions that they reach.[136] Like general rules in any area of law, the way the principles of rationality and proportionality work depends on the circumstances, including the legal and political context, of the case.

At the end of the day, then, there is good reason for the human rights activist to keep faith in the idea of judicial review and the principles of justice that it is designed to enforce. However much disappointment he or she may feel about the record of the Court, that record cannot be blamed on the law. Even though its jurisprudence is as uneven here as in its federalism decisions, it also shows that when the principles of rationality and proportionality are applied with vigilance and allowed to have their full effect, they can do a lot of good work. Even though they consist of nothing more than purely formal, abstract rules of logic and practical reasoning, constitutional rights can contribute to social and personal well-being in a community in important and meaningful ways. When the Court applied the tests in *Oakes* vigorously, women gained more control over their bodies, linguistic minorities secured additional space within which their cultural identities could flourish, and public servants had much more freedom to participate in the full political life of their communities. Cases like these show unambiguously that when law is invoked to protect human rights the quality of justice in a country will improve.

The reason that the Charter of Rights has not provided as much protection as it could is not the fault of the law. It is simply because a majority of the judges who sat on the Court in the time immediately following its entrenchment were not wholly committed to the idea of constitutional review. After an open and self conscious debate among themselves as to how the Charter should be interpreted and applied, the Court, as a collectivity,[137] deliberately chose a very cautious and conservative conception of the Court's powers of review and what the principles that it articulated in *Oakes* entailed. Responsibility for the limited impact of the Charter lies with a failure of human will rather than with the concept of constitutional rights.

To ensure that the law protects human rights as much as it can requires the same kind of institutional responses that we considered at the end of chapter 2, in examining the courts' role in federal-provincial relations. In the federalism cases, we saw that the courts did not discharge their powers of review in a way that supported the federal structure of the country when they were led by judges, such as Haldane and Laskin, who were inclined to rely on standards of constitutional validation that were much more stringent and rigid than the principles of rationality and proportionality. In its Charter jurisprudence, the Supreme Court has been distracted by judges such as Jean Beetz, Gerard LaForest, and William McIntyre, who went to the other extreme and advocated the use of doctrines and tests that offer considerably less protection for human rights than the standards that the Charter contains. In both cases, what is required, if the Court is to be an effective guardian of the constitution, is that those who are appointed to it understand that whenever the constitutionality of any law is challenged, they should always apply the principles of rationality and proportionality in a rigorous and uncompromising way.

4

Comparative Constitutional Law

INTRODUCTION

In the last two chapters, we have canvassed the major principles of law and the method of reasoning used by the Supreme Court of Canada (and the Judicial Committee of the Privy Council) in testing the constitutionality of whatever federal or provincial policies they have been asked to review. When one stands back from the jurisprudence that has been written by these courts, two characteristics of Canadian constitutional law stand out from all the rest. On the one hand, over the course of almost 125 years of judges' reviewing the constitutionality of thousands of pieces of law and administrative regulations, two tests of constitutional validation (rationality and proportionality) tower above the rest, whether an issue of federalism was involved or someone's human rights were at stake. On the other hand, as prominent and long-standing as these principles have been, experience shows that these rules, which provide the analytical framework for the courts, are extremely vulnerable to being manipulated and applied to suit the purposes (and philosophies of law) of individual judges.

After they have read all of the leading cases, few students take issue with the idea that Canadian constitutional law is less a story of judges adapting a century old constitution to the circumstances of a modern, post-industrial state by means of a creative, evolving interpretation of its text than it is about how two basic principles of rationality and proportionality have provided the Court with the same framework of analysis from beginning to end. Nor do they dispute the claim that these principles give expression to timeless ideals of equality, justice, and personal autonomy. The rationality requirement, which obliges all those entrusted with the legal powers of the state to use the most moderate means possible to pursue their political goals, maximizes the freedom of individuals and smaller communities to control their own destinies. And the ends-oriented principle of proportionality, or consistency guarantees a measure of equality of treatment by insisting that whatever restrictions are imposed on personal autonomy, or the sovereignty of one or other order of government, must be roughly equal to the kinds of constraints others have been made to endure.

Though the constitutional jurisprudence written by the Supreme Court and the Privy Council illustrates the formal, immutable character of law, it also shows that law is utterly dependent on humans to make it work. We have seen that the history of Canadian constitutional law is marked by periods in which the principles of review were applied by the courts in radically different ways. Canada's experience with judicial review teaches us that unless the principles are applied dispassionately, impartially, and in the utmost good faith, the integrity of the idea of the rule of law and constitutional order can quickly be lost.

In this chapter, I want to put the practice of Canadian constitutional law in a wider, global context. Studying the judgments of other courts entrusted with the powers of judicial review shows how the principles of rationality and proportionality are universal in space as well as in time. As with so much else of Canadian life, the way law is used to organize and regulate the powers of the state is pretty similar to the way in which constitutional law operates in other modern, free, and democratic countries.

Even though most students can see from the cases that constitutional law is mostly about principles of rationality and proportionality and about the duties and obligations that lawmakers and administrators owe to the public whose lives they control, many of them find this discovery strange, even counter-intuitive. Traditionally, human rights activists and others not trained in the law tend to think that, when the courts exercise their powers of review, their really critical job is interpreting the words and phrases that a constitution contains and figuring out exactly what rights and freedoms it protects. Especially among those weaned on American constitutional law, the view is widely shared that the only legitimate way judges can protect people's rights is by reading and elaborating the text of the constitution as sensitively as they can. That, and not requiring Governments to justify each and every initiative that they propose against general standards of justice, is how most lay people think courts go about their business of protecting human rights. Indeed, some American commentators[1] (and judges)[2] can be very critical of courts (and their colleagues) when it appears that principles of rationality and proportionality determine the outcome of a case.

In this chapter, I want to address this lack of familiarity and instinctive hostility with the idea that the most important part of constitutional law and human rights can be reduced to two elementary principles of justice or equality. In a summary (and therefore unavoidably incomplete) fashion, I want to describe the general framework of analysis and major doctrinal principles that have been developed by courts in other parts of the world that have also had extensive experience enforcing a constitutional bill of rights. A review of the jurisprudence written by the Supreme Courts of the United States, India, and Japan, by the European Court of Human Rights, and by the Constitutional Court of Germany shows that though each court has been influenced by a different set of institutional, political, and historical circumstances, and has developed its own unique style of review, all of them base their judgments on whether a law is constitutional or not on standards of rationality and proportionality. As a practical matter, it is principles of justification, much more than questions of interpretation, that determine how well human rights are protected. From a comparative perspective, even the jurisprudence of the U.S. Supreme Court can be seen to be grounded much more on a means-ends analysis of whatever law or administrative act it has been asked to review than on some elaborate exposition of what those who originally drafted or subsequently interpreted the Bill of Rights were trying to do.

The fact that principles of rationality and proportionality provide a common analytical framework for courts everywhere to identify human rights violations should provide considerable reassurance for students unaccustomed to thinking about human rights in this way. Showing judges employing the same process of reasoning no matter where they sit is a powerful piece of evidence in support of the integrity and the intelligibility of the law. The body of comparative jurisprudence written by these courts gives law and these legal principles a measure of objectivity and neutrality that transcends national borders and different cultures and environments.

The story of how the courts have protected human rights and exercised their powers of review is not one, however, that will give undisturbed comfort to human rights activists. Reading cases from these other jurisdictions shows that, like their counterparts in Canada, judges all over the world have, in different ways and to different degrees, displayed an unease with the role of measuring the decisions of the other two elected branches of government against broad standards of rationality and proportionality. Courts everywhere have, at one time or another, expressed doubts about the idea that lawmakers and administrators should have to meet these tests every time they exercise the powers of the state. The tension between the duties that the rules of constitutional law impose and the deferential mindset of the courts, which afflicts Canadian constitutional law, is one that is felt in every major national and international court in the world. For human rights activists who believe in the law, comparing how constitutional law has evolved around the world makes the idea of casting judges in the role of guardians of the constitution and defenders of human rights ambiguous at best.

Because the Americans have been at the job so much longer than anyone else, and because principles of rationality and proportionality are so alien to the way most people think of American constitutional law, it seems prudent to begin this comparative overview in Washington, DC. After seeing how these principles have been developed in U.S. constitutional law, we can move on to examine the most important parts of the constitutional jurisprudence written by the other major courts in Asia and Europe that are charged with protecting human rights. At the conclusion of the chapter, we should have a much better sense of how pervasive these norms of constitutional validation really are and how widespread the practice is of casting the concepts of human rights and judicial review in terms of the duties and obligations that lawmakers and their officials owe to those they represent. In the last chapter, with the benefit of this wider focus and understanding, we can stand back and reflect on what this comparative jurisprudence teaches us about the possibility of constitutional law and the intelligibility of the choice being made by numerous countries around the world at the close of the twentieth century, of entrenching a written bill of rights in the constitutional framework of their governments.

THE UNITED STATES

However foreign the principles of rationality and proportionality are to Americans' own understanding of what constitutional review is all about, to a comparativist they permeate every nook and cranny of American constitutional law. For example, the most fundamental rules that the U.S. Supreme Court has developed to define the reach of the constitution – to distinguish the public sector, where the Bill of Rights applies, from the private, where it does not – are simple analytical tools that allow it to catalogue and evaluate the societal and personal interests at stake.[3] Similarly, the principles and tests that it uses to mark out the division of responsibility between the three branches of government – such as the political-questions doctrine – are based on and give expression to standards of balance and proportionality.[4] But it is in the substantive rules and doctrines that the Court has developed to identify laws that are compatible with the constitution and those that are not that the principles of rationality and proportionality and the means-ends analysis are most pertinent and easy to spot.

There are three great pillars in the U.S. Bill of Rights on which almost all American constitutional law is built. Two are contained in the fifth and fourteenth amendments, and together they guarantee that neither the federal nor any state government can deprive anyone of 'life, liberty or property without due process of law' or deny them 'the equal protection of the law.' The third is made up of the fundamental rights of speech and religion, embedded in the first amendment. Almost all of the important doctrines that the U.S. Supreme Court has developed for protecting human rights have been built on one of these three cornerstones, and all of them rely on standards of rationality and proportionality to evaluate the ends and the means of whatever law or administrative act is under review.

Notwithstanding their very different texts, the way each of these constitutional guarantees protects human rights is basically the same. To justify laws that impinge on fundamental rights that fall within any of these entitlements, the state must show that the purposes or public interests that they serve are substantial and that the means – the particular policy instruments developed to realize those objectives – were no more restrictive than necessary to realize those ends.[5] When the Bill of Rights is defended most vigorously by the Court, lawmakers must prove that their purposes are 'compelling' relative to the measure of personal freedom that is at stake and that their policy choices (means) are drawn in a way that impinges as little as possible on constitutional guarantees. 'Compelling state interests' is the label used to describe purposes of state action that are more important (pressing, weightier) than any human rights violations that they inflict (proportionality), and 'least restrictive means' is the phrase that it uses to describe the most rigorous standard of rationality that it applies in evaluating the integrity of the policy instrument under review.

The way the U.S. Supreme Court has interpreted the first, fifth, and fourteenth amendments parallels closely the way the Supreme Court of Canada has come to read the major grants of power, such as 'trade and commerce' and 'peace, order and good government,' that are set out in section 91 of the original BNA Act. In both cases, the courts have defined the most important parts of the text in terms of rationality and proportionality, even though the words in the two documents probably have less in common than do gophers and the game of golf. Whether a claim is based on 'due process,' 'equal protection,' or one of the 'first amendment' rights, proportionality and rationality define the maximum protection for human rights that the American (or indeed any) constitution can provide.

What is striking about American constitutional law is not that the major doctrines that the Supreme Court has developed to give meaning to the most important parts of the Bill of Rights can be reduced to and are organized around these two principles and a means-ends framework of analysis. What is distinctive is that only a narrow range of public policy is subordinated to these rigorous standards of review. Essentially the Supreme Court has compartmentalized all the different areas of social policy in which governments are engaged into specific and discrete categories, only a select number of which are subjected to really searching review by the Court. For example, under the due process clause, only laws that affect fundamental values and interests related to personal matters such as marriage, procreation, and family life are required to meet the 'compelling state interest' – 'necessary means' – tests.[6] Even some of the most basic procedural rights such as the right to a hearing[7] or to a lawyer[8] are guaranteed only when the law threatens, in the first case, a benefit or advantage recognized in law and, in the second, a person's physical liberty.

The equal protection clause and the first amendment rights have been circumscribed and qualified in a similar way. According to the Supreme Court, the guarantee of equality applies only to a limited range of laws and administrative activity that affects 'fundamental rights' such as voting[9] and interstate travel[10] or that use 'suspect classifications' such as race[11] to restrict the benefits or assign the burdens of government programs, and then only if the discrimination is done quite intentionally.[12] Similarly, the first amendment's guarantee of freedom of speech is strictly enforced only when the law quite deliberately tries to control what people say and either the content of the communication is regarded as being especially closely connected with the values of personal autonomy, search for truth, promotion of democratic government, and so on that underlie the first amendment and/or a question of access to some public – governmental – forum is at stake.[13] Outside of intimate relations and associations formed to exercise other first amendment rights, freedom of association has received relatively little protection from the Court.[14] Even when rights of religious freedom are at stake, lawmakers do not always have to show that they have used the least restrictive policy to accomplish pressing political objectives.[15]

Though the range of government policy that may be measured against the principles of rationality and proportionality is relatively small, it is also characteristic of American constitutional law that within this select group of cases the Court does exercise its powers of review in a vigorous and uncompromising way. When rights and values central to the idea of a free and democratic society are at stake, there is probably no other Court in the world that applies these principles so severely. When the Court is of a mind to exercise its powers of review strictly, the standards of compelling state interests and least restrictive (necessary) means are invariably fatal in fact.[16]

'Strict scrutiny' by the Court means a searching evaluation of both the ends and the means of whatever law or administrative act is under review. Common to some of the most well-known cases in U.S. constitutional law, in which the Court invalidated a wide range of important state policies dealing with abortion,[17] the death penalty,[18] racial discrimination and affirmative action,[19] employment standards legislation,[20] voting rights,[21] and campaign financing[22] was a probing, exacting analysis of what the impugned law was trying to do and the way it went about its business. Like the Canadian Supreme Court, in a large number of cases in which the U.S. Court struck down a law as a violation of someone's constitutional rights it was the means-oriented principle of rationality or necessity that did most of the work.[23] Overbreadth, vagueness, less restrictive means are pervasive themes in the U.S. practice of constitutional review.[24]

What is quite idiosyncratic about the way the American Supreme Court exercises its powers of review when fundamental rights and core values are at stake is the demanding standards that it sets for the kind of policy objectives that lawmakers and administrators can legitimately pursue. When the scrutiny is strict, the Court is not shy about measuring the importance of the social objective promoted by a law against the restrictions of human rights that it causes and to find the resulting balance wanting.[25] In other cases, legislative goals that are lofty in theory have been dismissed in particular cases as having little or no basis in fact.[26] In its most bullish moments, the Court has even identified a list of policy objectives – including equalizing 'natural' disparities of wealth and social advantage,[27] deterring migration of indigents,[28] censoring the expression of particular points of view,[29] and any religious purpose whatsoever[30] – that are beyond the constitutional competence of any lawmaker or administrator to translate into law.

The exacting scrutiny of policy objectives which the U.S. Supreme Court undertakes when what it regards as fundamental rights or core values are at stake sets it apart from all the other major courts that enforce constitutional or international bills of rights. For most of its history, it also stands in sharp contrast with its own performance in other areas of government regulation, where it has virtually abdicated any supervisory role over the other two branches of government. Unquestionably the largest area of public policy that the Court has put beyond any meaningful review relates to social and economic programs. On labour laws,[31] business regulations,[32] Sunday shopping,[33] and welfare programs,[34] for example, the Court has defined a very marginal role for itself.

But the extent of the Court's abdication is much more pervasive than that. There is a whole range of laws and regulations dealing mainly with issues of foreign relations and national security that the Court has characterized as being 'political questions' and beyond its powers to review.[35] In addition, the Court has said that education is not a fundamental right or interest of a kind like voting or interstate travel that warrants its close attention.[36] Nor are laws dealing with private sexual relations[37] or people's personal appearance.[38] Poverty does not qualify as a suspect classification,[39] and all the procedural entitlements that the due process clause guarantees are available only to claimants who can show that the state has interfered with a right or interest that is recognized in law.[40] Even with the first amendment right of freedom of speech, the Court has embraced the technique of 'definitional' or 'categorical' balancing,[41] to exempt from any kind of searching evaluation laws that regulate speech and conduct that is inflammatory,[42] malicious,[43] libellous,[44] obscene,[45] pornographic,[46] or symbolic,[47] or that takes place in public places (such as jails), in which communicative activity may frustrate or interfere with the operation of some other aspect of community life.[48]

In all these areas of government activity, it is not that the Court has rejected the means-ends framework of analysis in favour of some other method of reasoning. Whether they are applied categorically to exclude different areas of social policy from review or are aimed more particularly at a specific law it has been asked to test, the principles of rationality and proportionality are still the Court's primary instruments for distinguishing laws that are faithful to the Bill of Rights from those that are not. What is different is the way in which these principles are applied.

In these areas of public policy, the Court has been willing to accept almost any 'public interest' as justifying whatever limitation of constitutional rights a law entails.[49] Simply proving that lawmakers had a 'legitimate interest' is all that is required. Any conceivable purpose might be accepted, even if it was not one that actually precipitated enactment of the law.[50] Other interests – such as the protection of children from sexual exploitation,[51] or regulation of the economy[52] – are weighted so heavily by the Court that Governments have been given discretion to regulate in these areas pretty much as they please.

Running parallel with this superficial analysis of legislative ends, the Court also gives lawmakers a lot of leeway in choosing which particular policy instruments – means – best suit their political agenda. The fit that is required between ends and means is much looser in these areas than when fundamental rights are at stake. Perfection – choosing the best, least restrictive policy option – is not the operative rule. Simply having a rational connection will do. Only laws that are 'substantially' broader, more restrictive, and so on than they need to be are vulnerable to being invalidated.[53]

The radical discontinuity between the two different levels or tiers of review that characterizes so much of U.S. constitutional law has been muted somewhat in recent years. Beginning in the 1970s, the Court created a third, or intermediate track for a small group of cases claiming violation of the equal protection clause and some first amendment rights. For example, laws that differentiated between the sexes[54] or singled out aliens[55] from the rest of the community sometimes have been given more rigorous scrutiny, under the equal protection clause, although not the demanding evaluation that strict scrutiny involves. Similarly, commercial expression, which was once declared to be outside the first amendment's protection has since come to be reviewed much more closely.[56]

To justify these sorts of laws, the Supreme Court has required Governments to establish that the purposes or public interest they are designed to promote are 'important' and 'substantial' – something between the 'compelling' and the 'legitimate' state interest standards that strict and minimal scrutiny imply. Similarly, the fit between ends and means has to be 'substantially related,' which means that while Governments do not have to prove that the particular policy instruments they choose are absolutely 'necessary' (are the least restrictive alternatives available), they do have to do a good deal more than simply show that the law is rationally related to its basic objectives.

When the judges work this middle ground, the principles of rationality and proportionality have had some real bite. For example, the Court has ruled that some purposes – like administrative convenience or efficiency – are not weighty enough to justify laws that discriminate against women and aliens.[57] Similarly, where the Court is satisfied that alternative, less drastic policies are available to the lawmakers to accomplish their purposes, that can be fatal as well.[58]

The development of three different tracks along which the principles of rationality and proportionality may be applied gives American constitutional law a character and style all its own. As interpreted by the Court, the sweeping and majestic phrases of the first, fifth, and fourteenth amendments have been transformed into a complex labyrinth of highly compartmentalized, categorical rules about what kinds of programs lawmakers can set for themselves in different areas of social policy. Even though nothing in the text authorizes it to read the Bill of Rights in this way, the Court has substantially reduced the protection of the constitution by ruling that the constraints that the Bill of Rights imposes on lawmakers vary enormously, depending on what aspect of community life is at stake. The Court has taken what is unquestionably the world's shortest and most laconic constitutional statement of human rights and engrafted on it a set of rules, and a framework of analysis, that is as complex and doctrinaire as the jurisprudence written by any court in the world.[59]

Indeed, the jurisprudence written by the American Supreme Court has been made even more complicated and difficult to follow because, beyond its preference for a highly categorical approach and for rules that draw bright lines around different areas of government policy, it is also (relative to the way constitutional law is practised in other countries) very fluid and open to change. More than their brethren in other parts of the world, American judges feel free to develop (and are often chosen to sit on the Court because of) their theories as to how these different tiers of review should be applied and over time, as different justices take their place on the Bench, the mind of the Court may change.[60] Judges can and do disagree and/or change their views as to what standard of review is appropriate in any area of social policy,[61] and even landmark cases are vulnerable to being overturned.[62]

When one compares the jurisprudence that the U.S. Supreme Court has written about the American Bill of Rights to the way other major courts have exercised their powers of review, the latter always seem quite simple and straightforward. In both Asia and Europe, the courts are inclined to apply the principles of rationality and proportionality in a way that is much more pragmatic and less doctrinaire.

INDIA

Though constitutional law in India, has developed a style all its own, in its broad outline and method of reasoning, it is pretty much like constitutional law anywhere else. Reading the judgments of the Supreme Court of India, one can see rationality and proportionality deeply embedded in the basic framework within which the constitutionality of law and administrative action is determined. Though the long and detailed text of the Indian constitution sometimes makes it difficult to spot the principles doing their work, on close reading one can see that they do provide the most important tests to differentiate laws that are constitutional from those that are not.

In fact, compared to the other major courts that practise constitutional review, the Indian Court has committed itself quite publicly and enthusiastically to defending human rights and to the principles of justice on which they are based. Its jurisprudence is distinguished by eloquent and impassioned calls to those exercising the powers of the state to respect the dignity and autonomy of those they rule.[63] At critical moments in the country's political history, the Court has resisted blatant attempts by the elected branches of government to restrict judicial review.[64] One of the recurrent themes of Indian constitutional law is that the socialist precepts of justice and economic security that lie at the heart of the Indian state can – and must – be pursued in a manner that respects the right of everyone to control as much of their own destiny as possible.[65]

When the judges in New Delhi have been confronted with laws that were overdrawn or overly burdensome, they generally have not been hesitant to declare them constitutionally infirm. In many of the Supreme Court's important rulings, it is easy to see the principles of rationality and proportionality at work, though they are known by other names. 'Arbitrariness,' 'reasonableness,' and 'fairness' are the labels under which these principles operate in Indian constitutional law.[66]

The means-oriented principle of rationality has figured prominently in major cases dealing with all the most important constitutional guarantees of equality (articles 14–18), freedom (articles 19, 25–6), and due process (article 21). Laws limiting freedom to publish,[67] engage in political demonstrations,[68] pursue vocations,[69] and live where one chooses[70] have all been struck down as contrary to article 19 when they were drafted in ways that were more absolute and extreme than their purposes required. University rules drawn so as to deny admission to certain individuals and groups who otherwise fell squarely within the mandate of the institution have been invalidated as failing to respect the right to equality.[71] And laws that made the death penalty mandatory for certain classes of offences[72] and made financial security an absolute condition for obtaining bail[73] were found to offend the due process clause because the Court considered that there were alternative, less drastic policies available to accomplish the desired purposes. When the Court was of the view that the political branches of government had drafted laws in ways that were too heavy-handed[74] or too vague,[75] or that allowed too much[76] or too little[77] discretion, it did act as an effective check against the powers of the state being exercised arbitrarily and overzealously.

As well as insisting on a modicum of rationality and a measure of precision in the relation between the ends and means of whatever law is under review, the Court has also required lawmakers to respect a degree of proportion and balance between the state's objectives and individuals' constitutional rights. All the major doctrinal threads that have been woven into the fabric of Indian constitutional law – arbitrariness (article 14), reasonableness (article 19), fairness (article 21), and so on – call for the Court to review every law by sizing up and comparing the costs and benefits that it involves.[78] In equality cases, in which affirmative action (reservation) programs are brought to the Court, measuring the public interest – in having the best possible educational, professional, and administrative services – against the claims of equal opportunity of the traditionally disadvantaged is particularly open and explicit.[79] It also has occupied centre stage in the right-to-freedom cases,[80] particularly those involving laws that were enacted to realize the social and economic objectives (such as education, living standards, nutrition, and peace) that are itemized in a list of Directive Principles that are entrenched in part IV of the constitution.[81] Requiring a measure of proportionality between costs and benefits, purpose and effects, was also decisive in some of the Court's leading due process cases, which fix the rights of those caught up in the criminal justice system to have access to their lawyers [82] and to have their legal fees reimbursed by the state when they cannot afford to pay them themselves.[83]

One of the striking features of many of these cases is how, in applying the principles of rationality and proportionality, the Court reasons analogically by looking to how comparable laws are drawn in other countries and states.[84] Laws that are imbalanced or that interfere with people's constitutional rights more than is necessary are often identified with reference to policies and programs that have been enacted in one or another of the states in India or in other free and democratic states. Rules of university admission are tested against procedures followed in recruiting people in other parts of the public service.[85] State laws prohibiting the slaughter of cattle are measured against laws of adjacent states.[86] Policies regulating when people who are being held in custody can have access to their lawyers are tested against opportunities available to other sectors of the inmate population.[87] In these cases, rather than simply judging the substance of the tradeoffs for itself, the Indian Court has endeavoured to make its analysis as objective as possible by using comparable laws of the state's own making as the relevant point of reference.[88]

The way in which the Supreme Court has exercised its powers of review for almost fifty years shows that it is every bit as strong a defender of personal freedom and human dignity as any of the major courts in the free and democratic world.[89] Though the Court can be – and has been – criticized for not always being as consistent and vigilant as it might have been,[90] on the whole it has been quite firm in making rationality and proportionality meaningful tests of constitutional validity. It has incorporated them into its central doctrinal precepts and has guaranteed their permanence by including them in the basic structure of the constitution, which cannot be altered even by formal amendment.[91] It has, for the most part, defined the reach of the constitution broadly, to include the whole of the broader public service,[92] though its application to the judiciary remains a matter of some ambiguity.[93] And its readings of the traditional, first-generation rights to life and liberty of the person to include basic entitlements to social and economic well-being are among the most progressive and innovative in the world.[94]

Cataloguing the cases and doctrines through which the Indian Supreme Court has pressed the principles of rationality and proportionality shows that it has taken its responsibility to guard the constitution and protect human rights very seriously. But it does not really convey how hard the Court has had to work checking arbitrary and abusive initiatives launched in the name of the State. What is perhaps the most impressive feature of the constitutional law of India is that it has been developed within the framework of a constitutional text that has made the work of the judges much more complicated and difficult.

The Indian constitution is one of the most detailed, dense, and prolix statements of how the powers of the state are to be organized and applied in the world, and the Indian Supreme Court has had to wrestle with it every step of the way. For those whose instincts might be to enhance the legitimacy of judicial review by describing the contours of the rights and freedoms in specific and precise terms (rather than with the grand, sweeping language that characterizes most constitutional texts), the experience of the Indian Supreme Court should caution further reflection. Paradoxically, the length and detail of its text have proven to be a minefield of interpretive dilemmas, which the Court has had to defuse in order that the principles of rationality and proportionality can have their day.

The distinctive style of the Indian constitution manifests itself throughout. The text consists of some 395 articles and ten schedules and has been amended over sixty-five times. The right to equality is divided into five separate articles; religious freedom is covered in four. All the other fundamental freedoms are guaranteed in one general article (19), in which very specific qualifying provisos are attached to each area of human activity (expression, association, mobility, vocation) that it protects. In addition, to give expression to the socialist aspirations of India as a modern welfare state, the constitution contains a long list of (non-justiciable) Directive Principles and Fundamental Duties to guide those who have been entrusted with the legislative and executive powers of the State.

The detail and density of this text have presented the Court a host of interpretive problems, which have frequently distracted and diverted it from its primary task of measuring laws and administrative acts against the yardsticks of rationality and proportionality. Oceans of ink have been spilled and forests of trees have been sacrificed figuring out how to reconcile the Directive Principles and Fundamental Duties of the state in parts IV and IVA of the constitution with the Fundamental Rights entrenched in part III.[95] The most famous case in this line of authorities runs in excess of five hundred (double-columned) pages.[96] Even within the parameters of Part III, the Court has had to struggle with the question of whether each article should be read as a discrete, watertight compartment or whether (and to what degree) the fundamental rights that it contains intersect and overlap. For example, the Court has had to decide whether the guarantee of life and personal liberty in article 21 – the 'due process' clause – covers the same set of activities as those protected by the list of fundamental freedoms (expression, association, mobility, and so on) that are itemized in article 19. Similarly, within article 19 itself, the Court has had to determine which limitation clause controls the constitutional validity of laws that impinge on more than one of the freedoms that it guarantees. Likewise, in applying the list of discrete entitlements in which the constitutional norm of equality is expressed, the Court has had to choose between reading all of the articles as integral parts of a common whole and defining some of them (e.g., those protecting affirmative action programs for disadvantaged individuals and groups) as exceptions or limitations on the general rule.

At first, when the Court was faced with such basic interpretive questions, it tended to follow a highly compartmentalized, categorical approach. In the same way the Privy Council once read the BNA Act, and the U.S. Supreme Court analysed its Bill of Rights, the instinct of the Indian Court was to define each right and freedom recognized in part III in terms of different interests and activities. Each right and freedom was regarded as providing an exclusive test of constitutional validity within the domain to which it applied. Bright lines were drawn and doctrines of exclusivity were developed to differentiate the protection that each entitlement secured.[97]

Initially the Court resisted the idea that the rights to equality (article 14), freedom (article 19), and due process (article 21) overlapped in any way.[98] Like the early judgments in Canadian federalism law, the Indian judges showed a strong preference for characterizing each section of their constitution as a discrete and watertight compartment. Separate doctrines of arbitrariness (article 14), reasonableness (article 19), and fair procedure (article 21) were articulated for each. Article 21, it was said, protected those who were subjected to physical restraint by the state, while article 19 guaranteed the freedom of those who were otherwise physically free to do as they pleased.[99]

Even within the guarantees of equality, freedom, and due process of law, the Court tended to read the text as marking out even finer lines of differentiation and categorization. For example, when it first turned its mind to the various equality rights in the constitution, it drew a sharp distinction between the general right to equality (article 14) and the rights of disadvantaged individuals and groups to receive preferential treatment from the state (articles 15[4], 16[4]). For a long time, the Court took the view that the provisions endorsing affirmative action (reservation) programs were the exceptions and the basic guarantees of equality were the rule, and on the basis of that characterization it held that affirmative action plans could never reserve more than 50 per cent of whatever benefits or opportunities were being allocated. When the text was broken down in this way, the 50 per cent limit was a logical imperative, or else, as the Court said more than once, the exception would swallow the rule.[100]

The way in which the text influenced the Court's perception of the constitution as a long list of discrete and independent rights is especially clear in its reading of article 19. Because the constitution specifies different objectives that the state can pursue (e.g., state security, public order, morality, and interests of the general public) when it passes a rule or law that restricts the various fundamental freedoms that article 19 guarantees, the Court has drawn very bright lines to mark off which sorts of interests and activities will receive protection and which will not.[101] For example, because the right of free speech (article 19[1][a]) can be limited only by laws passed for the purpose of protecting (among other things) the sovereignty or security of the country, public order, decency, or morality, the Court has felt constrained to embrace a rather narrow definition of the right and, on one occasion, ruled that commercial expression – such as advertising – did not fall within its terms.[102] On much the same reasoning, the Court has rejected the idea that each of the freedoms protects a series of 'concomitant' rights and has ruled that the right to freedom of association does not include the right to strike.[103] Major boundaries have also been staked out around (and interests and activities excluded from) the right to pursue a profession or trade[104] and the right to practise one's religion without interference from the state.[105]

The preference that the Indian Court has shown for sharp, categorical definitions of what interests and activities the constitution protects has carried over into the second phase of the review process when it focuses on the rule or law or administrative decision that it is asked to review. In the early years, the Court used a traditional 'pith and substance' analysis, looking almost exclusively at the purposes or objectives that the challenged law was meant to promote, and ignoring its indirect, consequential effects.[106] If a law were passed to pursue a purpose that was authorized by the constitution, for all practical purposes that would be the end of the matter, and the law would be validated on that basis alone.[107] The emphasis on purposes was particularly evident in equality cases, in which a very formal classification doctrine was applied.[108] Laws that indirectly or unintentionally[109] restricted rights were effectively immune from review. As long as the purposes of the law were legitimate, the Court did not worry about the means or the methods very much.

Another, quite similar line of reasoning that the Court has favoured is to play down or ignore the particular restriction that a law imposes on some constitutional guarantee and to concentrate on the ways in which those challenging the law were still free to do as they pleased. Laws which limited the bargaining rights of unions,[110] or authorized the dismissal of public servants who were members of the communist party,[111] were held not to violate the challengers' freedom of association because those affected were still free to form unions and join the political party of their choice. Like their brethren in Ottawa, anytime the judges in New Delhi were highly selective about which effects of a law should be influential in determining its constitutional validity, they could effectively put the law being tested beyond any meaningful review.[112]

The sort of categorical reasoning that runs through much of Indian constitutional law is not, on the whole, an approach that is very congenial to the protection of human rights. As happened early on in Canadian federalism law, and in the development of the U.S. Bill of Rights, reading the constitution as a set of discrete and disconnected entitlements has meant that each right or freedom acts as a check or limit on what any other provision can guarantee. Interests and activities that fall outside the scope of a constitutional right may receive less and in some cases no protection at all.[113] In addition, it has meant that the means oriented principle of rationality has played a much more limited role.[114]

As a practical matter, defining constitutional rights in this way has resulted in a system of tiered review in which the nature of the interests and activities regulated by a law has a very significant bearing on the kind of evaluation that it will undergo. In some cases – for example,social and economic laws passed to advance the Directive Principles – the Court's major concern seems to be the bona fides of those responsible for the law or rule under review.[115] In others – for example, when more than one constitutional right is at stake – the Court is prepared to engage in a more searching and rigorous review.[116] In many cases, as we have seen, the Court has evaluated the means or the method, as well as the purposes, of the law under review,[117] though even here there are certain types of laws (for example, rules and regulations implementing social and economic policy) where the Court has said that it will not apply the rationality standard very vigorously.[118]

Though Indian and American constitutional law have a lot in common, it is also the case that, over time, the Supreme Court of India has gradually moved away from a strictly categorical approach. After 45 years of constitutional review, many of the very bright lines that it painted early on have become blurred and begun to fade. Now the Court says that the three great guarantees of equality, freedom, and due process do overlap and that the doctrines of arbitrariness, unreasonableness, and unfairness actually mean very similar things.[119] Now the Court reads the principles of arbitrariness (article 14) and unreasonableness (article 19) into the definition of what constitutes 'due process' (article 21), even though it is known that those who drafted the constitution intended to avoid the problems the Americans have experienced by reading a substantive dimension into this universal precept of law.

The Court has also reconsidered other major boundaries and doctrines that it developed early on. Commercial speech, for example, has since been recognized as deserving some protection.[120] More generally, in equality cases, the Court now seems more inclined to include a means analysis in its assessment[121] and to read the articles dealing with equality as related and mutually reinforcing declarations of a larger principle or ideal, rather than as a series of separate clauses that might clash with each other, as it originally did.[122] Over time, the Court also abandoned the narrow pith-and-substance approach and now looks to both the purpose and effects of a law in determining its constitutional validity.[123] Even the Court's treatment of the relationship between the Directive Principles and the Fundamental Rights is not nearly as categorical and compartmentalized as it once was, and the Court has also analysed it within the overarching framework of ends and means.[124]

The way the Supreme Court of India has exercised its powers of review makes an interesting study for those learning about comparative constitutional law and the protection of human rights. It shows how a group of jurists, when they are so inclined, can adapt and convert a complicated and convoluted text to meet the needs of modern society in ways those who designed the original constitution could never have imagined, much less intended. The Court's extension of India's 'due process' clause to protect people's economic security and physical well-being is as bold and creative an act of constitutional interpretation as a comparativist will find.

At the same time, however, the Indian experience also cautions jurists against trying to protect human rights by loading up on words in the text. Indian constitutional law teaches that more words have tended to result in less, not more, protection for people's rights. It is no accident that many of the most creative and progressive decisions of the Indian Court are focused on article 21, where the text is uncharacteristically brief. Perhaps the most important lesson of Indian constitutional law is that words can only limit, never expand, the protection that a constitution can provide.[125]

JAPAN

If one compares the jurisprudence written by the major courts responsible for enforcing constitutional rights, in terms of the number of laws or acts of state officials that have actually been invalidated, the Supreme Court of Japan stands apart from the rest. Among comparativists, constitutional review in Japan is regarded as the most conservative and cautious in the world. The most powerful instinct of the Japanese judiciary seems to be to avoid confrontation and interference with the work of the other two, elected branches of government. In terms of influencing the policy-making process in Japanese government, the role of the third branch of government has been marginal at best. More than one commentator has observed that the Supreme Court has never said 'no' to any Government on any serious issue of social policy.[126] In almost fifty years of exercising the power of judicial review, the Supreme Court of Japan has struck down initiatives of the legislative and executive branches only six times. Even though the principles of rationality and proportionality are well-known and figure prominently in any description of Japanese constitutional law, the Supreme Court has developed a set of doctrines and provisos that substantially restricts their influence.

There is extensive reference to one and sometimes both principles in almost all of the Court's leading decisions. They go by various names. 'Reasonableness,' 'reasonable classification,' and 'reasonable distinction' are the most common expressions used by the Court when it evaluates whether a challenged law is balanced or proportioned in the way the constitution requires. 'Strict reasonableness' and 'necessity'[127] are the phrases one encounters most frequently when the Court is considering whether the means or method chosen by the Government to pursue its objectives is the most suitable of the available alternatives.

Both principles are grounded in the 'public welfare' standard that lies at the heart of Japanese constitutional law. In four separate articles, the Japanese constitution insists that assertion of fundamental human rights and freedoms must be consistent and reconciled with the public welfare of Japanese society as a whole. Articles 12 and 13 make the public welfare the litmus test – a general limiting condition – for the exercise of all the rights and freedoms that the constitution guarantees,[128] while articles 22 and 29 incorporate the public welfare standard in the constitutional guarantees to hold property and to choose one's profession and place of residence.

The relationship between the public welfare dimension of constitutional rights and the principles of reasonableness and necessity is immediate and direct. Reasonableness refers to the public interest that lies behind and motivates a challenged law and requires a measure of balance or proportionality between the benefits promoted and the burden that the law obliges certain individuals to bear. Necessity goes one step further and insists that laws must use means or methods that interfere with constitutional guarantees as little as possible.

In all the cases in which the Japanese Supreme Court has invalidated an act or initiative of one of the other two branches of government, one of these principles did the work. In three, the Court ruled that a law failed the means-oriented test of 'strict reasonableness' or 'necessity.' In the famous *Patricide* case,[129] for example, the Court accepted that the purpose of imposing more severe punishment on people who kill someone who was their direct lineal ascendant – protecting feelings of reverence and natural affection within families –

was perfectly legitimate but found that the degree of difference – the severity of the punishment – went too far.[130] The Court's decisions in the *Confiscation of Property* case[131]and the *Forestry* case[132] were based on the same line of reasoning. Again, the Court had no difficulty with the purposes the laws were designed to achieve; in the first case, to restrict illegal smuggling, and in the second, to protect the stability and productive capacity of the forest industry. The laws were found defective because the means employed – severely restricting the rights of innocent third parties and of people to divide property that they owned jointly with others – were more heavy handed than they needed to be.

In the other three cases that resulted in findings of constitutional invalidity, it was the ends, or public interest that the Court found wanting. In the *Pharmacy Law* case,[133] the Court struck down a zoning law imposing restrictions on where new pharmacies could be set up because the basis on which the law was enacted – the danger that defective medicines would be supplied if pharmacies were allowed to compete freely – was wholly speculative and contrary to proven fact.[134] In two *Malapportionment of Election District* cases,[135] although the Court acknowledged that there were important public interests – such as the size and history of electoral districts and the configuration of administrative units – that could justify departure from the constitutional guarantee of equal voting rights, it also said that there were limits – mathematical ratios – in how skewed and out of proportion the distribution could become.

Apart from the *Patricide, Forestry, Confiscation of Property, Pharmacy,* and *Malapportionment* cases, there were no other cases that resulted in the Court telling the other two branches of government what they could or could not do. The explanation for this remarkably close and cooperative relationship between the Court and the other two branches of government is not difficult to find. The reason why the overwhelming majority of cases that claimed a violation of human rights were ultimately dismissed had nothing to do with either the text of the constitution or with the sensitivity of Japanese legislators to constitutional standards and norms.[136] Japanese lawmakers have been successful in defending their laws and administrative rulings because of a conscious decision on the part of the Court to limit the number of cases in which a law will be subjected to rigorous evaluation. Unquestionably the most distinctive feature of the way the Japanese Supreme Court exercises its powers of constitutional review has been its adherence to a method of reasoning and a set of qualifying doctrines and provisos that limit the protection that the standards of reasonableness and necessity can provide.

None of the doctrines developed by the Court is idiosyncratic or indigenous to Japanese law. It is easy to identify parallel rulings and lines of reasoning being used by the other major courts with extensive experience in the enforcement of constitutional rights. What is distinctive about the jurisprudence that has been written in Japan is how important these limitations and restrictions are to the Court's process of reasoning and how frequently they carry the day.

Broadly speaking, three general strategies or lines of reasoning have been followed by the Japanese Court. Like so many of their colleagues around the world, the justices in Tokyo favour doctrines and rules that make sharp distinctions between and draw bright lines around different kinds of laws and areas of government policy and generally try to avoid detailed analysis of the law at hand. Collectively, these rules create different levels of review for different areas of government policy and weight the competing interests affected by a law very much in the Government's favour. First, as in Canada, an extensive doctrine of deference or legislative discretion has been recognized that effectively shields and in some cases completely excludes important areas of public policy from any form of independent, third-party review. Second, following Washington's lead, the Supreme Court has limited the range of cases in which the necessity test will be applied by drawing distinctions between various types of laws in terms of the kinds of purposes they pursue and effects they can have. Finally, and in a way that recalls the method of Laskin and Haldane, in many of the cases in which the proportionality test is applied, it seems to many people that the Court weighs the public interest and constitutional rights with its thumb on the scales.

Of the three lines of reasoning followed by the Court, granting the executive and legislative branches a significant discretion in how they pursue their political agendas is unquestionably the most important. Deference is the Court's normal posture when it exercises its powers of review. In many areas of public policy, either the Court has abandoned the principles of reasonableness and necessity in favour of such doctrines as 'political questions,' 'legislative discretion,' and the 'clarity test,' which render Government policy immune to review, or it has incorporated standards such as 'clearly unreasonable' and 'grossly inadequate' that are much easier for Governments to meet. On any of these tests, state action is vulnerable only if it is 'arbitrary in the extreme.'

When the Court has invoked the political questions doctrine or the principle of legislative discretion, the result has been to effectively immunize that area of public policy from any meaningful form of review. As a practical matter, these doctrines have allowed the Court to establish two levels or tiers of review.[137] Like the American doctrine of 'minimum scrutiny,' they do little more than confirm that the law in question relates to an area of public policy in which the Court concedes government discretion to be all-encompassing and practically unfettered.

The areas in which the Court has allowed the elected branches of government widest authority to act include foreign affairs, social and economic policy, and laws governing the ways the politicians are elected and organize their internal, institutional affairs. Questions about foreign policy, like the constitutionality of the Japanese-American Security treaty, have been designated as 'political questions' and, as in the United States, put completely beyond the Court's powers of review.[138] Social and economic policies such as welfare allowances,[139] school fees,[140] business[141] and tax[142] regulations, and restrictions on strikes[143] all have been designated as matters over which the executive and legislature have virtually exclusive responsibility and on which the Court should intervene only in the most extreme cases. Rules of Parliament and election laws have also been identified as areas falling within the discretion of the legislature even when the laws that have been challenged impose very substantial restrictions on the freedom of people to express themselves politically.[144]

In all these areas of government policy, the Court never questions the Government's assumptions and policy objectives. As a practical matter, the politicians have been given a licence to act virtually any way they please. Any legislative purpose falling within these broad areas of public policy is accepted as a sufficient justification for the Government to act.[145] On these issues the Court has insisted that the separation of powers between itself and the elected branches of government is practically absolute and inviolable. Even when, as in the malapportionment cases, the Court was of the view that the discretion of the legislature had been abused and the more lenient threshold of 'extreme' unreasonableness had been transgressed, it denied the challenger's request to invalidate the election and instead gave the politicians time to bring the rules into line.[146]

Alongside the principle of legislative discretion, the clarity test, and the political questions rule, the Supreme Court of Japan has also pursued two closely related lines of reasoning that have further diminished the influence that the standards of reasonableness and necessity can have. One line of cases has significantly reduced the number of laws required to satisfy the more rigorous 'necessity' (rationality) test.[147] In a series of decisions reviewing laws regulating zoning of business activities, the Court has drawn a distinction between laws passed for some 'negative' purpose – such as preserving public safety and order, protecting life and health – and those aimed at more positive socio-economic goals.[148] According to the Court, only negative laws have to stand scrutiny under the more rigorous necessity test. In addition, paralleling the distinction between different kinds of purposes government policies might promote, the Court has also differentiated laws in terms of their effects on constitutional rights. Like laws passed for positive socio-economic purposes, state initiatives that interfere with constitutional guarantees incidentally and indirectly are also not held to the stricter scrutiny that is implicit in the 'necessity' rule.[149]

At the same time that it has been restricting the range of cases in which the principle of necessity would apply, the Court has also demonstrated a discernible (and much criticized) tendency to apply the ends-oriented test of reasonableness with its 'thumbs on the scales.' Many reviewers have commented that the Court has shown a consistent bias in favour of weighting the public welfare promoted by a challenged law more heavily than the constitutional rights that are at stake. Even though laws restricting traditional rights and freedoms – such as expression, religion, and association - are said to attract more rigorous review, the Court has never invalidated a law restricting one of these fundamental guarantees.[150] Rather than investigating the details of a challenger's complaint, the Court just assumes that the public interest that motivated the government to act is paramount. In upholding a law that virtually banned all political activity by public servants, for example, the Court reasoned: 'Although freedom of expression is limited by this ban, interests which are gained by it (it preserves the political neutrality of public employees and the peoples' trust in unbiased administrative action) are far more important than interests lost by this ban. Thus, this ban is not disproportionate.'[151]

After almost fifty years of favouring doctrines and methods of reasoning that have reduced and restricted the impact of the standard principles of judicial review, the Japanese Supreme Court has reduced constitutional law to a matter of rhetorical flourish that offers little protection for human rights.[152] Its doctrinal standards have broken government policy down into rigid, almost watertight, compartments, only a very small number of which receive serious review. In almost all the cases that it has heard, the Court has ruled that the law in question affects a category of policy-making that is either completely beyond its competence or within the primary responsibility of the elected branches of government to control.

GERMANY

When one turns to inquire how courts in Europe protect human rights, one discovers a story that is very similar to the one we encountered in North America and Asia. Once again, judges use rules of rationality and proportionality to distinguish laws that are constitutional from those that are not, although here there seems to be a general tendency to run the two concepts together, and in tandem, rather than treating them as discrete tests and keeping them separate and apart. In contrast with the supreme courts in Canada and the United States, which, in different ways, have broken proportionality down into separate criteria of constitutional validity, in Europe proportionality is thought of more as a single measure of reasonableness, in which the ends and means of laws subjected to review are evaluated more or less simultaneously. As in North America and Asia, the courts in Europe have developed distinctive ways and patterns of applying these rules that give their jurisprudence a flavour and style all its own.

In Europe, as elsewhere, the records of the various courts can be differentiated according to how vigorously they enforce the standards of rationality and proportionality. At one end of the spectrum would be the Bundesverfassungsgericht – the German Constitutional Court – whose vigilance in the protection of human rights has been the equal of any in the world. At the other, the European Court of Human Rights has felt that its status as an international court, supervising the activities of independent, sovereign states, requires it to exercise its powers in a much more diffident, deferential way.

The German Constitutional Court exercises its powers of review over all three branches of government[153] using the same highly structured pattern of reasoning that is characteristic of so much of German law. For German jurists, constitutions have within them objective orderings of basic values and principles that control how the powers of the state can be exercised and enforced.[154] As they read Germany's Basic Law, all rights are perceived as being equal to each other,[155] and each is understood to cover a range of interests that are ranked according to their importance to people's dignity and freedom to organize their own lives.[156] Within this framework, the rules of rationality and proportionality are regarded as an integral part of the 'constitutional order,' working alongside and giving unity to such other fundamental values as popular sovereignty, separation of powers, and the basic rights themselves. Collectively, all of these values and principles promote the ideal of human dignity and personal development on which the foundations of the German state are based.[157]

As with every other constitution we have referred to so far, nowhere in the Basic Law is there any explicit reference to the 'proportionality principle.' Testing the limits of legitimate law-making against standards of necessity and proportionality follows logically from the Court's perception of the constitution as providing a coherent analytical framework within which the competing values that distinguish the German state can be organized and reconciled. For the Court, proportionality is implicit in and can be deduced from the Basic Law's characterization of the German state as a 'free liberal democratic order.' Proportionality is an idea inherent in the nature of rights.[158] It is an integral part of the German understanding of the Rechtsstaat principle, or rule of law.[159] From the premise that the dignity of each person is the supreme value protected in the constitution, it follows, for the Court, that its role is to ensure that everyone is guaranteed the largest possible scope to develop their personalities.[160]

Though the Bundesverfassungsgericht follows the approach that seems to be favoured in Europe of using a general 'reasonableness' standard of review, rather than sharply distinguishing between the norms of rationality and proportionality, it does make use of both criteria in testing the constitutional validity of the laws it is asked to review. On a close reading of the cases, it can be seen that in all of its most important rulings the German Court carefully evaluates both the ends and the means of whatever law or administrative act has been brought before it. In German constitutional law, the principle of proportionality refers to both tests,[161] and both have influenced the way the Court has interpreted the major rights and freedoms guaranteed in the Basic Law and how it has analysed cases when constitutional entitlements compete and collide. Indeed, on some occasions, the Court has pressed the logic of these criteria of constitutional validation to their limit by imposing positive duties on the state to initiate legislative policies and programs to protect the rights and freedoms that the Basic Law guarantees.

In marking out the boundaries of each right and freedom, the Court has made use of both principles. Because proportionality is understood to be inherent in the idea of 'constitutional order' (viz., the rule of law), it is thought of as part of each of the rights and freedoms that the constitution contains. In effect, proportionality has been read into all the major guarantees in the Basic Law, including the rights of property, occupational freedom, personal development, life, liberty, and human dignity. In the jargon of American constitutional law, proportionality is the German equivalent of 'substantive due process' of law.[162]

When the Court's attention is focused on the Basic Law and the rights and freedoms that it guarantees, the Court uses the 'proportionality principle' to rank the interests and activities affected by a law in terms of how important they are to people's ability to control their own development. Paralleling the way in which the Supreme Court of Canada has differentiated between types of expression in its analysis of section 2(b) of the Charter, the German Court has created a hierarchy of values and interests for each right and freedom. It has defined the basic rights as having a core, where protection is greatest, and peripheries or margins, where restrictions can be justified more easily.[163] Political speech that addresses issues of public importance,[164] or associations that have a close personal dimension, are examples of the kinds of interests and activities that have been placed at the centre of these first-generation guarantees.[165]

Rules of rationality (necessity) and proportionality (consistency) also organize the Court's thinking about laws that affect more than one right or freedom. They allow the Court to reconcile competing rights and freedoms when they collide. When one person claims the freedom to express him- or herself in ways that are harmful to the reputation, economic security, or personal integrity of others;[166] when property rights of investors and associational rights of workers clash;[167] when religious ideas and activities impinge on the educational, occupational, and/or religious rights[168] or even the life[169] of others; when the educational rights of faculty and students are opposed,[170] the Court's approach is to try to find a solution that reflects a measure of proportion that is faithful to the objective ordering of values that gives coherence to the Basic Law. Rationality and proportionality give a structural unity to the constitution that allows the Court to organize and harmonize the values and entitlements in the Basic Law in an objective and orderly way.

In both phases of the review process, the Bundesverfassungsgericht has pushed the logic of rationality and proportionality as far as any court with the power of judicial review and further than most. Though it has on occasion denied claims by individuals and groups that have been accepted by courts in other countries, these instances are quite rare.[171] Certainly when fundamental issues of privacy, personal development, equality, electoral reform, and even social and economic policy are at stake, it has provided as much protection as any court in the world.

In the first phase of the review process, the Court has defined the scope of the Basic Law and each of its rights and freedoms liberally and in an expansive way. It has ruled that the constitution takes precedence over and affects every other field of law, including 'private laws' governing personal relations and international treaties with foreign states.[172] German constitutional law does not recognize anything like a 'political question' doctrine, such as exists in the United States and Japan.[173] By reading the constitution's open-ended guarantees logically – in a deductive, purposeful way – and by rejecting an intent-based, originalist approach, it has recognized almost every form of human activity or belief as being covered by the text.[174] Interests and activities that do not fit within one of the more specific entitlements almost always can be included in article 2(1), which has been read by the Court as guaranteeing a general right to 'freedom of action.'[175] In the result, the Court has shown its willingness to intervene in almost every aspect of community life[176] and to invalidate any law that is arbitrary, excessive, or imbalanced.

The Court has been especially vigorous in reviewing laws that affect interests and activities that lie at the core of a person's autonomy and personal development. For example, in what are regarded as landmark rulings, the Court has invalidated parts of laws regulating abortion,[177] the judicial process,[178] census taking,[179] university admission,[180] and life imprisonment.[181] As well, and in contrast with the experience of courts in Asia and North America, the Bundesverfassungsgericht has consistently scrutinized laws regulating the political process and electoral policy with particular vigilance and care.[182] Even in the area of social and economic policy, though the Court has been sensitive to the separation-of-powers principle and has pulled back from issuing judgments that have substantial budgetary consequences, it has insisted that lawmakers design their programs to meet the standards of rationality and proportionality. Using one and usually both of these tests of constitutional legitimacy, the Court has invalidated important parts of the country's laws on taxation,[183] welfare,[184] copyright,[185] rent control,[186] professional organization,[187] and consumer protection.[188]

Though the German Court has always been willing to interpret the reach of the Basic Law broadly and to rely on tests of rationality and proportionality to identify laws that are constitutionally flawed, in some areas of public policy, rather than examining a particular program or instrument, the Court has concentrated its attention on the more basic question of whether the politicians could or should have acted at all. Again working from the idea that the values and principles in the Basic Law are organized objectively – according to how important they are to people's personal dignity and ability to control their own development, – the Court has developed a catalogue of 'dos' and 'don'ts' of legislative and executive authority.

Some policy objectives have been identified by the Court as entirely improper and inconsistent with the Basic Law's assumption that public officials have a limited capacity to affect the free will of the individual.[189] The don'ts include laws that seriously restrict people's freedom to develop their own personalities either because it is thought that such laws are in the best interests of those whose lives they control[190] or as a way of granting a privileged elite a monopoly on some form of human activity.[191] For example, laws that permitted the state to confine psychiatric patients in hospitals[192] or that encouraged women to stay in their homes,[193] on the basis that such laws were in the best interests of those they restrained, have been invalidated by the Court.

In other cases, the Court has followed the logic of reading the constitution as reflecting an objective, hierarchical ordering of values, in which a person's dignity and private development are taken to be, next to life itself, the highest value of all,[194] in the opposite direction. More than once, rather than restricting the kinds of laws and policies that lawmakers could enact, the Court has ruled that, if each individual is to enjoy the largest possible scope for his or her personal development, there will be many circumstances in which the state has a positive duty to act. Though the Court has generally been quite reluctant to dictate the precise policy that a Government must choose, it has been anything but hesitant in marking out broad areas where governments and even fellow judges[195] have a general duty to act.

The cases in which the Court has recognized such positive duties on Governments to enact laws to protect people's rights cover many of the major responsibilities assumed by modern, social-democratic states. In reviewing a series of laws regulating activities that can affect the environment, such as airport noise,[196] nuclear power,[197] and storage of chemical weapons,[198] the Court insisted that Governments have positive duties to enact (and continually reevaluate) laws that will respect people's physical well-being. To preserve the democratic character of the German state, the Court has ruled that Governments must take whatever initiatives are necessary to ensure that both the print and the electronic media are not monopolized by a narrow range of special interests[199] and remain accessible to a fully representative expression of views.[200] To meet its obligations in the area of public order and criminal law, the Court has held that the state must develop rehabilitative programs for those whom it incarcerates.[201] In other landmark rulings, the Court has held that the rights of unborn children and of families also have both a positive and negative dimension to them, which the state is obliged to respect,[202] and has interpreted the right of all Germans 'freely to choose their trade or profession' to impose significant obligations on the state to create adequate educational facilities and operate them to their maximum capacity.[203]

Though the Court has not been afraid to recognize that lawmakers have duties to take positive steps to protect the rights that are entrenched in the Basic Law, it has always been conscious of the principle of separation of powers and the limits of its own authority. Especially when the Court felt that the laws being reviewed were not susceptible to being measured against 'legally manageable criteria'[204] or had significant budgetary implications, or where Governments had several policy choices around which it might organize its law, the Court has allowed lawmakers considerable room to manoeuvre.[205] The 'form and manner' – the means – of such laws were, for the most part, left to the discretion of the politicians and their agents.[206] Only when the lawmakers' choice was 'totally inadequate'[207] or where the judges could say that they had 'manifestly violated their duty,'[208] does the Court intervene.

The major – and perhaps most controversial – exception to this posture of deferring to the legislative and executive branches of government in deciding how their positive constitutional obligations could and should be met was the Court's now-famous abortion decision of 1975.[209] In that case, in addition to telling the Bundestag that it had an obligation to pass a law regulating when women could have abortions, it actually dictated the type of policy response the lawmakers were required to adopt. To satisfy their positive obligations to protect the constitutional guarantee of 'life' in article 2(2), the Court said that the legislature had to use penal sanctions against those who performed and underwent an abortion in circumstances not permitted by the law.

When one stands back and considers the jurisprudence that the German Constitutional Court has built up around the Basic Law, the observation that the Bundesverfassungsgericht is in the business of determining the 'reasonableness' of almost all government activity regardless of whether that consists of positive initiatives or decisions not to act seems pretty close to the mark.[210] In discharging its responsibilities as guardian of Germany's constitution, the Court has been much more concerned with spelling out the general implications of the duties and obligations that the Basic Law imposes on those entrusted with the powers of the state than in categorizing and cataloguing a long list of personal entitlements that individuals can claim as their 'constitutional rights.' Though it has frequently resisted invitations to get involved in the nitty-gritty of policy formulation, across a broad spectrum of issues, it has insisted that lawmakers and administrators and even the judges themselves must respect basic tenets of rationality and proportionality.

The distinctive character of German constitutional law can be brought into sharper focus if one compares it with the way the European Court of Human Rights has come to exercise its powers of review. Though both courts are inclined to think of proportionality as a single, comprehensive test of both ends and means, the European Court has used a yardstick of reasonableness that is much easier for Governments to meet. As a practical matter, its standard of reasonableness has usually not proven to be a difficult hurdle for Governments and their officials to surmount.

THE EUROPEAN COURT OF HUMAN RIGHTS

Though they are members of a court whose existence grows out of an international treaty and that has jurisdiction over independent nation-states, the judges who sit on the European Court of Human Rights do exactly the same job as their colleagues who have responsibility for defending constitutional bills of rights. As a practical matter, in enforcing the guarantees in the European Convention of Human Rights and

Fundamental Freedoms (the Convention), the primary task of the Court is to analyse the ends and means of laws and administrative acts of the now more than thirty countries that belong to the Council of Europe. Established almost fifty years ago, at the end of the Second World War, the Court has now had an opportunity to review all the most important provisions of the Convention, and the definitional work of the judges is more or less complete.[211]

In giving meaning to the words of the European Convention, the Court has generally taken an expansive, activist approach.[212] It has, for the most part, had little sympathy for an originalist, intent-based approach and has usually favoured reading the Convention 'purposefully' to mark out the protection that it provides.[213] Because it has eschewed a formalistic, categorical approach,[214] few interests have been excluded and put beyond the reach of the Court's powers of review.[215] Instead, it has placed the principles of rationality and proportionality at the centre of all the major entitlements in the Convention. Regardless of which right or freedom is at stake it is these principles that distinguish laws that are consistent with the Convention from those that are not.

The Court has found grounding for the principles of rationality and proportionality all through the text. The idea that protection of human rights entails a compromise between the requirements for a democratic society and individual rights is said to be inherent in the Convention system,[216] and the Court has read each of the Convention's rights and freedoms as establishing tests of necessity and consistency that both politicians and their bureaucrats must respect. For such traditional civil liberties as freedom of conscience, religion, expression, association, and privacy, the Court drew the principles from the requirement that appears in articles 8 (privacy and family life) through 11 (assembly and association) that any limits on these basic guarantees must be shown to be 'necessary in a democratic society.' According to the Court, 'necessity' means that laws that impinge on these rights must meet 'a pressing social need,' be 'proportionate to the legitimate aim pursued,' and be supported by 'reasons which are relevant and sufficient.'[217]

Articles written in less explicit terms have also been read as imposing an obligation on politicians and administrators to explain both the goals of their initiatives and the particular policy instruments they have used. For example, the Court has interpreted the stipulation, in article 14, that all the rights and freedoms in the Convention must be secured 'without discrimination' to mean that all laws must pursue 'a legitimate aim' in a way that respects 'a reasonable relationship of proportionality between the means employed and the aim sought to be realized.'[218] Similarly, the guarantees of property,[219] education,[220] and free elections,[221] which were added in the first protocol in 1952, have been defined to require all laws and administrative action touching these interests to strike a 'fair,' or 'just,' balance between the 'general interests of the community and the protection of an individual's fundamental rights' and to reflect a 'reasonable relationship of proportionality between the means employed and the ends pursued.' In other provisions, extending protection to free elections,[222] marriage and family life (article 12),[223] and personal liberty and security,[224] the Court has introduced the concept of the 'essence' of a right, through which to undertake its ends-means analysis. Even its enforcement of the broad derogation clause in article 15[225] and of rights that are written in absolute terms – for example, against 'inhuman or degrading treatment' (article 3)[226] and 'forced or compulsory labour' (article 4)[227] – entails a close assessment of the ends and means of whatever state activity is under review.

The fact that the European Court of Human Rights is an international tribunal, created by an international treaty signed by independent states, has not affected its understanding that, in law, rights and freedoms are mostly about the duties and obligations that lawmakers and their agents must respect. As with all national courts that have been made guardians of a constitutional bill of rights, the most important part of the Court's work has been to ensure that politicians and administrators respect the principles of rationality and proportionality that are inherent in the Convention. The multinational character of the Court has, however, profoundly affected the way in which the judges think about their powers of review and the way these principles should be applied. Like all national courts, the European Court in Strasbourg has developed a distinctive style of its own.

In the Court's mind, the fact that its jurisdiction is international in scope, and involves the sovereignty of independent nation-states, has meant that it should apply the standards of rationality and proportionality with considerable caution and restraint. There is a very real sense among the judges that their authority is quite fragile and dependent on the good will of the national Governments whose policies and officials they review. The Court sees its role protecting the human rights and freedoms that the Convention guarantees as being a subsidiary one.[228]

It begins its work with the assumption that the national authorities are in a better position to assess what kinds of laws and policies are appropriate for their local communities than the members of an international court.[229] Together, the Court's instinct to respect the diversity and variation that exists among the different countries that belong to the Council of Europe, and its desire to promote effective and stable systems of government in all member states, have led it to take a very tentative and cautious approach in evaluating the various laws and administrative decisions it has been asked to review.

The Court's perception of its own limited authority permeates almost every aspect of its jurisprudence. As a practical matter, the Court has been willing to challenge national authorities only when it is able to identify a broad consensus – a European standard – among member states or when it believes that one of the essential tenets of democratic society or a fundamental right is at stake. In all other cases, the posture of the Court has been extremely deferential, and the principles of rationality and proportionality have been applied in only the most accommodating way.

In many of the most celebrated cases in which the Court has upheld a challenger's complaint, it was of the opinion that both fundamental rights and European standards were involved. In *Dudgeon*,[230] for example, the Court emphasized that Northern Ireland's law criminalizing private homosexual activities between consenting adults constituted a serious interference with one of the most intimate aspects of a person's life and was at odds with the tolerance that had developed for these activities in other member states. Similarly, in the *Sunday Times* case,[231] the Court concluded that Britain's common law rules dealing with contempt of court constituted a serious limitation on a freedom (of the press), which is one of the foundations of a democratic society, and was substantially more invasive than the methods used by other states to preserve the authority of and respect for their courts. Again, in *Abdulaziz*,[232] in striking down a provision of Britain's immigration laws that made it more difficult for women who had settled in the United Kingdom to marry and establish families with nationals from other states, the Court concluded that, despite considerable variation in the way member states controlled immigration, the importance of the right to gender equality and the fact that equality of the sexes was a major goal in all countries in Europe meant that the British rule could not survive.[233]

The importance to the Court of being able to point to a 'European standard' as a basis on which to challenge the sovereignty of a member state is evident in other landmark cases as well. In two important judgments, the Court defended the rights of children 'born out of wedlock' on the basis of a strong consensus that had emerged in both international law and the laws of member states.[234] Similarly, the Court's rulings striking down laws that imposed waiting periods before certain people could remarry,[235] restricted private reception of uncoded television signals,[236] and permitted infliction of corporal punishment[237] were justified, in the final analysis, on the fact that the laws in question were at odds with the ways state regulation had developed in the rest of the continent.

In all these cases, the reasoning of the Court was essentially the same and it was quite different from the method employed by the other courts we have examined. For the European Court, the principle of rationality, or alternative means, has not been nearly as vital as it has for most of the national courts which are in the business of defending human rights. Though it is an important part of the proportionality or necessity test, it has not exerted an independent force of its own.

When the European Court of Human Rights evaluates a law or an administrative act, it does not differentiate so sharply as do other courts between its ends and its means. The Court's definition of proportionality is broad enough to accommodate an analysis of both.[238] When it strikes down a law, the Court bases its judgment on a determination that on balance, and taken as a whole, the offending rule does not reconcile the various interests that it affects as sensitively as the policies that have been adopted in other member states. That is how the concept of the European standard works. For the Court, laws are defective when they fail to treat those they disadvantage as well as such people are treated by other member states – when they violate a basic test of equality.

In all the cases noted above, the Court followed this line of reasoning. For the European Court, proportionality is a rule of equal treatment that obliges signatory nations to respect the standards and policy options that have won general support among the other member states. Rather than trying to assess the balance struck by a challenged law in the abstract, the Court uses the European standard to test whether the law treats those it affects in a way that is similar to how others are treated elsewhere in their own countries[239] or in other member states. The existence of a European standard allows the Court to conclude that there could be no 'pressing social need' to justify whatever law is under review. Like their counterparts in New Delhi, the judges in Strasbourg use the experience of other states as proof that alternative policies are available that show more respect for people's freedom to control their own destinies without compromising the well-being of the community in any serious way. The European standard provides a neutral, objective benchmark – a litmus test – to identify laws that are more excessive or imbalanced than they need to be.[240]

In terms of positive law, the European Court is usually willing to challenge policy choices made by member Governments only when an analysis of the their ends and means can be translated into an 'equality' claim – when it can be shown that a law is more invasive and limiting of people's human rights than similar laws in other states. Beyond these limited circumstances (and occasionally not even when they prevail),[241] the Court has taken a deferential attitude towards the law-making powers of the national Governments. Except when issues of due process and the fairness of judicial and administrative procedures are at stake,[242] lack of a substantial consensus among member states is almost always fatal to a claimant's case.[243] According to the Court, the fact there is a divergence and plurality of views on what kinds of rules and regulations are appropriate on any issue of social policy argues for allowing local authorities a wide 'margin of appreciation' in formulating laws to suit their own needs.

'Margin of appreciation' is the doctrinal label used by the European Court to describe the deference that is so central to the Court's theory of its role.[244] With it, the Court has been able to develop different levels or degrees of review much like the Canadian, Japanese and U.S. Courts. The less uniformity there is among the member states on any issue of social policy, the wider the margin will be;[245] the more casual and less searching the review. In some cases, it has even led the Court to exclude an interest or activity from the protection of the Convention altogether.[246] On other issues, such as obscenity, that involve the moral ideas and character of a country, and in which cultures and histories can differ radically, the Court has said that member states are entitled to a wide margin of appreciation to develop policies that respect their communities' values and beliefs.[247] Similarly, on social and economic issues such as education,[248] environmental control,[249] election rules,[250] advertising,[251] licensing,[252] and nationalization of industry,[253] which require lawmakers to balance a number of competing interests and where the choice among policy instruments may be quite large, the Court has also given Governments a lot of room to manoeuvre. Even in its interpretation of when a country can invoke the derogation clause (article 15) to override the rights and freedoms that the Convention guarantees, the Court has been exceedingly deferential.[254]

On all these issues, the Court has said that it will not interfere where the Government can demonstrate some reasonable basis for its policy. In evaluating the particular means chosen by the government to realize its objectives, the rule is not one of 'strict necessity.'[255] Governments are free to choose the measures they think are most appropriate for their communities, so long as they are not 'so disproportionate to the public interest they are designed to promote.'[256] There is no obligation that lawmakers must choose the 'best solution'[257] – the policy that least interferes with the rights and freedoms in the Convention.[258] On these issues, the Court has said, local lawmakers must judge for themselves what particular policies 'necessity' requires.[259]

In evaluating the aims and objectives of laws that have been brought before it, the Court has also adopted a very deferential attitude. From its inception, the Court has favoured a hands-off approach. Unlike the U.S. Supreme Court, it has never been troubled by Governments trying to remedy social injustice and disadvantage[260] or teaching religion or secular ethics in their schools.[261] Only laws that are deliberately aimed at restricting the rights and freedoms that the Convention protects are regarded as illegitimate. Where European standards do not exist, the Court has generally been prepared to respect the lawmakers' judgment on the importance of the public interest promoted by the law, unless the law was 'clearly and manifestly unreasonable' and/or imposed 'excessive burdens' on particular individuals and minority groups.[262]

Though the record of the European Court in defending human rights is one of the most cautious in the free and democratic world, it is important not to lose sight of the fact that when it has exercised its authority to invalidate a law, the ideas of rationality and proportionality have done most of the work. The Court's jurisprudence teaches us not only that cultural and institutional factors can affect the way in which courts exercise their powers of review but, just as important, that the rules of constitutionality are concerned more with the duties and obligations that lawmakers and administrators must respect than they are with cataloguing and 'reifying' a long list of interests and activities as constitutional rights.

Indeed, the reasoning process followed by the European Court when it does intervene to protect the interests of some individual or group shows that, even when the Court evaluates the balance struck by a law between public and private interests, it can do so objectively and in a way that does respect the basic division (separation) of powers between the courts and the other two branches of government. The jurisprudence of the European Court provides a substantial body of law to counter the claims of those who argue that proportionality is a criterion of evaluation that is inherently subjective and without any objective standards.[263] The example of the European Court, using laws and policies in other free and democratic states to measure the balance of any law that it is asked to review, shows how courts can avoid the charge that when they test the proportionality of any law they are simply substituting their own views for that of the relevant legislature as to what the appropriate balance of interests should be.

5

Law and Politics

RIGHTS AND THE RULES OF LAW

In the last three chapters we covered a lot of constitutional law in a relatively short space. It is time to stand back and reflect on what we have seen. We must ask what lessons this body of comparative law teaches us about the integrity and efficacy of judicial review.

For many people, what is most arresting about a comparative study of how constitutional law is practised around the world is that wherever one looks, in Canada and abroad, the story is so strikingly similar. Two basic subplots or themes are repeated over and over again. First, in deciding whether a law is constitutional or not, every court works within the same basic framework of analysis. The reasoning process and the tests of constitutional integrity are exactly the same. Second, there are strong parallels psychologically as well. Instinctively, no matter where they sit, judges are wary of applying the tests that differentiate laws that are constitutional from those that are not strictly in every case.

For students who believe in the idea of human rights, the good news is that a comparative perspective provides strong confirmation that, as a matter of principle, constitutional law can be reduced to two basic rules or tests – rationality (necessity) and proportionality (consistency). They are at the centre of every important issue in constitutional law. The bad news is that, in practice, the principles have not always carried the day. Sadly (for human rights activists), judges all too frequently have abandoned the analytical framework through which these principles are applied. As in Canadian constitutional law, much of the comparative jurisprudence just reviewed is made up of doctrines and rulings that limit and constrain the protection that the standards of rationality and proportionality can provide.

After reading cases from around the world, many students have even more difficulty in making up their minds about whether judicial review is a good thing or not. When they focus on the cases in which relatively disadvantaged and powerless individuals and groups have succeeded in their claims, they find reason to be encouraged. Here one sees law at its best. Those entrusted with the powers of the state, from Delhi to Dublin, are obliged to justify their decisions against standards and tests that guarantee that people will be treated with a measure of equality and respect.

As one broadens one's vision, however, and looks across all the judgments handed down by the courts, there is just as good reason to doubt the possibility of law – whatever its theoretical attractions. For many people, the fact that each court, indeed each judge, seems to have so much control over how vigorously he or she will exercise his or her powers of review speaks volumes about the inherent subjectivity – and ultimately illegitimacy – of the law. From this perspective, judicial enforcement of national constitutions and international treaties seems an inherently undemocratic and ineffective way to protect human rights. If judges can choose when and how forcefully the rules of rationality and proportionality will be applied, the critics' fears that autocratic rule by judges will replace tyranny by majorities must be right.

To resolve this feeling of ambivalence and uncertainty, I advise students to concentrate on the verifiable fact that the principles of rationality and proportionality constitute the core of the protection that constitutions and human rights treaties guarantee all over the world. This body of comparative constitutional law provides compelling evidence for the coherence and integrity of judicial review. In an age plagued by postmodernist dogmas of relevatism and indeterminacy, it is remarkable that the same set of principles has been derived by courts all over the world from constitutions that differ radically in style and even in the rights and freedoms that they guarantee. Whether a constitution is written in a few hundred pages, as in India, or in a few dozen words as in the United States, and whether its focus is on intergovernmental relations or the relationship between the individual and the state, or both, principles of rationality and proportionality are at the core. Both of these tests of constitutional legitimacy have been deduced from and grounded in texts that are incredibly diverse. Rationality and proportionality are universal duties, which law takes to be the operative idea in the concept of rights. They are the logical derivatives of reading any liberal-democratic constitution in a holistic, 'purposeful' way.

In the cases in which these principles have carried the day, rights and freedoms have been turned into legal obligations that lawmakers and their agents are required to meet. It is these principles that determine whether a law is constitutional or not, not the words of the text. We have seen that in Canada few answers are given by the express words of the Charter and the same is true all over the world. Laws are invalidated because politicians did not live up to their duty to act rationally and/or consistently, not because of some proclamation or interdiction in the text.

As they read more judgments from around the world, most students are struck by how little the words of the text really matter. As we have seen, one of the important lessons of the Indian jurisprudence is that lots of evocative words and inspirational phrases often get in the way. Specificity and prolixity in the text just turn every dispute into a conflict of competing rights.

Brevity of text, on the other hand, has never been a problem for the U.S. Supreme Court. Even though they are written in a very abbreviated form, the rights to liberty (fifth and fourteenth amendments), equality (fourteenth amendment), and expression and religion (first amendment) cover as much ground and protect as many interests and activities as any constitution in the world. When the U.S. Supreme Court has pushed the purposeful, deductive method of reading these three great pillars of the U.S. Bill of Rights most assiduously, it has been able to imply, out of whole cloth, rights to privacy,[1] to associate,[2] and to travel[3] that are as extensive as any in the world. Similarly, the absence of express recognition of affirmative action (or reservation) programs in the text has not prevented the judges in Washington from understanding that preferential treatment of those who suffer some hardship or disadvantage is inherent in the concept of equality.[4] As we saw in the last chapter, when the U.S. Supreme Court has exercised its powers of review strictly, it has been able to advance the cause of minority groups on pressing issues such as language[5] and education[6] in important and meaningful ways.

The duties to which the principles of rationality and proportionality give rise relate mostly to how politicians translate the will of the people into law. Though courts have also recognized that lawmakers are under positive duties to initiate remedial measures to protect the essential cores of the rights and freedoms that constitutions guarantee, for the most part the duties to which the principles of rationality and proportionality give rise are concerned with the way in which social policies are put into law rather than with what the subject-matter or direction of those policies should be. Instead of prescribing what politicians should do, what purposes they should pursue, these principles impose restrictions on how Governments should act in pursuing whatever political program got them elected.

Rationality and proportionality and the duties that they impose on Governments work the same way all over the world. Not only are the principles neutral and objective in the sense that they can be grounded in a variety of very different constitutions which they envelop and extend – they also provide a method of reasoning that can generate concrete and determinate results. Comparing the substantive rules and doctrines of constitutional law that have been developed by courts around the world shows that these principles provide a comprehensive analytical framework by which any law or administrative action can be judged.

Rationality and proportionality are prescriptive rules that can be and (more often than not) have been applied in a logical and analytically coherent way. As we saw in our review of Canadian law, they can justify and/or explain all the landmark cases that have been decided to date. Where the courts have remained faithful to these two tests of constitutional validation and the values (of respect and consistency) that they protect, their decisions are easy to justify and invariably attract praise and support from students and professionals alike. On the other hand, when the courts have abandoned these principles, there is usually widespread recognition that a mistake has been made and that the judges have acted arbitrarily by claiming an authority for themselves that cannot be grounded in law.

Contrary to what critics and legal theorists frequently say, the cases show that, in deciding whether a law is constitutional or not, the principles never do run out. They are always there, and there is no reason in theory why they should ever conflict. In federalism and human rights cases alike, the principles ensure that both the motives and the methods of those entrusted with the powers of the state satisfy basic standards of reason and respect. They measure two different dimensions of government rules and regulations and so complement rather than contradict each other. Together they guarantee that anyone who is entrusted with powers of the state must act in a way that maximizes the freedom of each person that can be enjoyed equally by all.

It is true that these principles are not susceptible of being applied mechanically. They cannot be reduced to a set of mathematical formulae that could be made operational by a computer programmer. Reading constitutional law cases from Canada and around the world shows very clearly that individual judges and indeed entire courts can and do apply these principles in dramatically different ways. Some judges and some cultures believe that the job of the 'third branch' of government should be limited, and rationality and proportionality applied with caution and restraint. Others see their role as guardians of the constitution in much more positive, responsible terms. Even among those who are agreed as to how strictly the principles should be applied, there may be disagreements about what conclusions they point to in any given case.

But not all these differences justify fear (and loathing) about the subjectivity and indeterminacy of law. In every area of law, judges disagree about how particular cases should be decided, even when there is no dispute about which rules should be applied. In close cases, reasonable people, acting in good faith, may perceive the threat to the public welfare, or the viability of alternative policies, quite differently and so come to opposite conclusions about what the result of a case ought to be. As well, distinct societies and cultures do place different weights and values on various aspects of the human experience and life in their communities, and so what is well proportioned and evenly balanced in one society may appear to be quite distorted and skewed in another.

When judges and courts disagree on whether a law should be upheld as being constitutional in such circumstances, it is not because of the indeterminacy or subjectivity of the law. Everyone is agreed on what principles control the outcome of the case and what the content of those rules are. The divergences occur because of different perceptions that judges may take of the relevant factual (evidentiary) material and the legal and cultural background against which the principles are applied. The importance of tranquillity and civility in Japanese society, or of foetal life in the Irish Republic, for example, may justify laws restricting street demonstrations and door-to-door canvassing in Japan and abortions in Ireland, even though they might be struck down in other societies, such as Canada and Denmark, where these interests and activities have been valued quite differently. Equally, when a specific constitutional question is thought to be especially difficult, and likely to produce a divergent set of views, it is not because of the complexity or obscurity of the law involved but rather because the interests and values that the law is required to assess seem so evenly balanced.

The fact that law is sensitive to different ideas and values that distinguish cultures and countries is a point that should count in its favour not against it. Law is a method of reasoning that can be integrated into almost any political culture or system of government. The constitutional jurisprudence that has been written around the world illustrates quite powerfully the multicultural character of law and of the concept of rights. Except for their proscription against passing laws that serve no other purpose than denying people the freedom to choose how they will go about living their lives, the principles of rationality and proportionality impose almost no constraints on what goals and aspirations communities can pursue. They insist only that whenever lawmakers do act, they do not violate the most elementary rules of logical reasoning.[7] So long as Governments respect these basic rules of social ordering, they can define their own priorities and political program. They will be judged on their own terms.

RIGHTS AND DUTIES

Though there are many differences and disagreements among judges and courts that do not threaten the coherence and integrity of the law, the most sceptical students will want to insist that there are others that do. In particular, critics will point to the fact that however neutral and objective the rules of constitutional law may be in principle, in practice judges have retained an almost unlimited discretion in deciding when and how forcefully they should be applied. Even from our cursory summary of how constitutional law is practised around the world, it is evident that the recognition of different levels or tiers of review, or 'margins of appreciation,' is often crucial to the outcome of a case. Doctrines like these allow judges to be as deferential to lawmakers and their agents as they think appropriate in each case. Once it is accepted that judges have this kind of choice, it is hard to resist the critics' claim that the rules of constitutional law are just as indeterminate and subjective as any other branch of the law.[8] On an empirical level, the charge is irrefutable. The jurisprudence – right around the world – is there to read. Even members of the judiciary have called attention to the threat that is posed to the integrity of the process if judges are allowed to choose personally how rigorously the rules will be enforced.[9]

To defend the intelligibility and legitimacy of the law requires students to fine-tune their powers of critical analysis. Given the empirical reality of the case law we have read, the only way to salvage judicial review is to take issue with the practice of judges' arrogating to themselves the authority to decide in what circumstances and to what degree lawmakers and their agents will be held to account. One must test the force of the arguments that the judges and their defenders have advanced in justifying the tentative and deferential way in which they have gone about their work.

As we have seen in the preceding chapters, there are three sorts of reasons usually advanced in support of the idea that judges must be free to decide how forcefully and extensively the standards of rationality and proportionality should be applied in any case. Significantly, no one argues that a constitution explicitly gives judges a discretion to decide when and how rigorously these principles should be enforced. Concepts like tiers of review and margins of appreciation cannot be grounded in any text. There are no interpretive claims being made here. The justifications are rather of a theoretical and/or pragmatic kind. They are arguments about what judging and the judiciary are all about and their role in the operation of the liberal-democratic state and the realization of the just society.

First, it is commonly said that it is inconsistent with our ideas about democracy and the principle of separation of powers to insist that lawmakers and their agents be held strictly to account in every decision they make.[10] Where a law involves a delicate, political, balancing of competing interests (for example, in social and economic policy), the argument is that a degree of deference is owed to the elected branches of government that may not be appropriate in other circumstances, when different interests are involved. These kinds of decisions are at the core of the legislative function and must be left to the politicians to resolve.

In addition to the argument that courts must not usurp the role of the executive and the legislature, some say that there are sound practical reasons for courts' adjusting their approach to the type of policy issue at stake. As we saw at the end of chapter 3, some fear that if the courts were obliged to exercise their powers of review with the same intensity in every case, they would be swamped with petitions and would not be able to give sufficient reflection to the cases that matter the most. Even where the 'floodgates' argument is not a serious threat, others point out that judges are constrained by an adjudicative system of decision-making that is especially ill-suited to resolving the kinds of policy questions about which so much of modern regulatory law is concerned.[11]

Finally, in addition to questioning whether judicial review is compatible with the idea of popular sovereignty and is institutionally well suited to the task, some people think that it is actually inconsistent with the concept of rights for courts to hold every law or official action up to the same strict standard of review. Again, as we saw at the end of chapter 3, some people believe that such an approach would lead to judicial inquiries into the most intimate and personal aspects of individuals' lives, which the concept of rights was designed to protect. Others say that certain aspects of the human condition are more important than others and warrant stronger protection by the courts.[12] Still others worry that extending the same constitutional protection, regardless of whether the limit on personal freedom is trivial and insignificant or serious and substantial, will cheapen or devalue the protection that rights can provide in the cases where they are needed most.[13]

We have encountered all these arguments at one time or another in the preceding pages, and there is therefore no need to dwell on them again. We have seen how, in one way or another, all of them fall short of the mark. Dealing with the last argument first, one can only repeat what we earlier observed. Concerns that enforcing the strictures of rationality and proportionality rigorously in every case will weaken or undermine the value of rights in the cases we care about most have no basis in logic or in fact. Logically, duties are inextricably and unavoidably correlated to the concept of rights.[14] To have a right necessarily implies that someone else has a duty to recognize and respect it. Standards of rationality and proportionality are simply the duties that lawmakers and their agents owe to those whose lives they affect when they exercise the powers of the state. Holding politicians to these duties every time they propose to infuse some part of their political programme with the force of law maximizes the protection that rights can provide. Far from being inconsistent with the concept of rights, or undermining their integrity and coherence, insisting that lawmakers behave rationally and consistently every time they act promotes the underlying values of human dignity and personal autonomy on which all liberal-democratic constitutions are based. It guarantees that society will respect a person's authority to live his or her life as he or she sees fit as much as that is possible when society shows everyone the same concern.

There is also no evidence in the comparative case law that if politicians are required to act in accordance with these principles every time they exercise the powers of the state, courts will be flooded with cases that will overwhelm their resources and distract them from more menacing threats to constitutional rights. Even in a country such as Germany, where the Constitutional Court has recognized that virtually every interest or activity can be grounded in one or other of the rights and freedoms that the Basic Law guarantees (with the right of personal autonomy in article 2.1 acting as a kind of residual clause), people with complaints about laws that interfere with their lives in the most attenuated and insignificant ways have not rushed to court, and there is no reason, in logic (or economics), to expect that they will. Once people understand how these tests of constitutional validation work, the worry that the rigorous application of the principles of rationality and proportionality in every case will result in the courts' sometimes invading our personal freedom too deeply and other times not being protective enough should soon disappear.

When they are strictly enforced, the protection that the principles of rationality and proportionality provide varies directly with the importance of the interests at stake. Lawmakers must tell much more compelling stories to justify major restrictions of our most cherished freedoms (to express political, religious, and moral ideas) than they do when a law constrains a person's rights superficially and in trivial ways (e.g., freedom to express oneself violently and in socially harmful ways). Even though a politically motivated killing may be an act of expression or association designed to further the values on which liberal-democratic societies are based, few assassins should harbour any expectations that a constitutional challenge to a country's homicide laws would likely result in their early release. By contrast, those aspects of our private lives about which we care most should generally be much less vulnerable to detailed regulation by the state, precisely because this is where the core of personal autonomy resides and where considerations of self-actualization count the most.[15] It is implicit in the idea of proportionality that much more compelling reasons must be given to justify a law that impinges on an interest or an activity that is central to the idea of personal autonomy and self-determination than on aspects of personal freedom that are marginal or peripheral at best. Strictly applied, the principles of rationality and proportionality should give each part of each person's personal odyssey exactly the amount of protection it deserves.

The courts certainly have not had much difficulty distinguishing easy cases from those in which the justification is more difficult to assess. Governments everywhere have a much harder time justifying laws that restrict people's right to express themselves publicly and peacefully on current issues of the day than they do when, for example, purely commercial interests are at play.[16] Similarly, all over the world, courts demand more substantial explanations from politicians when they enact laws that limit individuals' freedom to enter a particular vocation or career opportunity than when they regulate the ways in which different occupational groups practise their trades.[17] Again, laws that tolerate or entail a degree of religious indoctrination or coercion are harder to justify in every country with a written bill of rights than general regulations that make it more difficult to engage in various exercises or activities that operate at the margins of a person's religion or faith.[18]

In addition to extending more protection to those human rights we traditionally value most, by requiring more substantial justification to be given for their limitation than for laws that interfere with people's freedom in less invasive and significant ways, the principles of rationality and proportionality are also entirely compatible with the idea of responsible government and democratic rule. After reading how constitutional law is being practised around the world, the argument that democracy and the principle of separation of powers require judges to apply these principles with caution and restraint seems impossible to defend. With only these two basic rules of how state power must be exercised, the courts pose little threat to the democratic character of government. Quite the opposite in fact. For the most part,[19] courts have not embraced criteria of constitutionality that restrict the policy objectives that politicians and their agents can pursue. In most countries, only initiatives that serve no other purpose than limiting basic constitutional guarantees have been ruled out of bounds. While the rules of constitutional law and politics regulate the same actors and behaviour and cover the same ground, there is a real division of responsibilities – separation of powers – in what they each do. Though the rules of constitutional law are supreme, sovereignty still resides in the people, and, because of that, politics is given jurisdiction over what policies and lifestyles a community may promote. Politics determines what direction a society will take; what, in philosophers' terms, is the content of the community's good. The rules of law are concerned with right conduct and are focused on the way Governments and their officials infuse their favourite policies with the authority of law. Law leaves the goals and aspirations to be chosen by the people.

Rationality and proportionality are concerned with the way in which lawmakers pursue their political programs, not with what the ends or objectives of social policy should or should not be. As they have been applied by most courts, the rules of constitutional law take the goals of whatever policy or program they are asked to review as a given and ask whether, on its own terms, the law is more restrictive and heavy-handed than it needs to be. What the rules of law really do is insist that lawmakers and bureaucrats act consistently with the standards they and their counterparts in other free and democratic societies have set for themselves when they faced similar issues in the past.

Comparing how courts exercise their powers of review establishes that, as an empirical matter, constitutional law is made up of a set of rules that are much more concerned with social obligations than with individual rights. Rather than marking off discrete spheres of personal and private autonomy and shielding them from any community influence or control, the central rules of constitutional law are concerned with the duties that lawmakers and their officials owe to those they represent. The basic rules of constitutional law enhance the integrity of the democratic process by ensuring that whatever their political philosophy or social agenda, lawmakers and their agents will act in a way that guarantees everyone a basic modicum of equality and respect. Far from resisting the will of the people to control their own destinies, rules of constitutional law ensure that lawmakers and administrators will show those they govern the same 'rights' that they give to others and demand for themselves.

Both rationality and proportionality are criteria of control that are 'internal' to the choice of the lawmaker.[20] Both test the policy instruments devised by Governments against standards or benchmarks of their own making. When a court measures a challenged law for its rationality, it takes the purposes and public interests promoted by the law as a given and asks whether there were alternative policies that could have been employed that would have restricted individuals' freedom less. In the case of the proportionality principle, as the doctrine of the European standard developed by the judges in Strasbourg makes so clear, the test is how a particular society and its neighbours have acted in similar circumstances. On both measures, the democratically elected representatives of the people control the substance and content of the criteria against which these measures of constitutionality are applied.

In the result, the principles of rationality and proportionality establish an analytical framework for the courts to follow that is acutely sensitive to ideas of popular sovereignty and the principle of majority rule. They direct the judges to follow a process of reasoning that has very little to do with textual exegisis of the constitution. Judges are supposed to apply the principles rigorously and to their full force and effect in every case. Their primary responsibility is not to search for definitions either from the original intention of the founding fathers or from their own ideas of what is politically or morally correct.

Most students see quite quickly the way in which the rationality principle works alongside and supports the democratic character of a constitution. Rationality allows the 'popular will' to seek almost any end or objective. The only constraint it imposes on the sovereignty of the people is a methodological one of not employing policies and regulations that interfere with anyone's life more than is necessary. Governments can do almost anything they want except be heavy-handed.

For many students, however, the way in which the proportionality principle promotes the virtues of popular sovereignty and democratic rule is not so readily apparent. As we noted back in chapter 1, proportionality is often referred to as a 'balancing principle,' and the image that it conveys is one of courts sitting in judgment on how a particular law or regulation reconciles the competing interests that it affects. On this characterization, when judges apply the proportionality principle they seem to be second-guessing the choices of legislators and interfering directly with the sovereignty of the popular will.

Though, as we have seen, there are many cases when courts have applied the proportionality principle in this way, that is not the way it is designed to work. Properly applied, proportionality acts as a consistency constraint in which Governments and their officials are made to respect a basic standard of equal treatment. Rather than permitting judges to weigh the competing interests affected by a law against some independent, external standards of their own, the proportionality principle asks how the particular balance that is struck by a law compares with how earlier legislators and Governments have reconciled similar interests in the past.

Three cases from the preceeding chapters illustrate how courts can employ this standard effectively and in a way that respects the democratic character of modern liberal states. In *McKay v. Queen,*[21] to return to a division-of-powers case first, it will be recalled that the Supreme Court effectively ruled that a law that prohibited people from putting up election posters on their lawns was beyond the powers of a municipality – or province – to pass. Though, as we saw, the judgment that was written by the Court leaves much to be desired, the decision can be justified on the ground that there was an element of inconsistency in the way the by-law was drawn. Although the municipality had a legitimate objective (the aesthetics of local neighbourhoods) in mind, the fact is that the by-law did allow certain individuals and groups (including doctors and real-estate agents) to spoil the view. When the by-law's proscriptions are measured against these exceptions – their own standards – and the relative importance of campaign posters in federal elections is given its due, the decision of the Court seems to promote values of democracy and justice simultaneously.

The Charter case of *Singh v. Minister of Employment and Immigration*[22] can be explained in exactly the same way. The constitutional failing in Canada's refugee law lay in the fact that those coming to Canada claiming that they were fleeing for their lives were not treated the same as refugee claimants in other free and democratic societies or even as ordinary Canadians faced with nothing more serious than a parking violation. The federal law failed the proportionality test because it denied refugee claimants the right to a hearing that Canadian law gives to others in similar and even much less extreme circumstances.

Finally, the decision of the European Court of Human Rights in *Dudgeon v. U.K.*[23] shows how proportionality can be reduced to a consistency or equality test and need not involve judges trying to balance competing interests on their own. In *Dudgeon*, the sodomy law in force in Northern Ireland was struck down because the only harm that Belfast could point to was relatively insignificant, on its own terms, when compared with the importance most people attach to their sexual relations. Once the Court had compared the law in Northern Ireland with those in force in the other free and democratic societies in Europe and elsewhere, its supporters could not defend it on the basis of preventing some social harm or securing some public good. The only ground on which it could be justified was the offence it gave to those who regard all homosexual behaviour as salacious and immoral.

While not denying that behaviour of this kind gives offence to people of various moral and religious views, the judges in Strasbourg – like most of my students – had little difficulty in seeing that, in relative terms, this harm is neither qualitatively nor quantitatively nearly as significant to the lives of those who experience it as the injuries suffered by those who are prevented from making what is a very intimate and personal choice for themselves. In the same way that the additional harm to the province's interest in *McKay*, in maintaining some environmental controls in its neighbourhood communities, did not compare to the importance of campaign posters in a federal election, so in *Dudgeon* the significance of private sexual activity in the lives of most everyone was seen to transcend the significance of these kinds of activities, and the harm they caused, in the lives of those who were offended by them.

McKay, *Singh*, and *Dudgeon* are important cases because they illustrate why holding Governments and their officials to a criterion of proportionality is not inconsistent with democracy or the sovereignty of the popular will. Rather than inviting judges to engage in a balancing exercise of the competing interests involved, proportionality directs the courts to evaluate the claims of those supporting and attacking a law in their own terms. Governments and their officials are tested not by what each judge thinks is proper and right but rather by how they and other free and democratic societies have treated others in similar circumstances.

Proportionality does not tell a court to put the public interest and constitutional rights that are affected by a law on opposite sides of a balance or scale and read off which is the more substantial (viz., weightier) of the two. Proportionality requires judges to examine the impact the law has on the various interests/rights that it affects separately. The idea is to measure how critical the law is to each of the interests/rights involved rather than judge their relative worth (weight) against each other. The critical judgment is more like one made by an inspector who examines how much wine has been decanted from two casks containing different vintages than a decision made by a taster whose job is to say something about the quality (worth, substance) of each. The really critical question for a court is how deeply the challenged law cuts into each interest or right – how much wine it draws off from each cask.

Claims that law and politics are in some sense antithetical or in tension with each other fail to understand the way principles of rationality and proportionality work. Arguments about the functional effectiveness of the courts also seem less persuasive when they are evaluated in the context of how judges around the world have exercised their powers of review. Reasoning analogically, and testing human behaviour against standards of necessity and consistency, are traditionally what courts do in every area of law, and our survey of how constitutional law formed by the courts when they exercise their powers of review over the activities of lawmakers and their officials. As a practical matter, in performing their role as 'guardians of the constitution,' a court's primary task is to compare the law that it has been asked to review against alternative policies that they and other lawmakers have tried elsewhere.

On almost every issue where one court or judge has argued that considerations of economy and institutional competence should encourage the law to be modest in its ambition, other courts and other judges have shown that they can apply the tests of necessity and consistency with care and sensitivity. For example, against the reluctance of the American, Japanese, and European courts to evaluate closely laws restricting the political rights of public servants, the Supreme Court of Canada has shown how rationality and proportionality can ensure that this sphere of community life is ruled with maximum fairness and toleration.[24] By contrast, when it comes to reviewing the constitutionality of labour and employment laws, Canadians have something to learn from both the Americans and the Europeans.[25]

In hundreds of cases, the courts have shown that they are capable of identifying policies that impose less drastic limitations on people's freedom to act, or that are more in keeping with how other lawmakers have acted in analogous cases, regardless of what kind of state regulation is at stake. Drawing sharp, categorical lines to distinguish areas of social policy where lawmakers will be held strictly to account from those in which looser standards will be tolerated proves to be as artificial and arbitrary here as in every other area of law. As we saw at the end of chapter 3, even the Supreme Court of Canada, which has shown some sympathy for the idea of being more deferential towards policies that attempt to balance competing interests than towards those in which the state speaks in a single, collective voice, has recognized that such a distinction is actually quite fuzzy and blurred.[26]

LAW AND POLITICS

At the end of the day then, none of the arguments about democracy, institutional competence, or the concept of rights supports the practice of judges' deciding for themselves when or how vigilantly the tests of constitutional validity should be enforced. As a matter of principle, populists and democrats who are sceptical about the virtues of law have nothing to fear. Law and politics are ways in which communities and countries organize their affairs that complement rather than conflict with each other.

Law and politics do not pertain to different areas or aspects of community life in which either one or the other but never both hold sway. There are no bright lines or sharp jurisdictional divisions that separate the two domains. Law and politics are different ways of ordering relations between people, but they do have a common core.

It is often said that politics is the art of compromise, which is a common-sense way of saying that in politics, as in law, one should always act with moderation, reserve, and consideration for the other side. The only difference is that in politics this standard of good behaviour is introduced through a process of negotiation and give and take, whereas in law proportionality is the product of logical analysis and is applied through a process of reasoning in which analogies and the demands of equality are expected to carry the day.

Though law and politics work the same turf, so to speak, the relationship is, as we have seen, unavoidably a hierarchical one. The rules of constitutional law are the ultimate criteria of what constitutes legitimate authority, and so in that sense politics is inevitably subordinate to the law. As part of every liberal constitution in the world, rationality and proportionality reign supreme over all other rules and institutions of the state. They control the way legal authority is exercised in every facet of a community's life.

As we have seen in the last three chapters, attempts to establish separate enclaves where the rules of constitutional law do not apply denies and runs counter to the supreme nature of constitutional law. When courts conclude that there are discrete spheres or categories of personal and/or community life where the rules of constitutional law do not prevail, they almost always make the same mistake. Instead of reading the constitution purposefully (deductively), they propose some other (historical, prudential) interpretation that is either conceptually and/or empirically flawed. The early attempts of the Supreme Court of Canada to divide jurisdiction between Ottawa and the provinces into very discrete, 'watertight' compartments, the different treatment social and economic laws have received around the world, the distinct categories of speech that characterized American first amendment law, and the distinctions the Japanese and Indian courts have drawn between laws that limit rights directly and indirectly are some of the more glaring examples we have encountered of courts reasoning in this way.

The categorical, dichotomous reasoning that is dominant on such occasions is antithetical to the principles of rationality and proportionality and the values on which they are based. It allows those entrusted with developing the rules and regulations governing these interests and areas of community life to exercise the coercive powers of the state arbitrarily, irrationally, and out of all proportion to whatever public purpose is being pursued. Categorical reasoning creates enclaves where the virtues of moderation and consistency no longer reign as the rules that certify the legitimacy – the inner morality – of law.

It has been my experience that the more judgments students read from other countries, the easier it is for them to see both the conceptual coherence and the practical possibilities of the law. However, invariably there are some students, usually those who are most committed to the protection of human rights, who have a harder time acclaiming the virtues of law. For them, the systematic failure of the courts to act consistently on a common understanding of their powers of review proves that conceptual clarity is not enough to guarantee that law will do the job it is designed to perform. They say that one cannot be optimistic about the future of human rights until those who are appointed to the Bench publicly commit themselves to enforcing the principles of rationality and proportionality as vigorously as possible.

From our review of cases in Canada and around the world, it is apparent that the plea of human rights activists for a more accountable and responsible process of appointing judges to a country's highest court has a good deal of empirical support. The jurisprudence we have reviewed demonstrates that much more important than the words that are used in a constitution is the process by which persons are appointed to the Bench. Study of the way in which rules of constitutional law have been developed and applied around the world reveals how infrequently the text controls the outcome of a case. It is the attitude of each judge to the way in which the rationality and proportionality principles should be applied that is decisive in determining how rigorous the protection of human rights will be.

In Canada, we have witnessed the consequences of judges' claiming the right to modify and vary the standards of review in a very dramatic way. Thus, as we followed the evolution of the Charter in chapter 3, although the Supreme Court applied the framework of analysis that it described in *Oakes* quite vigorously in the first two years, after that its approach became much more cautious and restrained. Had more judges been appointed to the Court who identified with the earlier approach, the record of protection of human rights in Canada would be much stronger than it is today. For those whose ambition is to entrench human rights in a constitutional document as powerfully as one possibly can, it is the method by which judges are appointed to the court, much more than the language used to describe the constitutional guarantees, that should be the primary focus of their attention. Only if methods of appointment are devised that can identify those whose commitment to the principles of rationality and proportionality is strong and uncompromising will constitutional protection of human rights realize its potential as an instrument of social justice.[27]

However, while the experience of the Canadian Supreme Court teaches us that it is the process by which judges are appointed, much more than the language of the text, that determines the extent to which constitutional rights will be respected, it would be wrong to leave the impression that what goes into a constitution does not matter at all. The lesson to be learned from how the Supreme Court of Canada and the other major courts around the world exercise their powers of review is, in fact, quite the reverse. To allay the doubts and concerns of the most committed human rights activists, we must also be careful about what we write. There are lessons to be learned from comparative jurisprudence about what constitutions should contain. There are real limits on what we can legitimately ask courts to do. The experience of the Indian Court shows how constitutions that try to cover too much ground can make the job of the judge more difficult.

Understanding that the essence of the review process is the evaluation of Government policies against broad principles of justice – of necessity and consistency – also explains why entrenchment of general guarantees of social and economic well-being is a risky venture. Allowing judges to define minimum conditions of social welfare would ask them to perform a function, and exercise a degree of control over the distribution of wealth in a community, that is qualitatively different from the task that constitutional bills of rights have traditionally called on the courts to perform. As the cases that have been highlighted clearly show, constitutional review is mostly a process in which the third branch of government tells the other two when they have gone too far – when they have drafted with too heavy a hand. Except in equality cases, the court's role has not been to tell legislators that they have or have not gone far enough. And, even in these cases, apart from requiring compliance with the equality norm, when courts have been asked to instruct a legislature on how far it should go, they have shown little inclination to accede to the request.[28]

Putting social and economic rights in a constitution encourages people to believe that it is within the mandate of the courts to make decisions of precisely this kind. It suggests that the judges should focus on the ends, not just the means, of Government policy. Rather than thinking about courts as an adjunct to, or monitor of, the legislative process, to guarantee a measure of moderation in the ways Governments go about transforming their election promises into law, judicial definitions of social and economic rights would assign the courts a different task, and one that lies at the core of the legislative function. Asking courts to concretize the substance of these 'second- and third-generation' rights would give judges a measure of control over the fiscal powers of the state, which, except in a limited and narrowly defined way,[29] is not part of the court's role when it assesses a Government's legislative choices against principles of rationality and consistency.

The essential core of the courts' job is to supervise the behaviour of lawmakers and their officials when they invoke the authority of the state. Except in delineating the broad circumstances in which lawmakers have a duty to take some initiative to protect basic rights, the courts' job is not to redress imbalances of power in private, interpersonal relations.[30] Even those courts that have required lawmakers to take some positive action to ensure that the overarching values of human dignity and personal autonomy are not undermined have not told politicians how far they must go or precisely what they must do. Even when the courts have insisted that Governments have a positive duty to act, the rules of constitutional law function more as general standards and obligations that politicians must meet than as claims of personal entitlement.[31] Adding social and economic guarantees to the traditional political and civil rights blurs the separation of powers between the courts and the two elected branches of government, which the principles of rationality and consistency are, by design, committed to respect. It would be a bit like asking a gopher to play a game of golf.

At the end of the day, the kind of protection that constitutions and courts can extend to human rights turns out to be quite limited. The rules of constitutional law can guarantee only that government regulation will satisfy two basic principles, justice and equality. As a practical matter, judges have no other tools to improve the moral integrity and democratic legitimacy of the state. While allowing the legislative and executive branches virtually unfettered discretion in the social objectives that they may pursue, the courts' task is to ensure that no one's freedom to live life as he or she sees fit will be interfered with gratuitously or in a way that is out of proportion with how others with similar interests have been treated. The means-oriented principle of rationality guarantees a degree of equality between all human beings by ensuring that no one's life will be interfered with by the state any more than is absolutely necessary to realize whatever social good is being pursued. The ends-oriented principle of proportionality insists that states respect a measure of equality or consistency in how similar interests are reconciled over time.

Together, the two principles are able to enhance the quality of social justice that a community is able to provide, without compromising, in any serious way, the sovereignty of the popular will and the democratic character of the state. They maximize the amount of personal choice that can be enjoyed equally in a society. Our own experience is quite unambiguous on this point. Thus, in striking down laws that unnecessarily restricted women's ability to control decisions about the uses to which their bodies could be put; denied older workers the right to collect unemployment insurance benefits; limited the opportunities of public servants to participate in the political life of their communities, or of other interest groups to communicate their ideas in public; and subjected people acquitted of criminal charges on the ground of insanity to the threat of indefinite detention, or exposed legitimate refugee claimants to serious risks to the security of their persons – to recall just a few of the cases in chapter 3 – the Supreme Court of Canada can fairly claim to have enhanced the quality of social justice in Canada.

Indeed, when constitutional review is thought of in this way, it becomes apparent that not only can the procedure of constitutional review enhance the moral character of a community but it does this in a way that promotes the idea of democratic decision-making as well. Understanding judicial review as a process in which the focus is on how Governments are able to defend the laws they enact against principles of necessity and consistency makes it easy to see constitutional litigation as a new way in which individuals, who perhaps have had little influence in the traditional processes and institutions of political life, can get the ear of their governors. Shifting the discourse of constitutional law from individual rights to principles of justice, political accountability, and social obligation shows that constitutional litigation can act as a vehicle for 'interest group' (as opposed to multi-interest, party) politics. In the way it has come to be practised around the world, constitutional review can be seen as a method by which those who, for one reason or another, have been ignored by their Governments can insist that valid explanations be provided for why they have been treated as they have.[32] It supports the idea, fashionable among some European scholars, of understanding rights in procedural and discursive terms.[33]

In the result, even though no court has exercised its powers of review as vigorously and vigilantly as human rights activists might like, the jurisprudence that has been written around the world does provide strong support for the conclusion that if constitutions are written in a simple and straightforward way, and if the people chosen to sit on the Bench are firmly committed to the rule of law and the concept of rights, the judiciary does have an important, if limited, role to play in the organization and operation of any socially responsible and democratically accountable state. There is no irreconcilable tension between law and politics, or between the courts and the two other elected branches of government, as many students of law and political science are taught. Rather, the experience in Canada and other countries that have some history with processes of constitutional review confirms the wisdom of those in central and eastern Europe, the former Soviet Union, and the Third, developing world, who, at the moment of their liberation from undemocratic and totalitarian regimes, have incorporated bills of rights into their constitutions. Even if the human rights activist has good reason to complain that the courts have applied the standards of rationality and proportionality too tentatively and erratically, their performance still provides compelling proof that extending the rule of law into the constitutional framework of government, through the process of judicial review, marks an improvement in, rather than a threat to, both the integrity and the efficacy of the modern nation-state.

Notes

CHAPTER ONE

1 *Stadium Corp. v. Toronto* 10 OR (3d) 203 (1993).
2 H.W. Arthurs, 'The Right to Golf: Reflections on the Future of Workers, Unions and the Rest of Us under the Charter,' *Queen's LJ* (1987) 17.
3 Jon Elster, 'Majority Rule and Individual Rights,' in S. Shute and S. Hurley, eds, *On Human Rights* (New York: Basic Books 1993), 175. For a review of some of the excesses of political power in Canadian history, see M. Trebilcock and N. Kelley, *The Making of the Mosaic: A History of Canadian Immigration Policy* (Toronto 1995). See also *Cunningham v. Tomey Homma* [1903] AC 151; *Quong Wing v. The King* (1914) 18 DLR 121.
4 In the original constitution of 1867, the democratic character of the Canadian state was expressed in the provision of elected legislative assemblies for both the provinces and the federal government and in the reference, in the preamble, to Canada's constitution being 'similar in principle to that of the United Kingdom.' See *Reference Re: Alberta Statutes* [1938] 2 DLR 81. In 1982, in the entrenchment of the Charter of Rights and Freedoms (sections 3–5), a series of 'democratic rights' to vote, stand for office and so on was added. See *Ref re: Electoral Boundaries Commission Act* (1991) 81 DLR (4th) 16.
5 Even in Canada, where there is no sharp differentiation between the executive and legislative branches, it is recognized that the function performed by the courts stands apart from other regulatory agencies. See P. Hogg, *Constitutional Law of Canada*, 3rd edition (Toronto: Carswell 1992), chap. 7.3. Even following entrenchment of the Charter, as we shall see in chapter 3, the courts have been quite insistent that their role is not to second-guess the merits or wisdom of the decisions of the other two branches of

government. See e.g. *Ref re: Section 94(2) of the Motor Vehicle Act (B.C.)* 24 DLR (4th) 536 (1985).

6 See Hogg, *Constitutional Law,* chap. 5.

7 In the Canadian constitution, the supremacy clause is contained in section 52 of the Constitution Act, 1982.

8 The provisions outlining the procedures and voting requirements for amending the Canadian constitution are found in part V (sections 38–49) of the Constitution Act, 1982. These provisions and the relevant case law are summarized in Hogg, *Constitutional Law,* chap. 4.

9 The federal government's powers over trade and commerce and criminal law are set out in sections 91(2) and 91(27) of the Constitution Act, 1867, while provincial responsibility for property and civil rights and matters of a local nature is set out in sections 92(13) and (16), respectively.

10 For descriptions of how 'executive federalism' has worked, see D. Smiley, *Canada in Question: Federalism in the Eighties,* 3rd edition (Toronto: McGraw-Hill Ryerson 1980) chap. 4; R. Simeon, *Federal Provincial Diplomacy* (Toronto: University of Toronto Press 1972).

11 See Hogg, *Constitutional Law,* chap. 6.

12 See K. Swinton, *The Supreme Court and Canadian Federalism* (Toronto: Carswell 1990), 40–52; see also A. Breton and A. Scott, *The Economic Constitution of Federal States* (Toronto: University of Toronto Press 1970).

13 Aboriginal peoples have been particularly aware of the possibilities of using law as a method of constitutional reform. See e.g. *R v. Sparrow* 70 DLR (4th) 385 (1990); *Delgamuukw v. A.G.B.C.* 104 DLR (4th) 470 (1993) (BCCA).

14 For a description of the rules of standing, governing who can initiate a constitutional challenge, see Hogg, *Constitutional Law,* chap. 56.2.

15 For a summary of the rules governing when and how the federal and provincial governments refer constitutional questions to the courts, see ibid, chap. 8.6.

16 For a description of the rules governing who can intervene and participate in a hearing, see ibid, chap. 56.6.

17 See e.g. ibid, chaps. 15.4 and 33.6.

18 For a discussion of how deductive and analogical forms of reasoning are used in law, see Steven J. Burton, *An Introduction to Law and Legal Reasoning* (Boston: Little, Brown 1985); cf Richard Epstein, 'A Common Lawyer Looks at Constitutional Interpretation,' *Boston ULR* 72 (1992) 699; see also Peter Westen, 'On "Confusing Ideas": Reply,' 91 *Yale LJ* 91 (1982) 1153. For a classic exposition on the importance of deductive, purposeful analysis in the interpretation of legal texts, see Lon Fuller, 'Positivism and Fidelity to Law: A Reply to Professor Hart,' *Harvard LR* 71 (1958) 630, 661–9.

19 W.R. Lederman, 'Unity and Diversity in Canadian Federalism: Ideals and Methods of Moderation' *Can. BR* 53 (1975) 597, 616–7; 'Comment' in J. Ziegal, *Law and Social Change* (Toronto: Osgoode Hall Law School 1973), 73.

20 Celebrated exceptions to this general practice underscore its widespread acceptance. In the United States, the best-known example is the Supreme Court's decision in *Brown v. Bd of Education* 347 US 483 (1954) reversing its earlier interpretation of the equal protection clause in *Plessy v. Ferguson* 163 US 537 (1896). In Canada, a parallel but less dramatic abandoning of an earlier decision is the Supreme Court's treatment of *Russell v. Queen* (1882) 7 AC 829 (JCPC), discussed in chapter 3.

21 See e.g. *Bedard v. Dawson* [1923] SCR 681, upholding a provincial law closing disorderly houses; and *A.G. P.Q. v. Kellogg's Co.* [1978] 2 SCR 211, upholding a provincial law prohibiting use of cartoons in advertisements aimed at children.

22 The rules of constitutional law and tort law have more in common than just their structure and mode of application. As we shall see, the rules of constitutional law are also very similar in substance to the rules of tort liability the courts have developed to evaluate the behaviour of public officials. See e.g. *Just v. British Columbia* (1989) 2 SCR 1228; *Swinamer v. Nova Scotia* [1994] 1 SCR 445. *Brown v. British Columbia* [1994] 1 SCR 420, and see generally D. Cohen and J.C. Smith, 'Entitlement and the Body Politic: Rethinking Negligence in Public Law' *Canadian BR* 64 (1986) 1.

23 See Paul Weiler, 'The Supreme Court and the Law of Canadian Federalism,' *UTLJ* 23 (1973) 307, 364; Patrick Monahan 'At Doctrine's Twilight: The Structure of Canadian Federalism,' *UTLJ* 34 (1984) 47, 50. See also M. Mandel, *The Charter of Rights and the Legalization of Politics* (Toronto: Wall and Thompson 1989); Allan Hutchinson, 'The Dilemma of Charter Legitimacy,' *UBCLR* 23 (1989) 531.

24 See e.g. Paul Weiler, *In the Last Resort* (Toronto: Carswell 1974), 172 ff; Monahan, 'At Doctrine's Twilight,' 95–96.

25 See e.g. Peter Hogg, *Constitutional Law*, 388 ff; Katherine Swinton, *The Supreme Court and Canadian Federalism* (Toronto: Carswell 1990) 55, 127, 210–17; R. Simeon, 'Criteria for Choice in Federal Systems,' *Queen's LJ* 8 (1982) 131; Lederman, 'Unity and Diversity,' 'Classification of Laws and the BNA Act,' in W.R. Lederman, ed, *The Courts and the Canadian Constitution* (Ottawa: Carleton Library, McLelland and Stewart) and 'The Balanced Interpretation of the Federal Legislative Powers in Canada,' in P.A. Crepeau and C.B. MacPherson, eds, *The Future of Canadian Federalism* (Toronto: University of Toronto Press, 1965).

26 Peter Russell, 'The Political Role of the Supreme Court of Canada in Its First Century,' *Can. BR* 53 (1975) 576, 591.
27 See Antonin Scalia, 'Federal Constitutional Guarantees of Individual Rights in the United States,' in D. Beatty, ed, *Human Rights and Judicial Review: A Comparative Perspective* (Dordrecht: Martinus Nijhoff 1994).
28 *R. v. Morgentaler* 44 DLR (4th) 385, 485 per Bertha Wilson. Cf. Robin West 'Adjudication Is Not Interpretation,' *Tenn. LR* 54 (1987) 203.
29 R. Dworkin, *Law's Empire* (Cambridge, Mass.: Harvard University Press 1986).

CHAPTER TWO

1 For many scholars of constitutional law, any theory that argues that courts have developed a set of neutral principles and standards that distinguish laws that are constitutional from those that are not is contested and controversial. See e.g. Paul Weiler, 'The Supreme Court and the Law of Canadian Federalism,' *UTLJ* 23 (1973) 307, 310, 328; Patrick Monahan, 'At Doctrine's Twilight: The Structure of Canadian Federalism,' *UTLJ* 34 (1984) 34, 47, 69–70, 74, 80; John Whyte, 'Constitutional Aspects of Economic Development Policy,' in R. Simeon, research coordinator, *Division of Powers and Public Policy* (Toronto: University of Toronto Press 1985), 29–31.
2 See e.g. *Ontario Public Service Employees' Union v. A.G. Ont* 41 DLR (4th) 1 (1987); *McKay v. The Queen* 53 DLR (2d) 532 (1965); *Oil Chemical and Atomic Workers' Union Local 16–601 v. Imperial Oil Ltd.* [1963] SCR 584.
3 *R. v. Morgentaler* 107 DLR (4th) 537 (1993).
4 *Toronto Electric Commissioners v. Snider* [1925] AC 396.
5 *Re Nova Scotia Board of Censors v. McNeil* 84 DLR (3d) 1 (1978).
6 *Westendorp v. Queen* 144 DLR (3d) 259 (1983); *Bedard v. Dawson* [1923] SCR 681.
7 *Lord's Day Alliance of Canada v. A.G. B.C.* [1959] SCR 497.
8 *Irwin Toy v. A.G. Quebec* 58 DLR (4th) 577 (1989); *A.G. Quebec v. Kellogg's Co* [1978] SCR 211.
9 *Citizens Insurance Company of Canada v. Parsons* (1881), 7 AC 96 (JCPC). On the Privy Council's earliest judgments, see W. Jennings, 'Constitutional Interpretation: The Canadian Experience,' *Harvard LR* 51 (1937) 1.
10 *Russell v. The Queen* (1882) 7 AC 829 (JCPC).
11 See Peter Hogg, *Constitutional Law of Canada*, 3rd edition (Toronto: Carswell 1992), 1288–90; Louis-Phillippe Pigeon, 'The Meaning of Provincial Autonomy,' *Can. BR* (1951) 1126; Katherine Swinton, *The Supreme Court and Canadian Federalism* (Toronto: Carswell 1990), chap. 4.
12 Even on an issue as basic as Canada's treaty-making powers, it is clear that

the framers of the original BNA Act did not contemplate the country's acting as an independent, autonomous state. For a discussion of the treaty-making power, see Robert Howse, 'The Labour Conventions Doctrine in an Era of Global Interdependence: Rethinking the Constitutional Dimensions of Canada's External Economic Relations,' *Can. Business LJ* 16 (1990) 160.

13 Compare G. Stevenson, *Unfulfilled Union*, 3rd edition (Toronto: Gage 1989), and A. Silver, *The French-Canadian Idea of Confederation 1864–1900* (Toronto: University of Toronto Press 1982). And see Alan Cairns, 'The Judicial Committee and Its Critics,' *CJPS* 4 (1971) 301.
14 See Swinton, *The Supreme Court*, chaps. 8 and 9.
15 P. Monahan, *Meech Lake: The Inside Story* (Toronto: University of Toronto Press 1991).
16 The classic description of constitutional law in nineteenth-century Britain is A.V. Dicey's *Introduction to the Study of the Law of the Constitution* (London: MacMillan 1939); see also *Reference re Alberta Statutes* [1938] 2 DLR 81 (per Duff CJC).
17 The idea that the two levels of government were independent, coordinate, and equal in their sovereignty over their respective areas of responsibility was recognized early and often by the Privy Council. See e.g. *Citizens Insurance Co. v. Parsons*; *Maritime Bank of Canada v. New Brunswick* [1892] AC 437.
18 K.C. Wheare, *Federal Government*, 4th edition (London: Oxford University Press 1963).
19 Hogg, *Constitutional Law*, chap. 5.
20 Peter Russell, 'The Political Role of the Supreme Court of Canada in its First Century,' *Can. BR* 53 (1975) 576, 585.
21 See e.g. Swinton, *The Supreme Court*, 200–1, 207, 217, 262; Monahan, 'At Doctrine's Twilight,' 83.
22 *Citizens Insurance Co. v. Parsons*, 108–9.
23 See e.g. Weiler, 'The Supreme Court'; A. Lajoie, P. Mulazzi, and M. Gamache, 'Political Ideas in Quebec and the Evolution of Canadian Constitutional Law 1945–85'; and G. Tremblay, 'The Supreme Court of Canada: Final Arbiter of Political Disputes,' both in I. Bernier and A. Lajoie, eds, *The Supreme Court of Canada as an Instrument of Social Change* (Toronto: University of Toronto Press 1986).
24 For example, repeated use of the word 'exclusive' in sections 91 and 92 to describe the powers of the federal and provincial governments seems to suggest a much more segregated, compartmentalized framework of intergovernment relations than 'concurrency' would imply.
25 W.R. Lederman, *Continuing Canadian Constitutional Dilemmas* (Toronto: Butterworths 1981), 243.

26 *Proprietary Articles Trade Assoc. v. A.G. Canada* [1931] AC 310.
27 *Reference re: Validity of s.5(1) of the Dairy Industry Act* (*Margarine Reference*) [1949] 1 DLR 433. See also *Thomson Newspapers v. Canada* 67 DLR (4th) 161 (1990).
28 *Ref re: Validity of s 5(1) of the Dairy Industry Act*; *Boggs v. The Queen* [1981] 1 SCR 49.
29 *Proprietary Articles Trade Assoc. v. Canada*; *Re Board of Commerce Act* [1922] 1 AC 191; *Ref re: Dominion Trade and Industrial Commission Act* [1936] SCR 379. And see generally Hogg, *Constitutional Law*, chap. 18.10.
30 *A.G. Canada v. A.G. Ontario* (Fisheries) [1898] AC 700; *A.G. Canada v. A.G. B.C.* (Fish Canneries) [1930] AC 111.
31 *A.G. Canada v. A.G. Ontario* (Labour Conventions) [1937] AC 326. See generally Howse, 'The Labour Conventions Doctrine,' and Lederman, *Continuing*, chap. 19.
32 *Ref re: Questions Concerning Marriage* [1912] AC 880.
33 *Commission du Salaire Minimum v. Bell Telephone Co. of Canada* 59 DLR (3rd) 145 (1966); *Commission de la Santé et de la Securité du Travail v. Bell Canada* 51 DLR (4th) 161 (1988). See also *Ontario Hydro v. Ontario Labour Relations Board* (107) DLR (4th) 457 (1993).
34 *Starr v. Houlden* 68 DLR (4th) 641 (1990); Hogg, *Constitutional Law*, chap. 19.7.
35 Hogg, *Constitutional Law*, chap. 24.3.
36 *Saumur v. City of Quebec* [1953] 4 DLR 641; *Switzman v. Ebling* 7 DLR (2d) 337 (1957).
37 See e.g. *Reference re Alberta Statutes* [1938] 2 DLR 81 (1938); *Winner v. S.M.T. (Eastern)* [1951] SCR 889.
38 For a description of how extensive the U.S. federal government's powers have proven to be, see A.B. Smith *Commerce Power in Canada and the United States* (Toronto: Butterworths 1963).
39 See e.g. B. Laskin 'Peace Order and Good Government Re-examined,' *Can. BR* (1947) 1054; W.P.M. Kennedy, 'The Interpretation of the BNA Act' (1943) *Cambridge LJ* 8 (1943) 156; D.G. Creighton, *Dominion of the North* (Boston: Houghton Mifflin 1944); R. MacGregor Dawson, *Government of Canada*, 4th edition (Toronto: University of Toronto Press 1963), 94–102.
40 *A.G. Ontario v. A.G. Canada* (Local Prohibition Reference) [1896] AC 348, 360–1.
41 *Russell v. The Queen*.
42 *Toronto Electric Commissioners v. Snider*.
43 *A.G. Ontario v. Canada Temperance Federation* [1946] AC 193.
44 *Re Board of Commerce Act*; *Toronto Electric Commissioners v Snider*.

45 *Reference re Anti Inflation Act*, 68 DLR (3d) 452 (1976).
46 *Johannesson v. West St. Paul* [1952] 1 SCR 292.
47 *Munro v. National Capital Commission* [1966] SCR 663.
48 *R. v. Crown Zellerbach Canada Ltd.* 49 DLR (4th) 161 (1988).
49 Although the court divided 4:3 in upholding the federal legislation, the judges differed chiefly on how the principles should be applied, rather than on which principles governed the outcome of the case.
50 See K. Swinton, 'Federalism under Fire: The Role of the Supreme Court of Canada,' *Law and Contemporary Problems*, 55 (1992) 121, 131–7; H. Brun and G. Tremblay, *Droit Constitutionnel*, 2nd edition (Cowansville: Yvon Blais 1990), 490–4.
51 In a way the Supreme Court of Canada was not! See *Severn v. Queen* [1878] 2 SCR 70.
52 *Citizens Insurance Co. v. Parsons*, 109.
53 Ibid, 112.
54 Ibid, 113.
55 See e.g. *Re Board of Commerce Act*; and *Toronto Electric Commissioners v Snider*,
56 See e.g. *Caloil Inc. v. A.G. Canada*, 20 DLR (3d) 472 (1971), *Re Agricultural Products Marketing Act*, 84 DLR (3d) 257 (1978), cf. *A.G. B.C. v. A.G. Canada* (Natural Products Marketing Act) [1937] AC 377.
57 *A.G. Ontario v. A.G. Canada* (Canada Standard Trademark) [1937] AC 405.
58 58 DLR (4th) 255 (1989).
59 *General Motors* was also handed down within weeks of another landmark ruling, *Irwin Toy v. Quebec* 58 DLR (4th) 577. The short period within which these three decisions were decided is reflected in the coincidence of principles and ideas on which they are based.
60 Peter Hogg, 'Subsidiarity and the Division of Powers in Canada,' *National Journal of Constitutional Law*, 3 (1993) 341; G.A. Bermann, 'Subsidiarity and the European Community,' *National Journal of Constitutional Law*, 3 (1993) 357, 'Taking Subsidiarity Seriously,' *Columbia LR* 94 (1994) 331; see also R. Howse, 'Subsidiarity in All but Name: Evolving Concepts of Federalism in Canadian Constitutional Law,' in P. Glenn, ed, *Droit Contemporain* (Cowansville, Que.: Yvon Blais Inc. 1994).
61 Louis-Phillipe Pigeon, 'The Meaning of Provincial Autonomy,' *Can. BR* 29 (1951) 1126, 1134.
62 See section 95, Constitution Act, 1867.
63 *Westendorp v. The Queen* 144 DLR (3d) 259 (1983).
64 *The King v. Eastern Terminal Elevator Co.* [1925] 3 DLR 1. See also *A.G. British Columbia v. A.G. Canada* (Natural Products Marketing Act (1937) 1, DLR 691 (JCPC). *A.G. Manitoba v. Manitoba Egg and Poultry Association* 19 DLR

(3d) 169 (1971); *Central Canada Potash Co. Ltd. v. Saskatchewan* 88 DLR (3d) 609 (1979).

65 *Multiple Access Ltd. v. McCutcheon* 138 DLR (3d) 1 (1982).

66 *Friends of the Oldman River Society v. Canada* (Minister of Transport) 88 DLR (4th) 1 (1992); see also Steven A. Kennett, 'Federal Environmental Jurisdiction after Oldman,' *McGill LJ*, 38 (1993) 181.

67 *Fowler v. The Queen* [1980] 2 SCR 213; *Northwest Falling Contractors v. The Queen* [1980] 2 SCR 292.

68 Hogg, *Constitutional Law*, chap. 15.5(c).

69 *Hodge v. The Queen* (1883) 9 App. Cas. 117.

70 The areas of social policy over which both the federal and provincial governments have explicitly been given joint responsibility include natural resources (92A), old age pensions (94A), and agriculture and immigration (95).

71 See Weiler, 'The Supreme Court, 349, 352, 361.

72 Hogg, *Constitutional Law*, chaps. 15.5, 15.9.

73 Ibid, chap. 15.9(c).

74 Ibid, chap. 16.

75 See e.g. Swinton, *The Supreme Court*, 41; cf K. Norrie, R. Simeon, and M. Krasnick, *Federalism and the Economic Union* (Toronto: University of Toronto Press 1986) 49–59.

76 See Hogg, *Constitutional Law*, chap. 16; see also W.R. Lederman, 'The Concurrent Operation of Federal and Provincial Laws in Canada,' *McGill LJ* 9 (1963) 185.

77 *Coughlin v. Ontario Highway Transport Board* [1968] SCR 569; *Peralta v. Ontario* [1988] 2 SCR 1045; and see generally Hogg, *Constitutional Law*, chap. 14.3; W.R. Lederman, 'Some Forms and Limits of Co-operative Federalism,' *Can. BR* 45 (1967) 409; Weiler, 'The Supreme Court,' 311.

78 *Re Canada Assistance Plan*, [1991] 1 SCR 525.

79 See e.g. *Labatt Breweries of Canada Ltd. v. The Queen* 110 DLR (3d) 594 (1980); *Dominion Stores v. The Queen* [1980] 1 SCR 844.

80 See e.g. *McKay v. The Queen*; *Winner v. S.M.T. (Eastern) Ltd.*

81 See e.g. *A.G. Alberta v. A.G. Canada* (Bank Taxation) [1939] AC 117; cf. *Bank of Toronto v. Lambe* (1887) 12 App. Cas. 575.

82 See e.g. *Starr v. Houlden*, cf. *Fraser v. The Queen* [1976] 2 SCR 9; *Di Iorio v. Warden of Montreal Jail* [1977] 2 SCR 152; *A.G. Quebec and Keable v. A.G. Canada* [1979] 1 SCR 218.

83 Swinton, 'Federalism'; Brun and Tremblay, *Droit Constitutionnel*.

84 See also *A.G. B.C. v. A.G. Canada* (Natural Products Marketing Act) [1937] AC 377.

85 See Howse, 'The Labour Conventions Doctrine.'

86 *Canadian Industrial Gas and Oil Ltd. v. Govt of Saskatchewan* 80 DLR (3d) 449 (1978); *Central Canada Potash Co. Ltd. v. Govt of Saskatchewan* 88 DLR (3d) 609 (1979).

87 *A.G. Manitoba v. Manitoba Egg and Poultry Association,*

88 *Re Public Service Board and Dionne* 83 DLR (3d) 178 (1978); *Capital Cities Communications Inc. v. C.R.T.C.* 81 DLR (3d) 609 (1977).

89 *Commisson du Salaire Minimum v. Bell Canada; Commission de la Santé du Travail v. Bell Canada;* cf. *Alberta Government Telephones v. Canada* [1989] 2 SCR 225, 275, *Ontario Public Service Employees' Union v. A.G. Ontario* 41 DLR (4th) 1 (1987) per Dickson CJC See also *Ontario Hydro v. Ontario Labour Relations Board* 107 DLR (4th) 457 (1993).

90 See Weiler, 'The Supreme Court,' 307, 364; Monahan, 'At Doctrine's Twilight,' 47, 50. See also Hogg, *Constitutional Law,* 15.5(c), 15.8 (e).

91 *Canadian Industrial Gas and Oil Ltd. v. Govt of Saskatchewan* 80 DLR (3d) 449 (1978); *Central Canada Potash Co. Ltd. v. Govt of Saskatchewan* 88 DLR (3d) 609 (1979).

92 *Westendorp v. Queen* 144 DLR (3d) 259 (1983); *Bedard v. Dawson* [1923] SCR 681.

93 Compare *Carnation Co. Ltd. v. Quebec Agricultural Marketing Board* 67 DLR (2d) 1 (1968); and *Central Canada Potash v. Saskatchewan,*

94 Compare *Ontario Public Service Employees' Union v. A.G. Ontario; Oil Chemical and Atomic Workers Union v. Imperial Oil Ltd.*; and *McKay v. The Queen,*

95 Compare *Westendorp v. The Queen;* and *Rio Hotel Ltd. v. New Brunswick* (Liquor Licensing Board) 44 DLR (4th) 663 (1987).

96 See e.g. Weiler, 'The Supreme Court'; Monahan, 'At Doctrine's Twilight.'

97 See e.g. *Ontario Public Service Employees' Union v. A.G. Ontario* per Dickson CJC See also Weiler, 'The Supreme Court,' 351.

98 Out-of-province consumers are not likely to be seriously burdened by any 'rent-seeking' behaviour by Quebec producers because substitute products are so readily available.

99 *Canadian Industrial Gas & Oil Ltd. v. Saskatchewan,* per Dickson J. (dissenting). See also Arne Paus-Jenssen, 'Resource Taxation and the Supreme Court of Canada: The Cigoil Case,' *Canadian Public Policy* 1 (1979) 45.

100 See F. Schauer, 'Easy Cases,' *Southern California LR* 58 (1985) 399.

101 Cairns, 'The Judicial Committee'; see also P.E. Trudeau, 'Federalism, Nationalism and Reason,' in P.A. Crepeau and C.B. MacPherson, eds, *The Future of Canadian Federalism* (Toronto: University of Toronto Press (1965), 30: 'It has long been a custom in English Canada to denounce the Privy Council for its provincial bias; but it should perhaps be considered

that if the law lords had not leaned in that direction, Quebec separation might not be a threat today; it might be an accomplished fact.'

102 For reviews of the work of Haldane and Laskin see R.J. Cheffins, *The Constitutional Process in Canada* (Toronto: McGraw-Hill 1969); J. Robinson, 'Lord Haldane and the British North America Act,' *UTLJ* 20 (1970) 55; F.R. Scott, *Canada Today* (London: Oxford University Press 1938); Swinton, *The Supreme Court*, chap. 8.

CHAPTER THREE

1 K.G. Banting and R.E. Simeon, *And No One Cheered* (Agincourt, Ont.: Methuen 1983); Alan Cairns, *Charter v. Federalism* (Montreal: McGill-Queen's University Press 1992).
2 *Reference re S. 94(2) of the Motor Vehicle Act (B.C.)* 24 DLR (4th) 536 (1985).
3 *Hunter v. Southam Inc.* 11 DLR (4th) 641 (1984).
4 Ibid; *Law Society of Upper Canada v. Skapinker* 9 DLR (4th) 161 (1984); *Singh v. Minister of Employment and Immigration* 17 DLR (4th) 422 (1985); *R. v. Big M. Drug Mart* 18 DLR (4th) 321 (1985); *R. v. Therens* 18 DLR (4th) 655 (1985); *Ref re S. 94(2) Motor Vehicle Act (B.C.)*; *R. v. Oakes* 26 DLR (4th) 200 (1986).
5 On the interpretive techniques relevant for constitutions and statutes, see R. Dworkin, *Law's Empire* (Cambridge, Mass.: Harvard University Press 1986), chaps. 9 and 10.
6 See e.g. *Hunter v. Southam Inc.; Ref. re S. 94(2) of the Motor Vehicle Act (B.C.)*; *Operation Dismantle Inc. v. R.* 18 DLR (4th) 481 (1985); *R. v. Big M. Drug Mart* 18 DLR (4th) 321 (1985); *R. v. Edwards Books and Art Ltd.* 35 DLR (4th) 1 (1986); *Ref. re Alberta Public Service Employee Relations Act* 38 DLR (4th) 161 (1987); *R. v. Turpin* [1989] 1 SCR 1296; *R. v. Raney* [1987] 1 SCR 598; *Andrews v. Law Society of B.C.* 56 DLR (4th) 1 (1989); *R. v. Keegstra* [1990] 3 SCR 697; *Comité pour La Republique du Canada v. Canada* 77 DLR (4th) 385 (1991). And see Peter Hogg, 'The Charter of Rights and American Theories of Interpretation,' *Osgoode Hall LJ* 25 (1987) 88.
7 *Ref. re S. 94(2) of the Motor Vehicle Act (B.C.)*; *Mahe v. Alberta* 68 DLR (4th) 69, 89 (1990).
8 The Supreme Court's interpretation in the '*Persons*' case [1928] 4 DLR 98 was reversed by the Privy Council in *Edwards v. A.G. Canada* [1930] 1 DLR 98. The literature on why the intention of those who wrote the constitution is an inadequate and inappropriate source of meaning is voluminous. Many of these essays and comments are collected and referred to in Peter Hogg, *Constitutional Law of Canada*, 3rd edition (Toronto: Carswell 1992), chap. 57.1(e), and David Beatty, *Talking Heads and the Supremes* (Toronto:

Carswell 1990), chap. 2 at notes 49 and 50.

9 In *Ref. re S. 94(2) Motor Vehicle Act (B.C.)*, the Court refused to read the reference in section 7 to 'principles of fundamental justice' as restricting its review to procedural matters, despite clear evidence that that was precisely what those who drafted the Charter intended those words to mean.

10 *Hunter v. Southam Inc.; R. v. Big M. Drug Mart; Ref. re S. 94(2) Motor Vehicle Act (B.C.); R. v. Oakes.*

11 26 DLR (4th) 200 (1986).

12 For the contrary view – that a purposive approach instructed the courts to read the rights and freedoms narrowly – see Hogg, *Constitutional Law*, chap. 33.7(c). For an argument that a deductive analysis of section 1 does not logically entail the 'proportionality principles' described in *Oakes*, see J. Bakan, 'Constitutional Interpretation and Legitimacy in Canadian Constitutional Thought,' Osgoode Hall LJ 27 (1989) 123.

13 *Irwin Toy v. A.G. Quebec* 58 DLR (4th) 577 (1989).

14 *Retail, Wholesale and Department Store Union Local 580 v. Dolphin Delivery Ltd.* 33 DLR (4th) 174 (1986); *Irwin Toy v. A.G. Quebec* ibid. See also *Young v. Young* 108 DLR (4th) 193 (1994) and *P.(D.) v. S.(C.)* 108 DLR (4th) 287 (1994), where the Court also excluded expression harmful to children.

15 *Retail, Wholesale and Department Store Union, Local 580 v. Dolphin Delivery Ltd.*

16 *R. v. Butler* 89 DLR (4th) 449 (1992).

17 *Ref. re SS. 193 and 195.1(1)(c) of the Criminal Code* [1990] 1 SCR 1123.

18 *Irwin Toy Ltd. v. A.G. Quebec,*

19 *R. v. Zundel* 95 DLR (4th) 202 (1992); see also *R. v. Keegstra* [1994] 3 SCR 697.

20 *R. v. Big M. Drug Mart Ltd.*

21 *R. v. Big M. Drug Mart Ltd. R. v. Edwards Books and Art Ltd.*

22 In parallel rulings, the Court has recognized that the other fundamental rights, such as freedom of expression and association, also have both a positive (freedom to) and a negative (freedom from) character as well. See e.g. *Slaight Communications Inc. v. Davidson* 59 DLR (4th) 416 (1989); *Lavigne v. Ontario Public Service Employees' Union* 81 DLR (4th) 545 (1991).

23 35 DLR (4th) 1 (1986).

24 18 DLR (4th) 321 (1985).

25 In addition to its large and generous interpretation of freedom of religion and expression, the Court has also read the protection provided by the words 'security of the person' and 'principles of fundamental justice' in section 7 in a sweeping and comprehensive way. See e.g. *R. v. Morgentaler* 44 DLR (4th) 385 (1988); *Ref. re S. 94(2) Motor Vehicle Act (B.C.)*. In the latter case, the Court explicitly embraced the deductive, 'purposeful' approach, even though that resulted in a definition of the 'principles of fundamental

justice' that contradicted the express intention of those who drafted section 7.

26 *R. v. Oakes.*

27 (1986) 26 DLR (4th) 200.

28 In *Oakes* itself the Court actually described a fourfold test that required those defending the constitutionality of a law or official action being reviewed to meet a purpose test and three proportionality principles, which focused on the means. In practice these tests can – and have been – reduced to two. See David Beatty, 'The End of Law: At Least As We Have Known It,' in Richard F. Devlin, ed, *Canadian Perspectives on Legal Theory* 1991, (Toronto: Emond Montgomery 1991) 391, 392–3. See also *Osborne v. Canada* (Treasury Board) 82 DLR (4th) 321 (1991).

29 For a chronological review of the first five years the Court worked with the Charter, see Beatty, *Talking Heads.* See also David Beatty, 'Human Rights and Constitutional Review in Canada: The First Decade,' Human Rights LJ 13 (1992) 185, and Patrick Monahan, 'The Charter Then and Now,' in Phillip Bryden, Steven Davis, and John Russell, *Protecting Rights and Freedoms* (Toronto: University of Toronto Press 1994), 105.

30 *A.G. P.Q. v. Quebec Association of Protestant School Boards* 10 DLR (4th) 321 (1984).

31 *R. v. Big M. Drug Mart.*

32 17 DLR (4th) 422 (1985).

33 *R. v. Morgentaler.*

34 *R. v. Zundel* 95 DLR (4th) 202 (1992).

35 *Ford v. A.G. Quebec* 54 DLR (4th) 577 (1988).

36 *Canada Employment and Immigration Commission v. Tétreault-Gadaury* 81 DLR (4th) 358 (1991).

37 *Andrews v. Law Society of British Columbia; Black v. Law Society of Alberta* 58 DLR (4th) 317 (1989); *Rocket v. Royal College of Dental Surgeons* 71 DLR (4th) 68 (1990); *R. v. Thibault* [1988] 1 SCR 1033.

38 *Osborne v. Canada (Treasury Board)* 82 DLR (4th) 321 (1991).

39 *Comité pour la Republique du Canada v. Canada* 77 DLR (4th) 385 (1991); see also *Ramsden v. City of Peterboro* 106 DLR (4th) 233 (1993).

40 See above, 50–4.

41 *A.G. Quebec v. Quebec Association of Protestant School Boards* 10 DLR (4th) 321 (1984).

42 *Ref. re S. 94(2) Motor Vehicle Act (B.C.)*; cf. *R. v. Goltz* [1991] 3 SCR 485.

43 *Hunter v. Southam Inc.*

44 *R. v. Big M. Drug Mart.*

45 *Singh v. Minister of Employment and Immigration.*

46 *R. v. Oakes.*

47 For an argument supporting the Court's different treatment of criminal law and laws regulating professional organizations, see Paul Weiler, 'The Charter at Work: Reflections on the Constitutionalizing of Labour and Employment Law,' *UTLJ* 40 (1990) 117.

48 *R v. Morgentaler.*

49 *R. v. Oakes*; *R. v. Smith* 40 DLR (4th) 435 (1987).

50 *R. v. Vaillancourt* 47 DLR (4th) 400 (1987); *R. v. Martineau* [1990] 2 SCR 633.

51 *R v. Swain* [1991] 1 SCR 933.

52 *Seaboyer v. The Queen* 83 DLR (4th) 193 (1991).

53 *R. v. Hess* [1990] 2 SCR 906.

54 See e.g. *R. v. Wong* [1990] 3 SCR 36; *R. v. Garofoli* [1990] 2 SCR 1421; *R. v. Koresch* [1990] 3 SCR 3; *R. v. Duarte* [1990] 1 SCR 30; *Thomson Newspapers v. Canada* 67 DLR (4th) 161 (1990); *Hunter v. Southam Inc.*; *C.B.C. v. New Brunswick* [1991] 3 SCR 459; *Societé Radio Canada v. Lessard* [1991] 3 SCR 421.

55 *Andrews v. Law Society of B.C.*

56 *Black v. Law Society of Alberta.*

57 *Rocket v. Royal College of Dental Surgeons.*

58 During the first ten years that the Court was deciding Charter cases, its membership changed almost completely. Only one member – the current Chief Justice, Antonio Lamer – was on it when the Court handed down its first decision, in *Skapinker v. Law Society of Upper Canada* 9 DLR (4th) 161 (1984). For a preliminary review of how the change in membership affected the Court's jurisprudence, see David Beatty, 'A Conservative's Court: The Politicization of Law,' *UTLJ* 41 (1991) 147; but see Robert J. Sharpe, 'A Comment on David Beatty's 'A Conservative's Court:' *UTLJ* 41 (1991) 469.

59 *Retail, Wholesale and Department Store Union, Local 580 v. Dolphin Delivery Ltd.*

60 *McKinney et al v. University of Guelph* 76 DLR (4th) 545 (1990); see also *Harrison v. University of British Columbia* 77 DLR (4th) 55 (1990); *Stoffman v. Vancouver General Hospital* 76 DLR (4th) 700 (1990).

61 *Lavigne v. Ontario Public Service Employees' Union.*

62 *Tremblay v. Daigle* 62 DLR (4th) 634 (1989). See also *Young v. Young* 108 DLR (4th) 193 and *P.(D.) v. S.(C.)* 108 DLR (4th) 287 (1994).

63 See e.g. *U.S.A. v. Cotroni* [1989] 1 SCR 1469; *R. v. Schmidt* 39 DLR (4th) 19 (1987); *Argentina v. Mellino* 40 DLR (4th) 74 (1987); *U.S.A. v. Allard and Charette* 40 DLR (4th) 102 (1987).

64 *Soering v. U.K.*, European Court of Human Rights, 26 Jan. 1989, Series A, No.161.

65 *Kindler v. Canada* [1991] 2 SCR 779; see also *Human Rights LJ* 14 (1993) 307. And see *Ref. re Ng Extradition* [1991] 2 SCR 858.
66 In addition to the extradition cases noted above in note 63, see *R. v. Spencer* 21 DLR (4th) 756.
67 *Re Operation Dismantle v. Queen* 18 DLR (4th) 481 (1985). For a criticism of the Court's decision in this case, see M. Rankin and A. Roman, 'A New Basis for Screening Constitutional Questions under the Canadian Charter of Rights and Freedoms: Prejudging the Evidence?' *Can. BR* 66 (1987) 365.
68 *MacKay v. Manitoba* 61 DLR (4th) 385 (1989).
69 See e.g. *Hunter v. Southam Inc.*; *R. v. Big M. Drug Mart*; *Singh v. Minister of Employment and Immigration*; *Ref. re S. 94(2) Motor Vehicle Act (B.C.)*; *R. v. Thomson* [1988] 1 SCR 640; *R. v. Morgentaler.*
70 Other cases in which the Court has rejected a constitutional claim on the basis that the challenger had not made out the factual foundation of his or her case include: *Societé des Acadiens du Nouveau-Brunswick v. Association for Parents for Fairness in Education* 27 DLR (4th) 406 (1968); *R. v. Schwartz* 55 DLR (4th) 1 (1988); *Moysa v. Alberta* 60 DLR (4th) 1 (1989); *R. v. Edwards Books and Art Ltd.*; and *Symes v. Canada* 110 DLR (4th) 470 (1994).
71 *Reference re Alberta Public Service Employee Relations Act*; *Public Service Alliance v. Canada* 38 DLR (4th) 249 (1987); *Retail, Wholesale and Department Store Union v. Saskatchewan* 38 DLR (4th) 277 (1987).
72 *Professional Institute of the Public Service of Canada v. Commissioner for the Northwest Territories* 72 DLR (4th) 1 (1990).
73 *Lavigne v. Ontario Public Service Employees' Union.*
74 See also *R v. Skinner* [1990] 1 SCR 1235, where the Court ruled that the contractual association between a prostitute and his or her customer lies outside the protection provided by section 2(d).
75 Patrick Macklem, 'Developments in Employment Law: The 1990–91 Term,' *Supreme Court LR* 3 (1992) 227.
76 *Irwin Toy v. A.G. Quebec*; cf. *Thomson Newspapers v. Canada* and *R. v. Wholesale Travel Group* [1991] 3 SCR 154.
77 *R. v. Edwards Books and Art Ltd.* See also *Ref. re SS. 193 and 195.1 of the Criminal Code* per Lamer J.
78 See e.g. *R.v. Morgentaler*; *Ref. re S. 94(2) Motor Vehicle Act.*
79 See in this book 92–4, and see generally Dale Gibson, 'The Deferential Trojan Horse: A Decade of Charter Decisions,' *Can. BR* 72 (1993) 417; Marc Gold, 'Comment: Andrews v. Law Society of British Columbia,' *McGill LJ* 34 (1989) 1063; W. Black and L. Smith, 'Andrews v. Law Society of British Columbia,' *Can. BR* 68 (1989) 591, 600. For the classic description of the way the 'similarly situated' test should be applied, see J. Tussman

and J. ten Broek, 'The Equal Protection of Laws,' *California LR* 37 (1949) 341.

80 *Andrews v. Law Society of British Columbia.*

81 *Ref. re Workers' Compensation Act* 56 DLR (4th) 765 (1989).

82 *R. v. Turpin* [1989] 1 SCR 1296; see also *R. v. S.(S.)* [1990] 2 SCR 254.

83 *Ref. re Electoral Boundaries Commission Act* 81 DLR (4th) 16 (1991).

84 *Societé des Acadiens du Nouveau-Brunswick v. Assoc. of Parents for Fairness in Education.*

85 See e.g. *B.C.G.E.U. v. A.G. B.C.* 53 DLR (4th) 1 (1988); *R. v. Simmons* 55 DLR (4th) 673; *R. v. Beare* 55 DLR (4th) 481; *R. v. Jones* 31 DLR (4th) 569 per Wilson J.; *R. v. Edwards Books and Art Ltd.* per Dickson CJC.

86 Though for the most part the Court relied on a balancing method to interpret the scope of these guarantees, it also, from time to time, made reference to the intention of the framers in defining the rights and freedoms it has been asked to apply. For a discussion of some of these cases, see Beatty, *Talking Heads*, 19 and 81. Compare also the judgment of the majority of the Court in *Ref. re Electoral Boundaries Commission Act* and the concurring opinion of John Sopinka.

87 For a discussion of the de minimis rule, see Beatty, *Talking Heads*, 63 and 100.

88 *Ref. re Electoral Boundaries Commission Act.*

89 *Lyons v. The Queen* 44 DLR (4th) 193 (1987).

90 *R. v. Simmons.*

91 *Comité pour la Republique du Canada v. Canada.*

92 An early case that provides a striking example of how different the Court's demands were on Governments proving the factual basis of their claims from what we have seen that it required challengers to prove is *R. v. Jones.*

93 This qualification on how the Court would apply the principles of *Oakes* received its earliest recognition in *Edwards Books and Art Ltd.* It was subsequently picked up and dealt with at greater length in *Irwin Toy v. Quebec*; *U.S.A. v. Cotroni* and *McKinney v. University of Guelph.*

94 *Irwin Toy v. A.G. Quebec.*

95 *R. v. Edwards Books and Art Ltd.*

96 *Irwin Toy v. A.G. Quebec.*

97 *McKinney v. University of Guelph.*

98 There have been exceptional cases in which, even applying a more relaxed standard, the Court has invalidated a law. See e.g. *Edmonton Journal v. A.G. Alberta* 64 DLR (4th) 577 (1989), ruling unconstitutional a provincial law limiting publication of legal proceedings related to matrimonial disputes; *Comité pour La Republique du Canada v. Canada*, ruling unconsti-

tutional an airport regulation prohibiting all 'leafletting' inside the terminal; and *Canada Employment and Immigration Commission v. Tétreault-Gadaury*, striking down a provision in the Unemployment Insurance Act limiting benefits to people under 65.

99 *R. v. Schwartz.*

100 *R. v. Cotroni.*

101 *R. v. Butler* 89 DLR (4th) 449 (1992).

102 *Ref. re SS. 193 and 195.1 Criminal Code.*

103 *R. v. Chaulk and Morrissette* [1990] 3 SCR 1303.

104 *Rodriguez v. B.C.(A.G.)* 107 DLR (4th) 342 (1994).

105 The so-called rape-shield laws are designed to limit the opportunity of an accused to adduce evidence about the complainant's past sexual activities. See *Seaboyer v. Queen.*

106 See e.g. Allan C. Hutchinson, 'Waiting for CORAF,' *UTLJ* 41 (1991) 332.

107 See David Beatty, 'Labouring Outside the Charter,' *Osgoode Hall LJ*, 29 (1991) 839.

108 A more extensive review of the errors and inconsistencies committed by the Court is contained in Beatty, *Talking Heads*, chap. 4.

109 See e.g. David Beatty, 'Constitutional Conceits: The Coercive Authority of the Courts,' *UTLJ* 37 (1987) 183; Brian Slattery, 'The Charter's Relevance to Private Litigation: Does Dolphin Deliver?' *McGill LJ* 32 (1985) 905; Allan Hutchinson and Andrew Petter, 'Private Rights/Public Wrongs: The Liberal Lie of the Charter,' *UTLJ* (1988) 288; Peter Hogg, 'The Dolphin Delivery Case: Application of the Charter to Private Action,' *Saskatchewan LR* (1987) 273; R. Elliott and R. Grant, 'The Charter's Application in Private Litigation,' *UBCLR* 23 (1989) 3; J. Manwaring, 'To The Bar of Justice: A Comment on ... Dolphin Delivery,' *Ottawa LR* 19 (1987) 413.

110 See e.g. Hogg, *Constitutional Law*, 844; J. Whyte, 'Is the Private Sector Affected by the Charter?' in L. Smith et al, eds, *Righting the Balance: Canada's New Equality Rights*; Canadian Human Rights Reporter, 1986 Saskatoon.

111 At common law there is no rule against people discriminating against others in the most personal aspects of their lives. See *Bhadauria v. Seneca College* (1981) 124 DLR (3d) 193.

112 See the essays listed in note 109 to this chapter.

113 Beatty, 'Constitutional Conceits.'

114 See Peter Hogg, *Constitutional Law of Canada*, 2nd edition (Toronto: Carswell 1985), 677–8.

115 Weiler, 'The Charter at Work.'

116 Hogg, *Constitutional Law*, 813, 844; Sharpe, 'A Comment,' 469.

117 See e.g. Richard Moon, 'Stop in the Name of Sense,' *UTLJ* 42 (1992) 228.
118 In *Professional Institute of the Public Service of Canada v. Northwest Territories* 72 DLR (4th) 1 (1990), the Court validated a law that allowed the Government of the Northwest Territories to pick the unions with which it would bargain, even though the parallel law in every other jurisdiction in the country respected the employees' right to make this choice.
119 Macklem, 'Developments,' 240.
120 *R. v. Keegstra* [1990] 3 SCR 697; *R. v. Zundel* 95 DLR (4th) 202 (1992).
121 89 DLR (4th) 449 (1992). Cf. *Young v. Young* 108 DLR (4th) 193 and *P.(D.) v. S.(C.)* 108 DLR (4th) 287. See also J. Cameron, 'Abstract Principles v. Contextual Conceptions of Harm: A Comment on *R. v. Butler*,' *McGill LJ* 37 (1992) 1135, and 'The Original Conception of Section One and its Demise: A Comment on *Irwin Toy v. A.G. P.Q.*' *McGill LJ* 35 (1990) 252; cf. K. Mahoney, '*R. v. Keegstra*: A Rationale for Regulating Pornography,' *McGill LJ* 37 (1992) 242.
122 See W.S. Tarnopolsky, *The Canadian Bill of Rights*, 2nd edition (Toronto: McClelland and Stewart 1975).
123 In numerous cases, the Court has stressed the importance of keeping the two phases of the review process separate and distinct. See e.g. *Ref. re S. 94(2) Motor Vehicle Act (B.C.)*; *R. v. Edwards Books and Art Ltd.*; *Andrews v. Law Society of B.C.*; *USA v. Cotroni*; *R. v. Turpin*; *Ford v. Quebec*; *R. v. Keegstra.* See also J. Cameron, 'The Original Conception,' 252, and 'The First Amendment and Section One of the Charter,' *Media and Communications LR* (1990–1) 59; and Dale Gibson, 'The Deferential Trojan Horse: A Decade of Charter Decisions,' *Can. BR* 72 (1993) 417.
124 *McKinney v. University of Guelph* 76 DLR (4th) 545 (1990).
125 81 DLR (4th) 545 (1991).
126 *Andrews v. Law Society of British Columbia.*
127 See Peter Westen, *Speaking of Equality* (Princeton, NJ: Princeton University Press 1990).
128 On the relationship of equality and proportionality in constitutional law, see E. Cheli and F. Donati, 'Methods and Criteria of Judgment on the Question of the Right to Freedom in Italy,' in D. Beatty, ed, *Human Rights and Judicial Review: A Comparative Perspective* (Dordrecht: Martinus Nijhoff 1994). For a more broad-ranging treatment of the ideas of equality, similarity, and proportionality and their relationship, see Westen, *Speaking of Equality.*
129 *Canada Employment and Immigration Commission v. Tétreault-Gadaury* 81 DLR (4th) 358 (1991).
130 But see *R. v. Hess* [1990] 2 SCR 906.

131 Compare *R. v. Drybones* [1970] SCR 282 and *A.G. Canada v. Lavell* [1974] SCR 1349.

132 One other doctrine formulated by the Court to limit the scope of the Charter warrants a brief note. In *New Brunswick Broadcasting v. Nova Scotia (Speaker of the House of Assembly)* 100 DLR (4th) 212 (1993), the Court held that the rules of proceedings of a legislative assembly are themselves part of the constitution and so are immune from Charter review. According to Beverley McLachlin, who wrote the majority opinion, it is a rule of constitutional law that one part of the constitution cannot be abrogated or limited by another part.

The decision strikes most students and commentators as odd and difficult to defend. See e.g. D. Gibson, 'The Deferential Trojan Horse: A Decade of Charter Decisions,' *Can. BR* 72 (1993) 417. It goes completely against the idea of mutual modification that the Court developed to reconcile the competing heads of federal and provincial powers in sections 91 and 92, or conflicting rights under the Charter, and is quite out of keeping with the way other courts around the world resolve conflicts between different constitutional entitlements and guarantees. On the practice of other courts, see Beatty, ed, *Human Rights.*

133 *Singh v. Minister of Employment and Immigration.*

134 On average, the judges in Ottawa consider 400–500 cases a year and write decisions in about a quarter of them. By comparison, their counterparts in Washington and Karlsruhe, Germany, receive between 3,500 and 4,500 petitions. See F. Morton, P. Russell, and M. Withey, 'The Supreme Court's First One Hundred Charter of Rights Decisions: A Statistical Analysis,' *Osgoode Hall LJ* 30 (1992) 1; see also Dieter Grimm, 'Human Rights and Judicial Review in Germany,' in David Beatty, ed, *Human Rights and Judicial Review: A Comparative Perspective* (Dordrecht: Martinus Nijhoff 1994).

135 Hogg, *Constitutional Law,* 813. See also Richard Moon, 'Stop in the Name of Sense.' *UTLJ* 42 (1992) 228.

136 One of the most striking recent examples is the very different conclusions of the US Supreme Court and the German Constitutional Court when they analysed laws restricting a woman's freedom to have an abortion. See D. Kommers, 'The Constitutional Law of Abortion in Germany: Should Americans Pay Attention?' *Journal of Contemporary Health Law and Policy* 10 (1994) 1.

137 Towards the end of her tenure on the Court, even Bertha Wilson embraced doctrines such as definitional balancing and flexible, multi-levelled tiers of review. See e.g. her judgments in *Lavigne v. Ontario Public Service Employees Union*; *R. v. Turpin*; *R. v. Hess.*

CHAPTER FOUR

1 A. Aleinikoff, 'Constitutional Law in the Age of Balancing,' *Yale LJ* 96 (1987) 943; J.H. Ely, 'Flag Desecration: A Case Study in the Roles of Categorization and Balancing in First Amendment Analysis,' *Harvard LR* 88 (1974) 1482; Hans Linde, 'Due Process of Lawmaking,' *Nebraska LR* 55 (1975–6) 197; Jerry L. Mashaw, 'The Supreme Court's Due Process Calculus,' *University of Chicago LR* 44 (1976–7) 28. See generally L. Tribe, *American Constitutional Law* (New York: Foundation Press 1988); but see G. Gunther, *Constitutional Law* (New York: Foundation Press 1991), 583–4; and M. Perry, *The Constitution in the Court* (Oxford: Oxford University Press 1994), especially chaps. 7–9; and see B. Jamie Cameron, 'The First Amendment and Section One of the Charter,' *Media and Communications LR* 1 (1990–1) 59.

2 See e.g. *Konigsberg v. California* 366 US 36 (1961) per Hugo Black; *Oregon v. Smith* 494 US 872 (1990) per Antonin Scalia.

3 See e.g. *Burton v. Wilmington Parking Authority* 365 US 715 (1961); *Jackson v. Metropolitan Edison Co.* 419 US 345 (1974); *Hudgens v. National Labour Relations Board* 424 US 507 (1976); and see generally Gunther, *Constitutional Law*, 891ff, 1348–50; and K. Swinton, 'Application of the Canadian Charter of Rights and Freedoms,' in W. Tarnopolsky and G. Beaudoin, eds, *The Canadian Charter of Rights and Freedoms: Commentary*, (Toronto, Carswell 1982).

4 See Gunther, *Constitutional Law*, 1651ff.

5 Re equal protection, see e.g. *Korematsu v. US* 323 US 214 (1944); *Loving v. Virginia* 388 US 1 (1967); *Brown v. Board of Education* 347 US 483 (1954). Re due process, see e.g. *Roe v. Wade* 410 US 113 (1973); *Zablocki v. Redhail* 434 US 374 (1978); and *Moore v. City of East Cleveland* 431 US 494 (1977). Re first amendment: see e.g. *Boos v. Barry* 485 US 312 (1988); *Austin v. Michigan* 494 US 652 (1990); US *v. O'Brien* 391 US 367 (1968) (freedom of expression); *Roberts v. US Jaycees* 468 US 609 (1984) (freedom of association); *Wisconsin v. Yoder* 406 US 205 (1972) (freedom of religion). See also *Lemon v. Kurtzman* 403 US 602 (1971), which, though it does not use the precise language of compelling state interests and necessary means, effectively invokes the same analytical structure.

6 See e.g. *Meyer v. Nebraska* 262 US 390 (1923); *Griswold v. Connecticut* 381 US 479 (1966); *Roe v. Wade.*

7 *Goldberg v. Kelly* 397 US 254 (1970); cf. *Board of Regents v. Roth* 408 US 564 (1972).

8 E.g. *Lassiter v. Dept. of Social Services* 452 US 18 (1981).

9 *Harper v. Virginia Board of Elections* 383 US 663 (1966); *Kramer v. Union Free School Dist. 15*, 395 US 621 (1969).
10 *Shapiro v. Thompson* 394 US 618 (1969); *Zobel v. Williams* 457 US 55 (1982).
11 *Korematsu v. US*; *Brown v. Board of Education*; *Bolling v. Sharpe* 347 US 497 (1954); *Regents of University of California v. Bakke* 438 US 265 (1978).
12 *Washington v. Davis* 426 US 229 (1976); *Personnel Administrator of Mass. v. Feeney* 442 US 256 (1979).
13 See e.g. *Konigsberg v. State Bar of California* 366 US 36 (1961); *United States v. O'Brien*; *Texas v. Johnson* 491 US 397 (1989); *Adderley v. Florida* 385 US 39 (1966); *Lehman v. City of Shaker Heights* 418 US 298 (1974); *US Postal Service v. Greenburgh Civic Associations* 453 US 114 (1981) *International Society for Krishna Consciousness v. Lee* 112 S.Ct. 2701 (1992); and see generally Gunther, *Constitutional Law*, chaps. 11–13, and A. Meiklejohn, *Political Freedom* (New York: Oxford University Press 1965).
14 *Roberts v. US Jaycees* 468 US 609 (1984); *Board of Directors of Rotary International v. Rotary Club* 481 US 537 (1987); *Dallas v. Stranglin* 490 US 19 (1989).
15 *Oregon v. Smith* 494 US 872 (1990).
16 G. Gunther, 'Forward: In Search of Evolving Doctrine on a Changing Court: A Model for a Newer Equal Protection,' *Harvard LR* 86 (1972) 1, 8.
17 *Roe v. Wade.*
18 *Furman v. Georgia* 408 US 238 (1972); *Coker v. Georgia* 433 US 584 (1977); *Thompson v. Oklahoma* 487 US 815 (1988); cf. *Gregg v. Georgia* 428 US 153 (1976); *Lockett v. Ohio* 438 US 586 (1978)
19 *Brown v. Board of Education*; *Regents v. Bakke.*
20 *Lochner v. New York* 198 US 45 (1905).
21 *Baker v. Carr* 369 US 186 (1962); *Reynolds v. Sims* 377 US 533 (1964); *Harper v. Virginia Board of Elections* 383 US 663 (1966).
22 *Buckley v. Valeo* 424 US 1 (1976); *First National Bank of Boston v. Bellotti* 435 US 765 (1978).
23 See e.g. *Griswold v. Connecticut*; *Roe v. Wade*; *Wygant v. Jackson Board of Education* 476 US 267 (1986); *Shapiro v. Thompson*; *Kramer v. Union Free School Dist. 15*; *Sugarman v. Dougall* 413 US 634 (1973).
24 Gunther, *Constitutional Law* 503–5, 601–7, 1191–1202.
25 See e.g. *NAACP v. Alabama* 357 US 449 (1958); *Wygant v. Jackson Board of Education*; *Boos v. Barry* 485 US 312 (1988); *Schneider v. State* 308 US 147 (1939); *Consolidated Edison v. Public Service Comm.* 447 US 530 (1980); *Roe v. Wade*; *Lochner v. New York*; *Shapiro v. Thompson*; *Mathews v. Eldridge* 424 US 319 (1976); *Goldberg v. Kelly* 397 US 254 (1970). Balancing is done on both a categorical and an ad hoc basis; see Aleinikoff, 'Constitutional Law.'

26 See e.g. *Regents v. Bakke*; *Buckley v. Valeo* 424 US 15 (1976); *Texas v. Johnson* 491 US 397 (1989).
27 See e.g. *Lochner v. New York*; *Buckley v. Valeo*; *Regents v. Bakke.*
28 *Shapiro v. Thompson.*
29 *Texas v. Johnson*; *R.A. Victor v. City of St. Paul* 112 SCt 2538 (1992).
30 *School District of Abington v. Shempp* 374 US 203 (1963); *Lee v. Weisman* 112 SCt 2649 (1992)
31 *West Coast Hotel v. Parrish* 300 US 379 (1937); *Mass. Board of Retirement v. Murgia* 427 US 307 (1976).
32 *Williamson v. Lee Optical* 348 US 483 (1955).
33 *McGowan v. Maryland* 366 US 420 (1961).
34 *Dandridge v. Williams* 397 US 471 (1970).
35 *Baker v. Carr* 369 US 186 (1962); see generally Thomas Franck, *Political Questions/Judicial Answers* (Princeton, NJ: Princeton University Press 1992).
36 *San Antonio School District v. Rodriguez* 411 US 1 (1973).
37 *Bowers v. Hardwick* 478 US 186 (1986).
38 *Kelley v. Johnson* 425 US 238 (1976).
39 *San Antonio School District v. Rodriguez.*
40 *Regents v. Roth.*
41 See e.g. Aleinikoff, *Constitutional Law*, 948; Gunther, *Constitutional Law*, 1004.
42 See e.g. *Brandenburg v. Ohio* 395 US 444 (1969).
43 See e.g. *Chaplinsky v. New Hampshire* 315 US 568 (1942); *R.A.V. v. City of St. Paul* 112 S.Ct 2538 (1992).
44 *N.Y. Times Co. v. Sullivan* 376 US 254 (1964).
45 *Roth v. United States* 354 US 476 (1957).
46 *New York v. Ferber* 458 US 747 (1982).
47 *US v. O'Brien.*
48 *Adderley v. Florida* 385 US 39 (1966); *Heffron v. Int'l Soc. for Krishna Consc.* 452 US 640 (1981); *US Postal Service v. Greenburgh Civic Assn.* 453 US 114 (1981).
49 *Nebbia v. New York* 291 US 502 (1934); *Goesaert v. Cleary* 335 US 464 (1948).
50 *Williamson v. Lee Optical*; *McGowan v. Maryland*; *US Railroad Retirement Board v. Fritz* 449 US 166 (1980).
51 *New York v. Ferber*, *Osborne v. Ohio* 492 US 904 (1989).
52 *Nebbia v. New York.*
53 See e.g. *US Railroad Retirement Board v. Fritz*; *Mass. Board of Retirement v. Murgia*; *Young v. American Mini Theatres* 427 US 50 (1976); *Ward v. Rock against Racism* 491 US 781 (1989); *S.U.N.Y. v. Fox* 492 US 469 (1989); *Broad-*

rick v. Oklahoma 413 US 601 (1973); *San Antonio School District v. Rodriguez.*

54 *Frontiero v. Richardson* 411 US 677 (1973); *Craig v. Boren* 429 US 190 (1976); *Mississippi University for Women v. Hogan* 458 US 718 (1982); *Michael M. v. Superior Court of Sonoma County* 450 US 464 (1981).

55 *Hampton v. Mow Sun Wong* 426 US 88 (1976); *Sugarman v. Dougall* 413 US 634 (1973).

56 *Central Hudson Gas v. P.U.C.* 447 US 557 (1980).

57 See e.g. *Frontiero v. Richardson; Craig v. Boren; Hampton v. Mow Sun Wong.* For a good summary of the development of a third tier of review, see Scott H. Bice, 'Standards of Judicial Review under the Equal Protection and Due Process Clauses,' *Southern California LR* 50 (1977) 689.

58 *Frontiero v. Richardson; Craig v. Boren; Hampton v. Mow Sun Wong; Schad v. Mt. Ephraim* 452 US 61 (1981); *Sugarman v. Dougall* 413 US 634 (1973).

59 See B. Jamie Cameron, 'The First Amendment and Section One of the Charter,' (1990) *Media and Communications LR* 1 (1990) 59.

60 Some judges, such as Felix Frankfurter and Antonin Scalia, have been inclined to exercise their powers cautiously and conservatively by subordinating the principles of rationality and proportionality to an overriding ethic of judicial deference and restraint and/or by taking a precise, categorical, rule-based approach. The instinct of others, such as William Brennan, Thurgood Marshall, and John Harlan, was to embrace a more open, balancing approach. Still others built their theory of judicial review and the protection of human rights on a text-bound, literalist approach; Hugo Black would be the most vigorous defender of this approach. For a brief description of these different methods, see G. Gottlieb, *The Logic of Choice* (London: Allen and Unwin 1968), chap. 10.

61 In commercial speech, for example, the Court has moved from a position in which it provided no protection (*Valentine v. Chrestensen* 316 US 52 [1942]) to a full, rigorous means-ends analysis (*Central Hudson Gas*) to something in between (*S.U.N.Y. v. Fox*). The Court has also changed its views about how carefully it should review laws establishing electoral boundaries (see e.g. *Baker v. Carr* 369 US 186 [1962]); affirmative action programs (see e.g. *Metro Broadcasting v. FCC* 110 SCt 2997 [1990]); and rules of access to places such as shopping plazas (see e.g. *Hudgens v. N.L.R.B.* 424 US 507 [1976]).

62 Two of the most discredited landmark cases are unquestionably *Plessy v. Ferguson* 163 US 537 (1896), and *Lochner v. New York* 198 US 45 (1905).

63 *Minerva Mills Ltd. v. Union of India* AIR 1980 SC 1789, pr 25; *Maneka Gandhi v. Union of India* AIR 1978 SC 597, pr 34; *Ajay Hasia v. Khalid Mujib* AIR 1981 SC 487 pr 15; *Bandhua Mukti Morcha v. Union of India* AIR 1984 SC

802; *Pradeep Jain v. Union of India* AIR 1984 SC 1420.

64 *Kesavananda v. State of Kerala* AIR 1973 SC 1461; *Indira Nehru Gandhi v. Raj Narain* AIR 1975 SC 2299; *Minerva Mills Ltd. v. Union of India.*

65 *Minerva Mills Ltd. v. Union of India* prs 39–61.

66 See e.g. *State of Madras v. V.G. Row* AIR 1952 SC 197; *Ajay Hasia v. Khalid Mujib*; *Maneka Gandhi v. Union of India.*

67 *Express Newspapers Ltd. v. Union of India* AIR 1958 SC 578; *Bennett Coleman and Co. Ltd. v. Union of India* AIR 1973 SC 106; *Prabha Dutt v. Union of India* AIR 1982 SC 6; *Indian Express Newspapers Private Ltd. v. Union of India* AIR 1986 SC 515.

68 *Kameshwar Prasad v. State of Bihar* AIR 1962 SC 1166.

69 *R.M.D.C. v. Union of India* AIR 1957 SC 628; *M.H. Quareshi v. State of Bihar* AIR 1958 SC 731; *Chintaman Rao v. State of M.P.* 1952 SCR 759; *R.C. Cooper v. Union of India* AIR 1970 SC 564; see also *Narendra Kumar v. Union of India* AIR 1960 SC 430.

70 *Ebrahim Vazir v. State of Bombay* AIR 1954 SC 229.

71 *Deepak Sibal v. Punjab University* AIR 1989 SC 903.

72 *Mithu v. State of Punjab* AIR 1983 SC 473.

73 *Hussainara Khatoon v. State of Bihar* AIR 1979 SC 1360.

74 *In Re Kerala Education Bill* AIR 1958 SC 956.

75 *K.A. Abbas v. Union of India* AIR 1971 SC 481 prs 46–8.

76 *Suman Gupta v. State of J & K* AIR 1983 SC 1235; *State of Madras v. V.G. Row*; *Ebrahim Vazir v. State of Bombay*; *State of West Bengal v. Anwar Ali Sarkar* AIR 1952 SC 75.

77 *Mithu v. State of Punjab.*

78 *Ajay Hasia v. Khalid Mujib*; *State of Madras v. V.G. Row*; *Narendra Kumar v. Union of India* AIR 1960 SC 430; *Maneka Gandhi v. Union of India.*

79 *Balaji v. State of Mysore* AIR 1963 SC 649, 664; *Fazal Ghafoor v. Union of India* AIR 1989 SC 48; *Pradeep Jain v. Union of India.*

80 See e.g. *Narendra Kumar* AIR 1960 SC 430 pr 19; *M.H. Quareshi v. State of Bihar*; *M.S.M. Sharma v. Sri Krishna Sinha* AIR 1959 SC 395.

81 *Minerva Mills v. Union of India.*

82 *Francis Coralie v. Union Territory of Delhi* AIR 1981 SC 746.

83 *Hussainara Khatoon v. State of Bihar* AIR 1979 SC 1369, 1377; *M.H. Hoskot v. State of Maharashtra* AIR 1978 SC 1548; *Ranjan Dwivedi v. Union of India* AIR 1983 SC 624; *Suk Das v. Union Territory of Arunachal Pradesh* AIR 1986 SC 991.

84 Cf. *Hamdard Dawakhana Wakf v. Union of India* AIR 1960 SC 554; see also *Fatehchand v. Maharashtra* AIR 1977 SC 1825.

85 *Ajay Hasia v. Khalid Mujib.*

86 *M.H. Quareshi v. State of Bihar.*
87 *Francis Coralie v. Union Territory of Delhi*; *Sheela Barse v. State of Maharashtra* (1987) 4 SCC 373.
88 See also *In Re Kerala Education Bill*; *K. Nagaraj v. State of A.P.* AIR 1985 SC 551, 556–7.
89 For a more cautious evaluation, see Marc Galanter, *Competing Equalities* (Delhi: Oxford University Press 1984), 484: 'The prevailing style of judicial work has impressed many foreign observers as less than optimal.'
90 Seervai, *Constitutional Law of India*, 4th edition (Bombay: N.M. Tripathi (1991), xv.
91 According to one of the Court's most prominent jurists, even laws passed in accordance with the directive principles that are expressly permitted to impinge on the rights to equality (14) and liberty (19) must meet the basic tests of rationality and proportionality. Bhagwati J. in *Minerva Mills Ltd. v. Union of India* pr 120.
92 *M.C. Mehta v. Union of India* AIR 1987 SC 1086; *Ajay Hasia v. Khalid Mujib* pr 9; *Ramana v. I.A. Authority of India* AIR 1979 SC 1628; *Sukhdev Singh v. Bhagatram* AIR 1975 SC 1331, 1342.
93 See e.g. *Naresh v. State of Maharashtra* AIR 1967 SC 1 and generally Seervai *Constitutional Law*, 390–9.
94 See e.g. *Maneka Gandhi v. Union of India*; *Bandhua Mukti Morcha v. Union of India*; *Francis Coralie v. Union Territory of Delhi*; *M.C. Mehta v. Union of India* AIR 1987 SC 1086; *Olga Tellis v. Bombay Municipal Corp.* AIR 1986 SC 180.
95 *State of Madras v. Sm. Champakam Dorairajan* AIR 1951 SC 226; *Golak Nath v. State of Punjab* AIR 1967 SC 1643; *Kesavananda v. State of Kerala*; *Indira Nehru Gandhi v. Raj Narain*; *Minerva Mills Ltd. v. Union of India.*
96 *Kesavananda v. State of Kerala.*
97 See e.g. *Gopalan v. State of Madras* AIR 1950 SC 27; see also *Maneka Gandhi v. Union of India* prs 54–5.
98 *Gopalan v. State of Madras*; *Kharak Singh v. State of U.P.* AIR 1963 SC 1295.
99 *Gopalan v. State of Madras* pr 120.
100 *Devadasan v. Union of India* AIR 1964 SC 179; and see generally Galanter, *Competing Equalities*, chap. 12.
101 See generally *Maneka Gandhi v. Union of India* pr 80.
102 See *Hamdard Dawakhana Wakf v. Union of India.* But now see also *India Express Newspapers (Bombay) Ltd v. Union of India* AIR 1986 SC 515 pr 91.
103 *All India Bank Employees Association v. National Industrial Tribunal* AIR 1962 SC 171 pr 20.
104 *R.M.D.C. v. Union of India*; *Cooverjee v. Excise Commissioner* AIR 1954 SC

220; see also *Fatehchand v. Maharashta.*

105 *Commissioner, Hindu Religious Endowments v. L.T. Swamiar* AIR 1954 SC 282; *Yagnapurushdasji v. Muldas* AIR 1966 SC 1119; *M.H. Quareshi v. State of Bihar.*

106 See e.g. *Gopalan v. State of Madras*; *Hamdard Dawakhana Wakf v. Union of India*; *Jamuna Prasad v. Lachhi Ram* AIR 1954 SC 686.

107 *Ibid.*

108 *Chitra Ghosh v. Union of India* AIR 1970 SC 35; *Lachman Dass v. State of Punjab* AIR 1963 SC 222.

109 See *Budhan Choudhry v. State of Bihar* AIR 1955 SC 191, 195; *State of J & K v. Ghulam Rasool* AIR 1961 SC 1301 pr 6; *Narain Dass v. Improvement Trust, Amritsar* AIR 1972 SC 865 pr 6–7; *Maneka Gandhi v. Union of India* pr 67–8.

110 *All India Bank Employees Ass'n v. National Industrial Tribunal.*

111 *Balakotaiah v. Union of India* AIR 1958 SS 232.

112 *Charanjit Lal v. Union of India* AIR 1951 SC 41; *Jamuna Prasad v. Lachhi Ram*; cf D. Beatty, *Talking Heads and the Supremes* (Toronto: Carswell 1990), 88–99.

113 See e.g. *Hamdard Dawakhana Wakf v. Union of India*; *All India Bank Employees Ass'n. v. National Industrial Tribunal.*

114 See e.g. *Chitra Gosh v. Union of India*; *Lachman Dass v. State of Punjab.*

115 See Mr Justice B.P. Jeewan Reddy and Rajeev Dhavan, 'The Jurisprudence of Human Rights,' in D. Beatty, ed, *Human Rights and Judicial Review: A Comparative Perspective* (Dordrecht: Martinus Nijhoff 1994), 175.

116 *M.H. Quareshi v. State of Bihar*; *Ajay Hasia v. Khalid Mujib.*

117 See e.g. the cases referred to in notes 67–83.

118 See e.g. *Chitra Ghosh v. Union of India* pr 9; *Cooverjee v. Excise Commissioner* pr 2; *Glass Chatons Importers v. Union of India* AIR 1961 SC 1514.

119 *Ajay Hasia v. Khalid Mujib* pr 15; *Maneka Gandhi v. Union of India* prs 54–6; *R.C. Cooper v. Union of India* AIR 1970 SC 564.

120 *India Express Newspapers (Bombay) Ltd. v. Union of India.*

121 *Ajay Hasia v. Khalid Mujib*; *Suman Gupta v. State of J. & K.*

122 *State of Kerala v. Thomas* AIR 1976 SC 490; *K.C. Vasanth Kumar v. State of Karnataka* AIR 1985 SC 1495, 1523–7, 1551–7.

123 *Maneka Gandhi v. Union of India* pr 68.

124 *Minerva Mills v. Union of India* per Bhagwati J.

125 The experience of the Indian Supreme Court also shows that no matter how strongly a constitution speaks to the economic security and well-being of its people, the only powers available to the Court lie in the principles of rationality and proportionality. Contrary to the belief of many human rights activists, the Supreme Court of India has generally been as conservative and cautious as any court in reviewing laws dealing with

social and economic policy (see e.g. *Bearer Bonds* AIR 1981 SC 2159; *Glass Chatons*; *C.B. Boarding and Lodging v. State of Mysore* AIR 1970 SC 2042 pr 9; Seervai, *Constitutional Law*, 529, 637, 856) and just as reluctant to assume responsibility for the budget of the Indian state (*Ranjan Dwivedi v. Union of India*). Though the Court has insisted that lawmakers must face the financial implications of the constitutional right of equality (see Seervai *Constitutional Law*, 458), it has always resisted any suggestion that it should take over the task of setting benefit levels. See generally D. Beatty, 'The Last Generation: When Rights Lose Their Meaning,' in Beatty, ed, *Human Rights and Judicial Review*, 321.

126 See e.g. N. Urabe, 'Rule of Law and Due Process: A Comparative View of the United States and Japan,' *Law and Contemporary Problems* 53 no. 1 (1990) 70; M. Nakamura, 'Quarante ans de controle judicaire de la constitutionnalité des lois,' *Annuaire international de Justice constitutionnelle* 3 (1987) 691. Although the Supreme Court of Japan has shown a strong aversion to actually invalidating initiatives of the two elected branches of government, on several occasions it has used the cosmetically softer device of 'reading down' laws that were broader and more heavy handed than they needed to be. See e.g. the *Court Worker Incitement* case (1969) 25 Keishu 685, reported in part in H. Itoh and L. Beer, *The Constitutional Case Law of Japan: Selected Supreme Court Decisions, 1961–1970* (Seattle: University of Washington Press 1978).

127 M. Nakamura, 'Freedom of Economic Activities and the Right to Property,' *Law and Contemporary Problems* 53 no. 2 (1990) 1, 8.

128 See e.g. S. Matsui, 'Freedom of Expression in Japan,' *Osaka University LR* 38 (1991) 13, 14–18.

129 *Aizawa v. Japan (Patricide* case*)* (1973) 27 Keishu 265, reproduced in part in W.F. Murphy and J. Tanenhaus, *Comparative Constitutional Law: Cases and Commentaries* (London: St Martin's Press 1977), 359.

130 For a discussion of the *Patricide* case, see H. Tomatsu, 'Equal Protection of the Law,' *Law and Contemporary Problems* 53 no. 2 (1990) 109, 111–14.

131 *Nakamura et al v. Japan* (1962) 16 Keishu 1593, reproduced in part in Itoh and Beer, *The Constitutional Case Law of Japan.*

132 *Hiraguchi v. Hiraguchi* (1987) 41 Minshu 408 is discussed in Nakamura 'Freedom.'

133 *Sumiyoshi v. Governor of Hiroshima* (1975) 29 Minshu 572 reported in part in Murphy and Tanenhaus, *Comparative Constitutional Law*, 258.

134 For comments on the *Pharmacy* case, see M. Nakamura 'Freedom,' 6 and T. Kamata, 'Adjudication and the Governing Process: Political Questions

and Legislative Discretion,' *Law and Contemporary Problems* 53 no.1 (1990) 182, 189.

135 *Kurokawa v. Chiba Election Commission* (1976) 30 Minshu 223; *Kanao v. Hiroshima Election Management Comm.* (1985) 39 Minshu 1100. An earlier decision of the Supreme Court, upholding a previous apportionment of candidates among electoral districts, *Koshiyama v. Tokyo Metropolitan Election Supervision Commission* (1964) 18 Minshu 270, is reproduced in part in Itoh and Beer, *Constitutional Case Law of Japan.* All three cases are discussed by H. Hata, 'Malapportionment of Representation in the National Diet,' *Law and Contemporary Problems* 53 no. 2 (1990) 157; see also Tomatsu 'Equal Protection,' 116.

136 Nakamura 'Quarante ans,' See also J. Mark Ramseyer, 'The Puzzling (In)dependence of Courts: A Comparative Approach,' *Journal of Legal Studies* 23 no.2 (1994) 721.

137 Y. Okudaira, 'Forty Years of the Constitution and Its Various Influences: Japanese, American and European,' *Law and Contemporary Problems* 53 no.1 (1990) 17, 25; Nakamura 'Quarante ans.'

138 See *Sakata v. Japan* (*Sunakawa case*) (1959) 13 Keishu 3225, reproduced in part in John M. Maki, *Court and Constitution in Japan* (Seattle: University of Washington Press 1964), 298. See generally Kamata, 'Adjudication,' and James Auer, 'Article Nine of Japan's Constitution: From Renunciation of Armed Force "Forever" to the Third Largest Defense Budget in the World,' *Law and Contemporary Problems* 53 no.2 (1990) 171.

139 See *Japan v. Nakano* (1948) Keishu 1235 reproduced in part in Maki, *Court and Constitution in Japan; Asahi v. Japan* (1967) 21 Minshu 1043, reproduced in part in Itoh and Beer, *Constitutional Case Law of Japan*, 130. And see generally A. Osuka, 'Welfare Rights,' *Law and Contemporary Problems* 53 no.2 (1990) 13.

140 *Kato v. Japan* (*Textbook Fee* case) (1964) 18 Minshu 343, reproduced in part in Itoh and Beer, *Constitutional Case Law of Japan*, 147.

141 See e.g. *Shimizu v. Japan* (*Fukucka Bathhouse* case) (1955) 9 Keishu 89; *Japan v. Marushin Industries Inc.* (1972) 26 Keishu 586. Both cases are discussed in Nakamura, 'Freedom,' and I. Sonobe, 'Human Rights and Constitutional Review in Japan,' in Beatty, ed, *Human Rights and Judicial Review*, 135.

142 *Oshima v. Hamaguchi* (1985) 39 Minshu 247, discussed in Kamata, 'Adjudication,' 183–4. See also *Joint Income Tax* case (1961) 15 Minshu 2047, reproduced in part in Murphy and Tanenhaus, *Comparative Constitutional Law*, 342.

143 *Tsurozomo v. Japan* (1973) 27 Keishu 547 (*Zennorin* case); *Japan v. Osawa*

(1974) 28 Keishu 393 (*Sarafutsu* case). Both are discussed in Kamata 'Adjudication,' and in L. Beer, 'Freedom of Expression: The Continuing Revolution,' *Law and Contemporary Problems* 53 no.2 (1990) 39. For an earlier case, in which the Supreme Court took a less deferential approach, see *Toyama v. Japan* (*Tokyo Central Post Office* case)(1966) 20 Keishu 901 reproduced in part in Itoh and Beer, *Constitutional Case Law of Japan*, 85.

144 *Taniguchi v. Japan* (1967) 21 Keishu 1245 reproduced in part in Itoh and Beer, *The Constitutional Case Law of Japan*, 149; *The Right of Suffrage of Election Law Violators*, reproduced in part in Maki, *Court and Constitution in Japan*, 182. And see generally Kamata, 'Adjudication,' 184; M. Usaki, 'Restrictions on Political Campaigns in Japan,' *Law and Contemporary Problems* 53 no. 2 (1990) 133; Hata, 'Malapportionment'; Matsui, 'Freedom of Expression.'

145 Kamata, 'Adjudication.'

146 Hata, 'Malapportionment.'

147 This approach, of exercising its powers of review in a partial or modified (intermediate) way, is discussed by many commentators. See e.g. Beer, 'Freedom of Expression'; Matsui, 'Freedom of Expression'; Nakamura, 'Freedom'; and Sonobe, 'Human Rights.'

148 Nakamura, 'Freedom'; Sonobe, 'Human Rights.'

149 See Kamata, 'Adjudication'; Usaki, 'Restrictions'; Nakamura, 'Quarante ans'; Beer, 'Freedom of Expression'; Matsui, 'Freedom of Expression.'

150 Matsui, 'Freedom of Expression'; Nakamura, 'Quarante ans'; Beer, 'Freedom of Expression.'

151 *Japan v. Osawa* (*The Sarafutsu case*), cited in Kamata 'Adjudication,' 197–8.

152 Urabe, 'Rule of Law,' 69: 'In practice, the rule of law in Japan does not work as a principle to protect the rights and liberties of the people. Rather, it is no more than an ideology to legitimize domination.'

153 *Luth* case (1958) 7 BverfGE 198, reproduced in part in D. Kommers, *The Constitutional Jurisprudence of the Federal Republic of Germany* (Durham, NC: Duke University Press (1989), 368.

154 See e.g. *Luth* case, 370.

155 A partial exception to this approach is the Court's treatment of the right to free development of one's personality (article 2.1 of the Basic Law). See *Luth* case, 358; *Mephisto* (1971) 30 BverfGE 173, reproduced in part in Kommers, *Constitutional Jurisprudence* 309, and see generally Kommers, *Constitutional Jurisprudence*, 323. The *Mephisto* case is also referred to in W.F. Murphy and J. Tanenhaus, *Comparative Constitutional Law, Cases and Commentaries* (New York: St Martin's Press 1977), 581.

156 A particularly poignant example of how the German court evaluates different interests and activities that fall within one of the guarantees in the Basic Law is the *Abortion Decision* (1975) 39 BVerfGE 1, which is reported in *John Marshall Journal of Practice and Procedure* (1976) 605. And see the cases listed in note 163 below.

157 For a description of the overall structure and organizing principles contained in the Basic Law, see D. Kommers, 'The Basic Law and Its Interpretation,' in Kommers, *Constitutional Jurisprudence*, 35; J. Ipsen, 'Constitutional Review of Laws,' in C. Starck, ed, *Main Principles of the German Basic Law* (Baden–Baden: Nomos Verlagsgesellschaft 1983). See also *Socialist Reich Party* case (1952) 2 BVerfGE 1 (1952), reproduced in part in Murphy and Tanenhaus, *Comparative Constitutional Law*, 602.

158 See e.g. *Census Act* case (1983) 1 BvR 209, reproduced in part in *Human Rights LJ* 5 (1984) 94.

159 *Privacy of Communication* case (1970) 30 BVerfGE 1, reproduced in part in Murphy and Tanenhaus, *Comparative Constitutional Law*, 659. See also David Currie, 'Lochner Abroad: Substantive Due Process and Equal Protection in the Federal Republic of Germany,' *Supreme Court Review* (1989) 333, 353; and F. Neumann, *The Rule of Law* (Leamington Spa: Berg Publishers 1986).

160 See e.g. *Life Imprisonment* case (1977) 45 BVerfGE 187; *Mephisto* case; *Elfes* case (1957) 6 BVerfGE 32, reproduced in part in Kommers, *Constitutional Jurisprudence*, 316, 306, and 327, respectively. See also Currie, 'Lochner Abroad,' 359.

161 See Kommers, 'The Basic Law.'

162 See Currie, 'Lochner Abroad,' 159.

163 *Luth* case; *Abortion* case; *School Book* case (1971) 31 BVerfGE 229 and *Co-Determination* case (1979) 50 BVerfGE 290, reproduced in part in Kommers, *Constitutional Jurisprudence*, 271 and 278, respectively.

164 *Luth* case.

165 *Co-Determination* case; *Investment Aid* case (1954) 4 BVerfGE 7, reproduced in part in Kommers, *Constitutional Jurisprudence*, 249.

166 See e.g. *Luth* case; *Mephisto* case; *Blinkfuer* case (1969) 25 BVerfGE 256; *Picture Postcard* case (1984) 68 BVerfGE 226; *LeBach* case (1973) 35 BVerfGE 202, reported in part in Kommers, *Constitutional Jurisprudence*, 381, 393, and 414, respectively.

167 *Co-Determination* case.

168 See e.g. *School Prayer* case (1979) 52 BVerfGE 223; *Interdenominational School* case (1975) 41 BVerfGE 29; *Rumpelkammer* case (1968) 24 BVerfGE 236; *Sex Education* case (1977) 47 BVerfGE 46, reproduced in part in Kom-

mers, *Constitutional Jurisprudence*, 466, 473, 447, and 498, respectively. See also *Catholic Hospital* case (1987), *International Labour Law Reports* 5 (1987) 112.

169 See e.g. *Blood Transfusion* case (1971) 32 BVerfGE 98, reproduced in part in Kommers, *Constitutional Jurisprudence*, 451.

170 *Group University* case (1973) 35 BVerfGE 79, reproduced in part in Kommers, *Constitutional Jurisprudence*, 437.

171 See e.g. *Homosexuality* case (1957) 6 BVerfGE 389, reproduced in part in Murphy and Tanenhaus, *Comparative Constitutional Law*, 403; cf. *Dudgeon v. U.K.* (1981) 4 EHRR 149.

172 *Luth* case; *Basic East-West Treaty* case (1973) 36 BVerfGE 1, reproduced in part in Murphy and Tanenhaus, *Comparative Constitutional Law*, 252; *Pershing 2 and Cruise Missile* case 1 (1983) 66 BVerfGE 39 reproduced in part in Kommers, *Constitutional Jurisprudence*, 164.

173 See Thomas M. Franck, *Political Questions/Judicial Answers* (Princeton, NJ: Princeton University Press 1992), chap.7.

174 See e.g. *Life Imprisonment* case (1977) 45 BVerfGE 187, reproduced in part in Kommers, *Constitutional Jurisprudence*, 314; *Rumpelkammer* case; and see generally Dieter Grimm, 'Human Rights and Judicial Review in Germany,' in D. Beatty, ed, *Human Rights and Judicial Review: A Comparative Perspective* (Dordrecht: Martinus Nijhoff 1994), 267.

175 *Elfes* case; *Census Act* case; Currie, 'Lochner Abroad,' 359–61.

176 One exception, explicitly provided for in the Basic Law, where the Court has refused to intervene, is the internal affairs of churches. See *Evangelical Church* case (1965) 18 BVerfGE 385, reproduced in part in Kommers, *Constitutional Jurisprudence*, 487; *Catholic Hospital* case. See also the dissenting opinion of Mr Justice Dieter Grimm in (1989) 1 BVR 921/85 (6 June).

177 *Abortion* case (1975).

178 See e.g. *Josef Franziska* case (1959) 10 BVerfGE 200; *Disciplinary Court* case 18 BVerfGE 241 (1964); *Lawyer's Disciplinary Court* case 26 BVerfGE 186 (1961); *Social Court* case 27 BVerfGE 312 (1969), noted in Kommers, *Constitutional Jurisprudence*, 141. But see *Klass* case (Privacy of Communication) (1970) 30 BVerfGE 1 (1970), in Murphy and Tanenhaus, *Comparative Constitutional Law*, 659.

179 *Census Act* case.

180 *Numerus Clausus* case (1972) 33 BVerfGE 303, reproduced in part in Kommers, *Constitutional Jurisprudence*, 295 and note 302–4.

181 *Life Imprisonment* case (1977) 45 BVerfGE 187, reproduced in part in Kommers, *Constitutional Jurisprudence*, 314.

182 See e.g. *Green Party Exclusion* case (1986) 70 BVerfGE 324; *Apportionment*

case (1963) 16 BVerfGE 130; *Party Tax Deduction* case (1958) 8 BVerfGE 51; *Party Finance* case (1966) 20 BVerfGE 56; *West German Media* case (1962) 14 BVerfGE 121; *Radical Groups* (1978) 47 BVerfGE 198; all reported in part in Kommers, *Constitutional Jurisprudence*, 192, 202, 205, 218, 240, respectively. See also *Socialist Reich Party* case (1952) 2 BVerfGE 1 and *Communist Party* case (1956) 5 BVerfGE 85 (1956), both reported in part in Murphy and Tanenhaus, *Comparative Constitutional Law*, 602 and 621, respectively.

183 See e.g. *Joint Income Tax* case (1957) 6 BVerfGE 55, reproduced in part in Kommers, *Constitutional Jurisprudence*, 493. See also Kommers, *Constitutional Jurisprudence*, note at 252–4. See Currie, 'Lochner Abroad,' 368.

184 See Currie 'Lochner Abroad,' 345, 369, and Kommers, *Constitutional Jurisprudence*, 497.

185 *School Book* case, 272.

186 Kommers, *Constitutional Jurisprudence*, 264.

187 *Pharmacy* case (1958) 7 BVerfGE 377, reproduced in part in Kommers, *Constitutional Jurisprudence*, 285; see also note 293 and Currie, 'Lochner Abroad,' 249.

188 *Chocolate Candy* case (1980) 53 BVerfGE 135, reproduced in part in Kommers, *Constitutional Jurisprudence*, 292.

189 *Joint Income Tax* case.

190 See e.g. ibid and *Mental Hospital* case (1967) 22 BVerfGE 168, noted in Currie, 'Lochner Abroad,' 353.

191 See e.g. *Numerous Clausus*; *Pharmacy* case. See also *Taxicab* case (1960) 11 BVerfGE 168, noted in Kommers, *Constitutional Jurisprudence*, 294.

192 *Mental Hospital* case.

193 *Joint Income Tax* case.

194 *Elfes* case, 327; *Life Imprisonment* case, 316; *Mephisto* case, 306. For a review of how the Court relied on an objective order of values and in particular the relationship between the right to life and the right to personal autonomy in its analysis of Germany's abortion laws, see Donald Kommers, 'The Constitutional Law of Abortion in Germany: Should Americans Pay Attention?' (1994) 10 *Journal of Contemporary Health Law and Policy* 10 (1994) 1.

195 *Princess Soraya* case (1973) 34 BVerfGE 269, reported in part in Kommers, *Constitutional Jurisprudence*, 131, and in R. Schlesinger, H. Baade, M. Damaška, and P. Herzog, *Comparative Law* (Mineola, NY: Foundation Press 1988), 622.

196 *Aircraft Noise Control* case (1981) 56 BVerfGE 54, reproduced in part in Kommers, *Constitutional Jurisprudence*, 137.

197 *Kalker* case (1978) 49 BVerfGE 89, reproduced in part in Kommers, *Constitu-*

tional Jurisprudence 150, and see note on 344.

198 See *Chemical Weapons* case (1987) 77 BVerfGE 170, noted in Kommers, *Constitutional Jurisprudence,* 364. See also Currie, 'Lochner Abroad,' 355.

199 *Spiegel* case (1966) 20 BVerfGE 162, reproduced in part in Kommers, *Constitutional Jurisprudence* 397.

200 *First Television* case (1961) 12 BVerfGE 205 and *Third Television* case (1981) 57 BVerfGE 295, reproduced in part in Kommers, *Constitutional Jurisprudence* 404 and 409, respectively.

201 *Life Imprisonment* case, 314.

202 *Abortion* case (1975); *Joint Income Tax* case, 493.

203 *Numerous Clausus* case; *Group University* case (1973) 35 BVerfGE 79, reproduced in part in Kommers, *Constitutional Jurisprudence,* 437. See also Currie, 'Lochner Abroad,' 338.

204 *Pershing 2 and Cruise Missile* case.

205 *Numerous Clausus* case, 300; *Co-Determination* case; *Aircraft Noise Control* case; *Kalker* case; *Schleyer Kidnapping* case (1977) 46 BVerfGE 160, reproduced in part in Kommers, *Constitutional Jurisprudence* 362 and notes 247–9, 252–4. And see generally Grimm, 'Human Rights.'

206 *Aircraft Noise Control* case, 139.

207 *Chemical Weapons* case.

208 *Numerous Clausus* case; *Aircraft Noise Control* case.

209 In the summer of 1993, following reunification of East and West Germany, the Court handed down a second landmark ruling on abortion. For a discussion of both decisions, see Kommers, 'The Constitutional Law.'

210 Currie, 'Lochner Abroad,' 371.

211 See R. St J. Macdonald, E. Matscher, and H. Petzold, eds, *The European System for the Protection of Human Rights* (Dordrecht: Martinus Nijhoff 1994), J.G. Merrills, *The Development of International Law by the European Court of Human Rights* (Manchester: University Press 1988), 233.

212 As note 211.

213 *Re Belgian Language in Education* (1968) 1 EHRR 252; *Traktorer Aktielbelag v. Sweden* (1991) 13 EHRR 309; *Airey v. U.K.* (1987) 8 EHRR 42. And generally see Rudolph Bernhardt, 'Human Rights and Judicial Review: The European Court of Human Rights,' in D. Beatty, ed, *Human Rights and Judicial Review: A Comparative Perspective* (Dordrecht: Martinus Nijhoff 1994), 297.

214 *Airey v. U.K.*; *Young, James and Webster v. U.K.* (1981) 4 EHRR 37.

215 But see *Kosiek v. Germany* (1986) Series A, No. 105, 28 Aug.; *National Union of Belgian Police* (1975) Series A, No. 19, 27 Oct.; *Le Compte, Van Leuven and De Meyere v. Belgium* (1981) 4 EHRR 1; *Van Marle et al v. Nether-*

lands (1986) Series A, No. 101, 26 June.

216 *Klass et al v. Federal Republic of Germany* (1972) 2 EHRR 214 pr 48–9; *Brogan et al v. United Kingdom* (1982) 2 EHRR 215 pr 62.

217 *Barthold v. Germany* (1985) 7 EHRR 383 pr 55; *Sunday Times v. United Kingdom* (1982) 2 EHRR 215 pr 62.

218 *Abdulaziz, Cabales and Balkandali v. United Kingdom* (1985) Series A, No. 94, 28 May, pr 72; *Marckx* case (1979) Series A, No. 31, 13 June, pr 33; *Rasmussen* case (1984) Series A, No. 87, 28 Nov., pr 38.

219 *Sporrong and Lonnroth v. Sweden* (1982) Series A, No. 52, 23 Sept.; *Fredin v. Sweden* (1991) Series A, No. 192, 18 Feb.

220 *Re Belgian Language in Education.*

221 *Mathieu-Mohin and Clerfayt v. Belgium* (1988) 10 EHRR 1.

222 First Protocol to the Convention, 20 March 1952, article 3. See *Mathieu-Mohin v. Belgium.*

223 *F. v. Switzerland* (1987) Series A, No. 128, 18 Dec.

224 *Brogan et al v. United Kingdom* prs 48, 62.

225 *Ireland v. United Kingdom* (1970) Series A, No. 25, 18 Jan.

226 *Tyrer v. United Kingdom* (1978) 2 EHRR 1.

227 *Van Der Mussel v. Belgium* (1984) 6 EHRR 163.

228 *Handyside v. United Kingdom* (1979–80) 1 EHRR 737. See also H. Petzold, 'The Convention and the Principle of Subsidiarity,' in Macdonald, Matscher, and Petzold, *European System for the Protection of Human Rights*, 41. And see Bernhardt, 'Human Rights.'

229 *Muller v. Switzerland* (1991) 13 EHRR 212; *James v. United Kingdom* (1986) 8 EHRR 123; *Ireland v. U.K.*

230 *Dudgeon v. United Kingdom* (1981) 4 EHRR 149.

231 *Sunday Times v. United Kingdom* (1982) 2 EHRR 215.

232 *Abdulaziz et al v. United Kingdom* (1985) Series A, No. 94, 28 May.

233 Cf. *Rasmussen* case.

234 *Marckx* case, pr 41; *Johnston et al v. Ireland* (1986) Series A, No. 112, 18 Dec.

235 *F. v. Switzerland.*

236 *Autronic A.G. v. Switzerland* (1990) Series A, No. 190, 22 May.

237 *Tryer v. United Kingdom* pr 31.

238 See e.g. *Dudgeon v. U.K.; Sunday Times v. U.K.; Young, James and Webster v. U.K.; Barthold v. Germany.*

239 *Young, James and Webster v. U.K.*

240 Even when a European standard was identified in areas in which the Court was normally inclined to exercise its powers quite deferentially, it determined the outcome of the case. See e.g. *Dudgeon v. U.K.; Marckx v. Bel-*

gium; *Sporrong and Lonnroth v. Sweden*; *Abdulaziz et al v. United Kingdom*; *Johnston v. Ireland.*

241 *Handyside v. United Kingdom.*

242 See e.g. *Olsson v. Sweden* (1988) Series A, No. 130, 24 March; *Konig v. Federal Republic of Germany* (1970) Series A, No. 27, 28 June; *Le Compte Van Leuven and De Meyere v. Belgium*; *Fredin v. Sweden*; *Feldebrugge v. Sweden* (1986) Series A, No. 99, 29 May.

243 But see *B. v. France* (1992) Series A, No. 232, 25 March; *Sporrong and Lonnroth v. Sweden*; *Barthold v. Germany*; *Golder v. United Kingdom* (1975) Series A, No. 18, 21 Feb. In all four cases, the claimants were successful even in the absence of a European standard.

244 *Lawless v. Ireland* (1979–80) 1 EHRR 15 (Series A, No. 3, 1 July 1961); *Handyside v. United Kingdom*; and see generally R. St J. Macdonald, 'The Margin of Appreciation,' in Macdonald, Matscher, and Petzold, eds, *European System for the Protection of Human Rights*, 83.

245 Macdonald, 'Margin of Appreciation'; Merrills, *Development*, 146. And see the cases cited in note 240 above.

246 *National Union of Belgian Police.*

247 *Handyside v. United Kingdom*; *Muller v. Switzerland.*

248 *Re Belgian Language in Education*; *Kjeldsen, Busk, Madsen and Pedersen v. Denmark* (1976), Series A, No. 23, 1 Dec.

249 *Fredin v. Sweden; Powell and Raynor v. U.K.* (1990) Series A, No. 172, 21 Feb.

250 *Mathieu-Mohin and Clerfayt v. Belgium.*

251 *Markt Intern and Beerman v. Germany* (1990) 12 EHRR 161.

252 *Traktorer v. Sweden.*

253 *Lithgow et al v. United Kingdom* (1986) 8 EHRR 329.

254 *Lawless v. Ireland*; *Ireland v. United Kingdom.*

255 *James v. United Kingdom* pr 51.

256 *National Union of Belgian Police* pr 47; *Re Belgian Language in Education* pr 10.

257 *James v. United Kingdom*; *Klass v. Federal Republic of Germany*; *Powell and Rayner v. United Kingdom.*

258 *Traktorer v. Sweden.*

259 See e.g. *Lithgow v. United Kingdom*; *Traktorer v. Sweden*; *Fredin v. Sweden*; *Klass v. Federal Republic of Germany*; *James v. United Kingdom* pr 46; *Handyside v. United Kingdom.*

260 *James v. United Kingdom*; *Mellacher et al v. Austria* (1989) Series A, No. 169, 19 Dec.

261 *Kjeldsen, Busk et al v. Denmark.*
262 *Traktorer v. Sweden*; *James v. United Kingdom*; *Powell and Rayner v. United Kingdom.* And see the cases collected in note 240 above.
263 See notes 1 and 2 to this chapter. See also Richard Moon, 'Stop in the Name of Sense,' *UTLJ* 42 (1992) 228.

CHAPTER FIVE

1 *Roe v. Wade* 410 US 113 (1973).
2 *NAACP v. Alabama* 357 US 449, 460 (1958), and see generally T. Emerson, 'Freedom of Association and Freedom of Expression,' *Yale LJ* 74 (1964) 1.
3 *Shapiro v. Thompson* 394 US 619 (1969).
4 *Regents of the University of California v. Bakke* (438) US 265 (1978); *United Steelworkers v. Weber* 443 US 193 (1979).
5 *Meyer v. Nebraska* 262 US 390 (1922).
6 *Yoder v. Wisconsin* 406 US 205 (1972); *Brown v. Board of Education* 347 US 483 (1954); *Bakke v. Regents of the University of California.*
7 S.J. Burton, *An Introduction to Law and Legal Reasoning* (Boston: Little, Brown 1985).
8 See e.g. J. Bakan 'Constitutional Arguments: Interpretation and Legitimacy in Canadian Constitutional Thought,' *Osgoode Hall LJ* 27 (1989) 123.
9 R. St. J. Macdonald, 'The Margin of Appreciation,' in R. St J. Macdonald, E. Matscher, and H. Petzold, eds, *The European System for the Protection of Human Rights* (Dordrecht: Martinus Nijhoff 1993), 83. See also the concurring opinion of Spielmann J. in *Muller v. Switzerland* (1991) 13 EHRR 212. Cf. Gerard LaForest, 'The Balancing of Interests under the Charter,' *National Journal of Constitutional Law* (1992–3) 133.
10 The claim that judicial review is inconsistent with the principle of democratic decision-making and popular sovereignty is made by many critical scholars on the left. See e.g. M. Mandel, *The Charter of Rights and the Legalization of Politics in Canada* (Toronto: Wall and Thompson 1989) and A. Petter, 'The Politics of the Charter,' *Supreme Court LR* 8 (1968) 473. It has also been put forward by members of the bench, see LaForest, 'Balancing.'
11 Paul Weiler, 'The Charter at Work: Reflections on the Constitutionality of Labour and Employment Law,' *UTLJ* 40 (1990) 117; Robert J. Sharpe, 'A Comment on David Beatty's 'A Conservative's Court: The Politicalization of Law,' *UTLJ* 41 (1991) 469.
12 See e.g. Patrick Monahan, *Politics and the Constitution* (Toronto: Carswell

1987), R. Moon, 'Stop in the Name of Sense,' *UTLJ* 42 (1992) 228.

13 See e.g. *R.A.V. v. City of St. Paul* 112 SCt 2538 (1992) per White J.; *Comité pour la République du Canada v. Canada* 77 DLR (4th) 385 (1990) per McLachlin J.

14 R. Flathman, *The Practice of Rights* (Cambridge: Cambridge University Press 1976).

15 Of course, there are legitimate reasons for some public regulation of even the most intimate aspects of our lives, as the laws of abortion and sexual assault illustrate. See above, 86.

16 See e.g. *Central Hudson Gas and Electric Co. v. P.U.C. of N.Y.* 447 US 557 (1980); *Irwin Toy v. A.G. Quebec* 58 DLR (4th) 577 (1989); *India Express Newspapers (Bombay) Ltd. v. India* AIR 1986 SC 315; *Markt Intern and Beerman v. Germany* (1990) 12 EHRR 161; *Chemist Advertising* case 53 BVerfGE 96 (1980), noted in D. Kommers, *The Constitutional Jurisprudence of the FRG* (Durham, NC: Duke University Press 1988), 386.

17 See e.g. *Sumiyoshi v. Governor of Hiroshima* (1975) 29 Minshu No.665, reported in W.F. Murphy and J. Tanenhaus, *Comparative Constitutional Law* (New York: St Martin's Press 1977), 285; *Pharmacy* case 7 BVerfGE 377, reported in part in Kommers, *Constitutional Jurisprudence*, 285.

18 See e.g. *Kjeldsen, Busk, Madsen and Pederson v. Denmark* ECHR Series A, vol. 23, 7 Dec. 1976. *School Prayer* case (1979) 52 BVerfGE 223, reported in Kommers, *Constitutional Jurisprudence*, 466.

19 The major exception would be the US Supreme Court. See above, 106–13.

20 See E. Cheli and F. Donati, 'Methods and Criteria of Judgment on the Question of Rights to Freedom in Italy,' in D. Beatty, ed, *Human Rights and Judicial Review: A Comparative Perspective* (Dordrecht: Martinus Nijhoff 1994), 227.

21 *McKay v. The Queen* 53 DLR (2d) 532 (1965).

22 *Singh v. Minister of Employment and Immigration* 17 DLR (4th) 422 (1985).

23 *Dudgeon v. U.K.* (1981) 4 EHRR 149.

24 Compare *US Civil Service Commission v. National Association of Letter Carriers* 413 US 548 (1973); *Court Worker Incitement* case (1969) 23 Keishu, 685 reported in part in H. Itoh and L. Beer, *The Constitutional Case Law of Japan* (Seattle: University of Washington Press 1978), 103; *Kosiek v. Germany* (1986) 9 EHRR 328; and *Civil Servant Loyalty* case (1975) 39 BVerfGE 334, reported in Kommers, *Constitutional Jurisprudence* 323, with *Osborne v. Canada (Treasury Board)* 82 DLR (4th) 321 (1991).

25 Compare *Abood v. Detroit Board of Education* 431 US 207 (1977); *Young, James, and Webster v. U.K.* (1981) 4 EHRR 38; *Workers' Chamber* case (1978) 1 ILLR 27; and *Co-Determination* case (1979) 50 BVerfGE 290, reported in

part in Kommers, *Constitutional Jurisprudence* 278; with *Ref. re Alberta Public Service Employee Relations Act* 38 DLR (4th) 161 (1987); *Lavigne v. Ontario Public Service Employees Union* 81 DLR (4th) 545 (1991).

26 See e.g. *Seaboyer v. Queen* 83 DLR (4th) 193 (1991), and see above, 82–4.

27 For a brief discussion of an appointment procedure appropriate for a federal state, see D. Beatty, *Talking Heads and the Supremes* (Toronto: Carswell 1990), chap. 10. For a comparison of how different appointment procedures affect decision-making by US and Japanese courts, see J. Mark Ramseyer, 'The Puzzling (In)dependence of the Courts: A Comparative Approach,' *Journal of Legal Studies* 23 no.2 (1994) 721.

28 D. Beatty, 'The Last Generation: When Rights Lose Their Meaning,' in D. Beatty ed, *Human Rights and Judicial Review: A Comparative Perspective* (Dordrecht: Martinus Nijhoff 1994), 321.

29 It may be the case that in ruling that a law violates the principles of rationality or consistency the effect of the court's decision is to require a government to spend substantial sums to remedy the defect. A clear example of a case of this kind in Canada is *Singh v. M.E.I.* 17 DLR (4th) 422 (1985), where the Supreme Court required the Government to establish a refugee review process that guaranteed refugee claimants certain procedural rights, including an oral hearing. See also *R v. Askov* [1990] 2 SCR 1199. In most cases of this kind, however, the Court's ruling is restricted to requiring Governments to put institutions and procedures in place – such as legal aid schemes – on which other constitutional guarantees depend. Even here, however, it is never the case that the courts will dictate to the legislature the precise details of the institution or procedure required. See e.g. *Airey v. Ireland* (1977) 8 ECHR 42.

30 Cf. Allan Hutchinson, 'Waiting for CORAF,' *UTLJ* 41 (1991) 332.

31 See e.g. *Asahi v. Japan* (1967) 21 (5) Minshu 1043, reported in part in Itoh and Beer, *The Constitutional Case Law of Japan*, 103; *Olga Tellis v. Bombay* AIR 1986 SC 180; *Airey v. U.K.*; *Aircraft Noise Control* case (1981) 56 BVerfGE 54, and *Chemical Weapons* case (1987) 77 BVerfGE 170, portions of which are translated in D. Kommers, *Constitutional Jurisprudence*, 137, 139, 364. And see D. Grimm, 'Human Rights and Judicial Review in Germany,' and E. Cheli and F. Donati, 'Methods and Criteria of Judgment on the Question of the Right to Freedom in Italy,' both in Beatty, ed, *Human Rights and Judicial Review*, 227, 267.

32 For a series of examples of how this method of interest group politics has been played out in Canada, see Beatty, *Talking Heads*, 123–245.

33 See e.g. Robert Alexy, 'Basic Rights and Democracy in Jürgen Habermas's Procedural Paradigm of the Law' *Ratio Juris* 7 (1994) 227–38.

Index

abortion, 20, 22, 40, 62, 65, 73, 83, 86, 109, 130, 132–3, 143, 145
adjudication. *See* legal reasoning
advertising, 40, 44, 65, 67, 83, 102, 138; *see also* fundamental freedoms
affirmative action, 109, 114–15, 117–18, 143
age discrimination, 73, 93; *see also* *McKinney* case
Andrews case, 93–4
Anti-inflation case, 38, 169n45
assisted suicide. *See* *Rodriguez* case

Big M Drug Mart case, 68, 72

Canadian Bill of Rights, 63–4, 90
Carnation case, 25–6
Citizens Insurance Co. v. Parsons case, 23, 27, 35–7
concurrent powers, 28–9, 40–2, 45–6, 48, 51–2, 54, 56, 69, 71, 100
constitutional law: as analytical framework, 10–13, 26, 29, 69–70, 77–8, 82, 90, 96–7, 103–5; as method of constitutional reform, 9–10, 20, 59; constitutional conventions, 180n132; objectivity and determinacy, 13–15, 20, 29, 50, 54, 56–8, 84, 97–9, 103–5, 127–8, 140, 142–7; *see also* legal reasoning; proportionality principle; rationality principle
constitutions: amending, formal, 5–6, 115; amending, informal, 8, 60; purpose, 3–5, 25; scope, 77–82, 85–93, 107, 110, 116, 124–5, 130, 134; style, 5–6, 62, 93, 116–17, 143; supremacy, 5, 85, 87–92, 94–5, 98, 150, 156; underlying values, 24–5, 62, 65–6, 68, 89–90, 100, 109, 128, 131, 148
criminal law, 7, 21–2, 30–1, 41–2, 44–5, 53, 75, 79, 83, 97, 114–15, 132
Crown Zellerbach case, 34–5, 50

deference principle, 82–4, 88, 91–2, 96, 99–100, 105–6, 111–12, 124, 132, 135–6, 138–9, 146–7, 155
delegation, 47
de minimis rule, 80–1
democratic rule, 4, 25, 32, 48, 82–3, 85, 99–100, 132, 134, 142, 147, 150–4, 160–1
discrimination. *See* equality
Dolphin Delivery case, 76, 85

double aspect, 44–5, 47–8, 53, 60, 71
Dudgeon case, 136, 153

Eastern Terminal Elevator case, 41, 43, 51
Edwards Books and Art Ltd. case, 67
election laws, 20, 40, 49, 54–5, 73–4, 78–80, 109, 119, 123, 125–6, 130, 135, 138, 152–3
environmental law, 22, 42–4, 132, 138, 154
equality, 79–80, 87, 92–4, 107–8, 111, 114, 117–20, 134–5, 138, 158
European standard, 136–9, 151
expression. *See* fundamental freedoms
extradition. *See* foreign policy

federal principle, 5, 25–9, 32–8, 40–1, 45–8, 65–6, 100
fisheries, 30, 42–4, 45
floodgates arguments, 87–8, 95, 147, 149
foreign policy, 77–8, 81, 84, 110, 125, 130; *see also* political questions doctrine
Fowler case, 42–4, 49
fundamental freedoms: association, 62, 78, 80, 87, 91, 109, 117–19, 125, 129, 134, 143, 173n22; commercial speech, 67, 73, 83, 111, 118, 120, 150, 184n61; expression, 108, 110, 114, 125, 129, 132, 134, 150; hate speech, 67, 73, 90; political speech, 67, 78, 114, 129; religion, 66–8, 109–10, 119, 125, 129, 134, 139, 150

General Motors case, 37–8

Haldane, Lord, 34, 36, 60, 102, 124
human rights, 5; as duties of lawmakers, 17, 104, 106, 129, 131–2, 135, 139–40, 142–4, 146–55, 159; implied bill of rights, 31–2; limits, 68–9, 122, 134

immigration law, 74, 110–12, 136; *see also Singh* case
interjurisdictional immunity, 31, 52
interpretation: balancing (prudential) approach, 80–2, 89–90, 96, 110, 152; doctrinal (precedential) approach, 11–12, 23, 63–4; historical (intention) approach, 23–4, 32, 35, 40–1, 44, 47, 64–5, 120–1, 130, 134, 152, 156, 177n86; literal (plain meaning) approach, 21–2, 32, 35, 40–4, 87, 89; purposeful (logical) approach, 11, 25–8, 31–2, 34–9, 54, 65–9, 71, 78–80, 87–9, 130, 134, 143, 156

Labatt Breweries case, 49
labour law, 21–2, 44, 52, 62, 67, 76, 78, 81, 85, 88–9, 91–2, 97, 109–10, 118–19, 125, 129, 155
language rights, 72–4, 79–81, 143
Laskin, Bora, vii, 32, 60, 102, 124
Lavigne case, 76, 92
LeDain, Gerald, 34
legal reasoning: analogical, 11, 16, 52, 97, 115, 154–5; categorical, 28, 40–1, 43, 51–3, 108–10, 112–13, 117–21, 124, 127, 132, 134, 155–6, 167n24; deductive, 11, 24–5, 30–2, 34–9, 40, 42, 52, 54–5, 65–9, 78–9, 87–90, 128, 142; transcultural, 105, 145–6
life, liberty, and security of the person, 62, 72, 78–80, 87, 107–8, 116–

17, 120, 124, 129, 132–3, 135, 173n25
Local Prohibition case, 33–4

McKay case, 20, 49, 54–5, 58, 152
McKinney case (mandatory retirement), 76, 83, 91–2
mandatory retirement. *See McKinney* case
Manitoba Egg case, 51, 55–6
margin of appreciation, 83, 138, 146–7
minimal scrutiny, 83, 110–11, 125
mutual modification, 27–30, 35–6, 48, 54, 69, 71, 180n132

Northwest Falling case, 43–4, 49

Oakes case, 65, 68–70, 82
overbreadth. *See* rationality principle

paramountcy rule, 46–7
'peace, order and good government' (POGG), 32–5, 48, 50, 108
'*Persons*' case, 65, 172n8
pith and substance rule, 45–8, 52–3, 71, 119–20
political questions doctrine, 107, 110, 124–5, 130
popular sovereignty. *See* democratic rule
pornography, 7, 20–1, 24, 40, 44, 65, 67, 83–4, 110
principles of fundamental justice, 79, 173n9
professional occupations, 73, 75–6, 83, 104, 123, 131, 150
property and civil rights, 7, 21–2, 31–2, 37, 42
proportionality principle, 15–17, 26–7, 32–5, 37–9, 43–6, 48–52, 54–60, 69–75, 81, 86, 91–4, 103–6, 106–13 (United States), 113–21 (India), 121–7 (Japan), 127–33 (Germany), 133–40 (European Court of Human Rights), 141–6, 152–4, 159–60
prostitution, 7, 21–2, 24, 40–1, 52–3, 56, 65, 67, 84
provincial inability test, 34–5, 38, 50, 60
public/private, 76–7, 85–7, 107, 116, 127, 130, 136, 149, 159

rationality principle, 15–17, 34–9, 43–6, 48–52, 54–60, 69–75, 81, 86, 91–2, 96, 99–102, 103–6, 106–13 (United States), 113–21 (India), 121–7 (Japan), 127–33 (Germany), 133–40 (European Court of Human Rights), 141–6, 159–60
religion. *See* fundamental freedoms
Rodriguez case, 92, 178n104
Russell case, 33–4

Saumur case, 55, 168n36
separation of powers, 4, 81–2, 125, 128, 130–2, 140, 147–8, 150–1, 158–9
Singh case, 72, 74, 153, 180n133; *see also* immigration law
social and economic law, 79, 83, 97, 110–11, 115, 120, 125, 130–1, 138, 147, 155–6, 158, 187n125
spending powers, 47
state action, 76–7, 85–7, 107, 116
strict scrutiny, 75, 109–10, 126, 143, 149
strikes and picketing. *See* labour law
subsidiarity, 38, 135
Sunday shopping, 21–2, 24, 40, 44, 62, 65, 67–8, 72, 74, 77, 83, 110
supremacy. *See* constitutions

tiers of review, 82–4, 91–2, 96, 108–12, 120, 125, 138, 146–7
trade and commerce, 7, 21–2, 27, 36–9, 41, 45, 48, 50, 108
treaties, 30, 51, 125, 166n12

union dues. *See Lavigne* case
U.S. Bill of Rights, 106–13; as source of reasoning for Canadian courts, 63–4

vagueness. *See* rationality principle
voting rights, 79–81, 108–9

Watson, William, 34
Westendorp case, 21, 53, 56, 58, 169n63

Lightning Source UK Ltd.
Milton Keynes UK
UKHW012031200722
406142UK00001B/19